face to face

Three Centuries of Artists' Self~portraiture

AF372100

face to face

Three Centuries of Artists' Self~Portraiture

Xanthe Brooke

Catalogue to accompany an exhibition
Walker Art Gallery, Liverpool
28 October 1994 ~ 8 January 1995

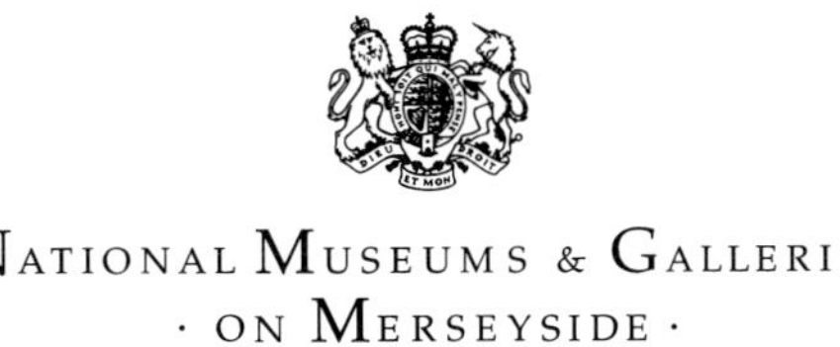

NATIONAL MUSEUMS & GALLERIES
· ON MERSEYSIDE ·

cover photograph Elizabeth Louise Vigée Le
Brun, *Self-portrait in a Straw
Hat* (National Gallery,
London)

back cover Rembrandt van Rijn, *Self
portrait* (English Heritage,
(The Iveagh Bequest,
Kenwood, London))

published by The Bluecoat Press
for NMGM

designed by March design

© Board of Trustees of the
National Museums &
Galleries on Merseyside

All rights reserved. No part
of this publication may be
reproduced, stored in a
retrieval system, or
transmitted in any form or
by any means, electronic,
mechanical, photocopying,
recording or otherwise,
without prior permission
from the publisher.

ISBN 0 906367 71 9

Contents

Preface

Face to Face is one of the Walker Art Gallery's series of exhibitions focusing on well-known pictures in the collection. Each of these exhibitions (the first on Murillo's *Virgin and Child in Glory*, the second on W.F. Yeames' *And when did you last see your father?*) was larger than the previous one, and this, the third in the series, is larger still. Originally proposed by Xanthe Brooke, Curator of European Art, as a small exhibition comparing the Walker's distinguished self-portraits by Rembrandt and Mengs, it has developed, through her enthusiasm and scolarship, into and exploration of a far larger theme, the genre of self-portraiture itself.

Seven self-portraits from the collections in the care of NMGM and included in the exhibition; from the Lady Lever Art Gallery comes a rare George Stubbs self-portrait on a Wedgwood ceramic plaque; from the Walker, besides the Rembrandt and the Mengs, there are self-portraits by the Pre-Raphaelite painters Millais and Madox Brown, and a self-portrait recently acquired from a local source, painted by William Davis, a Liverpool follower of the Pre-Raphaelites. To these and others have been added a magnificent group of self-portraits, spanning three centuries in date, by many of the great names of British and European Old Master painting.

We have been fortunate in being able to borrow these pictures from collections throughout the British Isles, and we owe a considerable debt of gratitude to all the lenders who have generously agreed to part with their pictures during the exhibition. We are also grateful to the curators of local and national collections for all the suggestions and advice given to Xanthe whilst she was researching the exhibition.

Special thanks should go to those artists whose informal comments did much to shape the discussion on the nature of self-portraiture in the catalogue and exhibition. Particular thanks are also due to the staff of NMGM, first of all Xanthe Brooke, but also many others, including the Art Galleries Registrar, David McNeff, members of the Conservation Division, and Kathryn Smith of the Press Office.

Self-portraiture and the construction and 'de-construction' of the image of the artist, male or female, has recently gained an increasing interest among artists, academics and the media. Concepts such as imaging the 'self' and 'the other' have become commonplace in art-historians' discussions and writings. But questions such as what artists looked like, how they saw themselves, whether their image measured up to popular expectation and why they created self-portraits have equally intrigued the public at least since 1568, when Giorgio Vasari illustrated the second edition of his best-selling book *Lives of the Artists* with a portrait of each of his subjects.

We believe that this exhibition should satisfy both academic and popular curiosity and provide enjoyment to all our visitors. The inscription on Augustus Egg's *Self-portrait* speaks not just for the one picture but for the whole exhibition: 'In every scene some moral let it teach, And if it can at once both please and preach.'

Richard Foster,
Director,
National Museums & Galleries on Merseyside

Julian Treuherz,
Keeper of Art Galleries,
National Museums & Galleries on Merseyside

Face to Face

The nineteenth-century French painter Henri Fantin-Latour (1836-1904) once said of self-portraits: 'The model is always ready and offers all sorts of advantages; he is exact, submissive, and one knows him before painting'.[1] For a socially timid young portraitist like Fantin-Latour, often ill at ease with unknown sitters, the utility of self-portraiture was obvious. The mundane truth, even for some of the greatest of painters like Rembrandt, was that the cheapest and easiest model to hand was often the artist. A more spirited commentary on the attraction of self-portraiture for artist and viewer alike was given by the popular British painter of Victorian life W. P. Frith (Cat.no.46) in his *Reminiscences*, (1888). For Frith the student need never be at a loss for a model 'so long as he possesses a looking-glass. Better practice than the reproduction of his own features cannot be followed. He is sure of a patient sitter, and he has the example of nearly all the great painters, whose "very form and feature" have come down to us limned by their own hands'. Having listed the famous artists whose finest works were portraits of themselves, including Rembrandt, Reynolds, Titian, Rubens, Van Dyck, Raphael and Leonardo, 'to say nothing of nearly - if not all - the great Dutchmen' Frith then continued 'I share - in common with all my fellow creatures - the eager curiosity that everyone feels respecting the outward and visible form of the producer of works of genius'. That curiosity was evident also in the second half of the sixteenth century when the artist biographer Giorgio Vasari introduced engraved portraits to the second edition of his *Lives of the Artists* (1568) and in the second half of the seventeenth century when Cardinal Leopoldo de' Medici established the first purposely created collection of artists' self-portraits in the Uffizi, Florence.

Frith himself found that transcribing his own features frequently defied him: 'In my youth, in the absence of a better model, I spent hour after hour staring into a mirror, with results unrecognisable by my friends as likenesses of myself.'[2] Other nineteenth-century artists also disliked painting themselves and not necessarily because of their lack of facility in portraiture. The society portrait-painter Sir Thomas Lawrence never contributed his portrait to the Uffizi collection despite promising one and when it was observed that his Royal Academy self-portrait had a melancholy expression he replied that 'you would surely not have a man look smirkingly at himself in a glass; and you seem to forget what an irksome task it is to me'.[3] The reluctance of some artists to depict themselves suggests that those who painted self-portraits repeatedly were folowing an impulse as ancient as that encapsulated in the classical tale of Narcissus, the mythical originator of painting, who so fell in love with his image reflected in water that he decided to paint it.

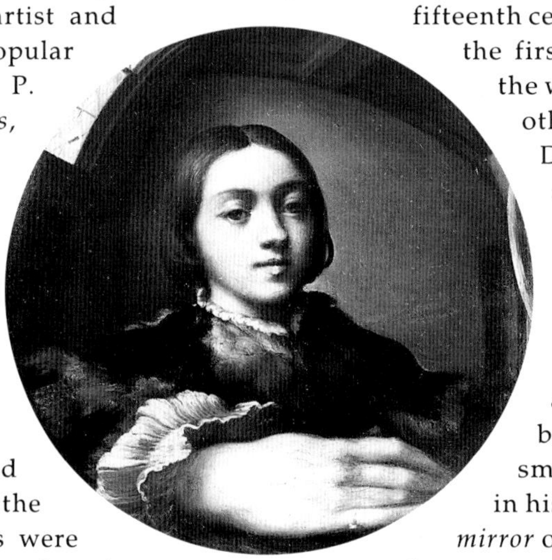

The Practice of Self-portraiture

Before the invention of photography the artist relied on mirrors to help in the task of painting his portrait and until the late medieval period mirrors were pocket sized and convex rather than flat. The manufacture in quantity of larger non-distorting flat mirrors began early in the fifteenth century in Venice, which retained its renown for the high quality of its mirrors into the seventeenth century. It is, therefore, no accident that the development of the full-frontal scrutiny of the autonomous self-portrait coincided with technological progress in the fifteenth century. Albrecht Dürer (1471-1528), the first outstanding self-portraitist, led the way in isolating his image from any other historical or religious theme. Dürer painted two of his three major self-portraits after his first visit to Venice in 1494. The blown glass mirrors familiar to Dürer in Germany magnified whatever was nearer their surface and miniaturised what was further away. It was precisely this contrast between the exaggeratedly large and small that Parmigianino manipulated in his celebrated *Self-portrait in a convex mirror* of about 1523 (fig.1), one of the best documented self-portraits of the sixteenth century. The optical distortion captured on the small panel of wood made to the same size as the barber's mirror in which Parmigianino's image was reflected, fascinated and astonished contemporary and later commentators and collectors. The huge elongated hand thrust towards the viewer was meant to startle, and the small, precious seeming image was obviously intended as a collector's piece, to show off the skills of an artist still in his early twenties. The use of disturbing anatomical distortions was one of the key effects of the Mannerist style that Parmigianino helped create and develop. His self-portrait thus acted, as many others were to do in the future, as an excellent promotion for a new style and an advertisement for the talent and imagination of a young artist. The painting's success in advancing Parmigianino's career can be gauged by the extensive and sensitive description in Vasari's *Lives of the Artists* and by the admiring reception which it and the artist gained at the court of the newly installed Medici Pope Clement VII, to whom he presented his self-portrait and from whom he later gained commissions.[4] The painting was successively passed on as a valued gift to the poet Aretino and the sculptor Vittoria before ending up in the prestigious collection of Emperor Rudolph II in Prague.

Mirrors were a long sanctioned feature of artists' studios. Their use to check on the accuracy of a work's representation of nature had been advised as early as 1435 by Leon Battista Alberti in his treatise on painting.[5] The practice was still being employed in the late

*Fig. 1: Francesco Parmigianino **Self-portrait in a convex mirror**, about 1523 (Vienna, Kunsthistorisches Museum)*

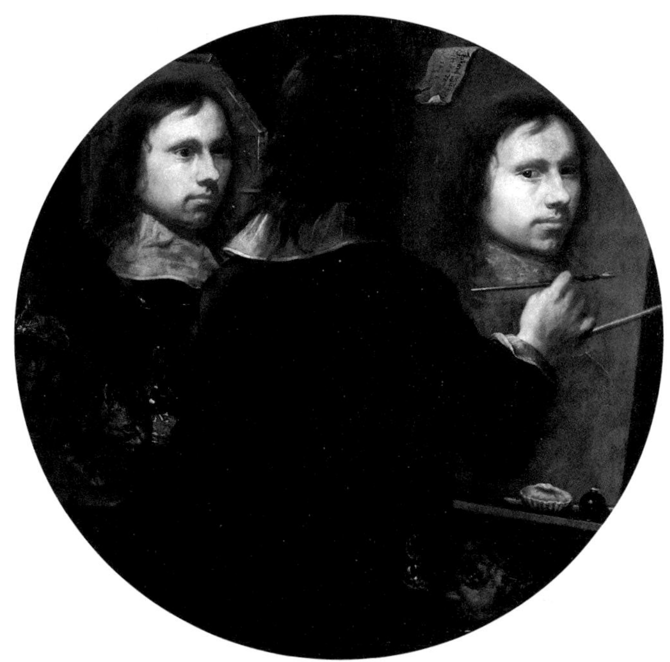

*Fig. 2: Johannes Gumpp **Triple Self-portrait**, 1646 (Florence, Uffizi Museum)*

eighteenth century by Elisabeth Vigée Le Brun (Cat.no.35): 'You should always have a mirror positioned behind you so that you can see both the model and your painting at the same time; ... it is the best guide and will show up faults clearly'.[6] A mirror positioned in just such a way can be seen in James Sant's nineteenth-century *Self-portrait in a Studio* (Cat.no.52). To produce a self-portrait the most common place for the mirror was demonstrated in Johannes Gumpp's *Triple Self-portrait* (fig.2), where viewers find themselves face to face with the artist's features twice over, on the canvas and in the octagonal mirror placed at an angle to the canvas on which he shows himself, from the back, at work. This clever 'party-trick' enabled Gumpp, a relatively obscure artist from Austria, to attract the attention of the prestigious Uffizi collection and have his work hung alongside self-portraits by Dürer, Rembrandt, Van Dyck and Guercino. The picture's illusionistic representation of three views of the painter, a painted one, a 'reflected' one and a 'real' one, may also invoke the famous artistic dispute comparing painting and sculpture which claimed that with the aid of mirrors painting could match the three-dimensionality of sculpture. Gumpp's picture does not reveal all the tricks of the trade, for it does not show the positioning of the mirror that he must have used to paint his back view. It does, however, show the reason for the 'typical' self-portrait pose which recurs throughout the centuries: the sideways glance out of the picture at the spectator. Some artists successfully masked what could be an awkward, stiff pose; others turned it to their advantage. By exaggerating the turn of the body Van Dyck (Cat.no.4) created an elegant twist of the head as he looks at us over his shoulder. Other artists made use of the sideways flick of the eyes to create the impression that the viewer was a distracting intruder into the artist's presence, reinforcing the self-portrait's illusion of intimacy that we are in fact face to face with the artist.

Recreating a three-dimensional likeness on a two-dimensional surface was not easy and the difficulty of reproducing it in a three-dimensional form was even harder. For this reason sculpted self-portraits were a relatively rare form of the genre, although paradoxically the Renaissance polymath artist and theorist Alberti's self-portrait medal (fig.3), sculpted in low relief in about 1435, was one of the earliest autonomous self-portraits. Alberti would have needed two or even three mirrors to create his portrait in profile on a bronze medallion, the form of which deliberately aped classical Roman coins and cameos. The profile pose is one of the most 'objective' views of a head. Lacking the interaction between sitter and viewer introduced by eye contact the head is treated purely as an object, a symbolic representation of the person portrayed. Alberti's use of the pose and the accompanying personal mottoes and hieroglyphic

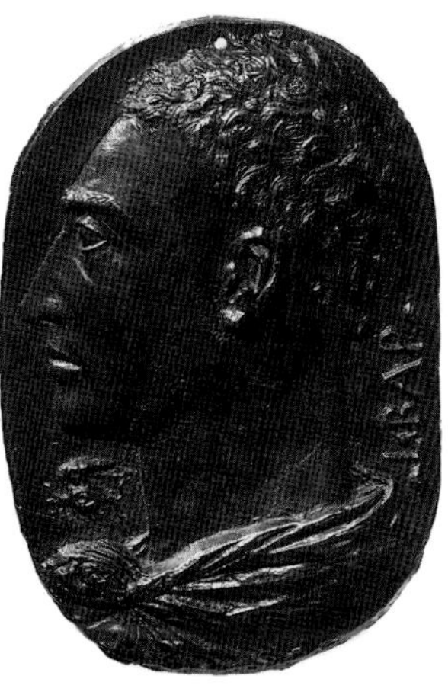

*Fig. 3: Leon Battista Alberti, **Self-portrait in profile** bronze medal, about 1435 (Washington, National Gallery of Art, Samuel H. Kress Collection)*

emblems create an abstracted schematised 'portrait' of the artist emphasising his intellectual identity rather than recording his features for future generations. Alberti recognised the commemorative aspect inherent in all portraiture, the wish to live on after one's death which was also an important element in all artists' desire to portray themselves.

When it came to producing a likeness of yourself as others saw you and correcting the reversed mirror image, even an expert self-portraitist late in his career, like Rembrandt, could begin by placing his brushes in the wrong, non-painting hand, as x-rays of the Kenwood canvas have revealed (Cat. no.16). An artist could use two mirrors to avoid the problem of reversed image but this may have inhibited further the spontaneity of composition and execution. The problems created by the mirror's reversed image were particularly acute when artists painted or drew their hands, in any case one of the most difficult parts of the anatomy to represent. It may be significant that Rembrandt's earliest self-portraits were etchings so that the process of printing reversed the mirror-image drawn on the plate whilst his earliest painted self-portraits were bust-length and avoided showing his hands altogether. The active hand with which the artist was working on the self-portrait was often problematic and artists frequently sought solutions by hiding it with the turn of their body or under clothing or palette. Artists who produced a series of self-portraits might eventually feel confident enough to show their hands. Van Dyck, whose hands were often the most expressive feature of his work, began as a teenager by painting only his head on a small scale, and developed as he matured through half- and three-quarter length views on larger canvases, first omitting his hands altogether, then showing only one (his non-painting)

hand, then including both hands elegantly but simply posed, and finally reaching the complexity of gesture demanded by the *Self-portrait with a sunflower* (Cat.no.4).

Alberti knew that the viewer's attention is always engaged by contact with a person's eyes and suggested that there should always be a figure staring out and beckoning the viewer into the narrative of any story picture.[7] Artists often introduced themselves as such figures in the large fresco cycles of the early Italian renaissance or the crowded gothic altarpieces of northern Europe. The otherwise anonymous painter of the Master of the Aachen Altarpiece triptych of *Christ's Passion and Crucifixion* (Liverpool, Walker Art Gallery) is believed to have pictured himself in the background looking out at the viewer over Pilate's shoulder (fig.4). The artist acted as a contemporary 'witness' to the historic, religious or legendary events which he had depicted, emphasising the continuing relevance of the story by using himself as a modern-day bystander and allowing the viewer through interaction with his gaze to enter imaginatively into the scene. Rembrandt used himself in that way in some of the earliest of his narrative pictures.

The artist's features also acted as a telling 'signature' exemplifying his or her skills. The 'signature' featured in the first literary reference to a self-portrait, Plutarch's description of how the ancient Greek architect and sculptor Phidias had sculpted his portrait on the shield of the cult statue of Athena in the innermost shrine of the Parthenon. The self-portrait continued to be employed in this way throughout the medieval period, most notably in Lorenzo Ghiberti's double self-portrait on the Baptistry doors in Florence and most commonly in the form of cathedral sculpture such as that on the pulpit of St. Stephen's in Vienna. But long after the rise

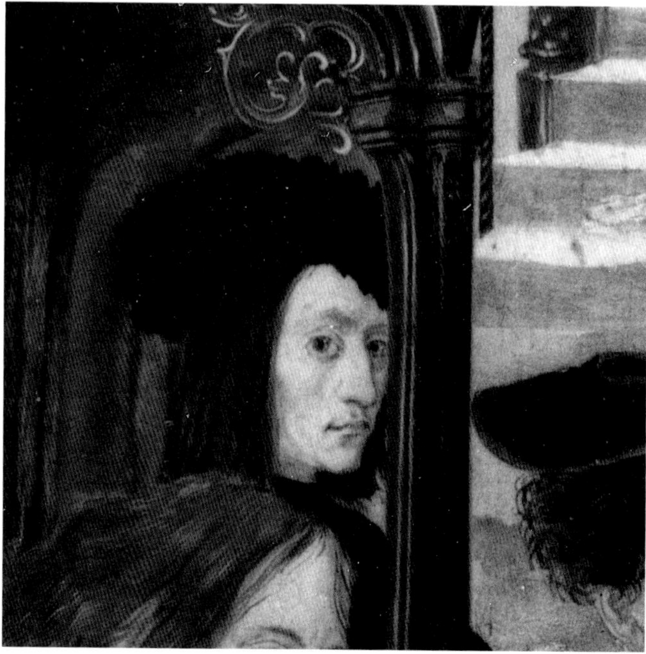

*Fig. 4: Detail from the Master of the Aachen Altarpiece's, **Triptych with scenes of Christ's Passion and Crucifixion**, about 1500 (Liverpool, Walker Art Gallery)*

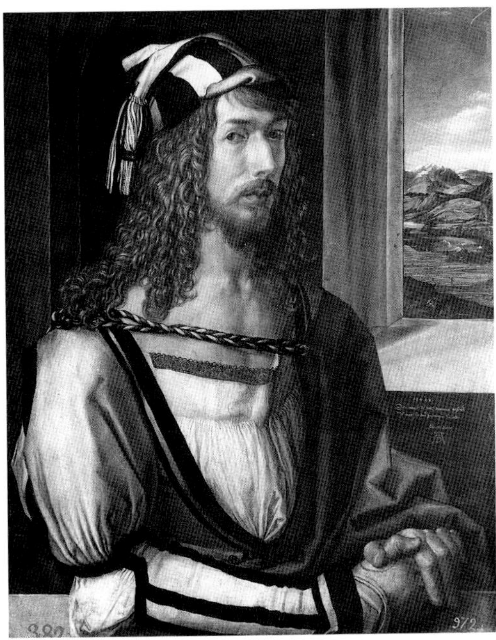

*Fig. 5: Albrecht Dürer, **Self-portrait**, 1498 (Madrid, Prado Museum)*

of the autonomous self-portrait artists were still posing as witnesses to religious events or 'signing' their work with their own features, as can be seen somewhat surprisingly in two late eighteenth-century *Adoration of the Shepherds* by artists as disparate as Mengs (Madrid, Prado Museum) and Reynolds (painted glass window in New College Chapel, Oxford). Any image which focussed on the eyes in particular also implied contact with the deep recesses of the mind. Sixteenth- and seventeenth-century philosophy considered the eyes to be the 'mirrors of the soul'.[8] The intense stare that often resulted from the concentrated scrutiny that the artist needed to give the face as it was recreated on the canvas or paper also created the impression that a self-portrait did more than merely reflect exterior features but that it must also reflect and reveal the interior mind; that a self-portrait was as much a mode of confession as a method of display. This reflected a late-medieval notion that mirrors made possible a special sort of awareness and encouraged self-criticism. The symbolic attribute of the allegorical figure of Prudence was, after all, a mirror into which one might stare in order to know oneself and 'reflect' upon one's actions. In certain artists' hands the self-portrait could become an intimate interrogation of the self but it could equally well conceal as much as it revealed, presenting to the viewer a mask-like persona in place of the person.

Dürer was the first to develop, as a significant part of his creative activity, the autonomous self-portrait for its own sake. In doing so he began the process of making self-portraiture a contemplative self-revelatory act, expressing a wide range of moods. Their status as self-portraits, distinguished for the first time from other types of portrait, was attested to by the inscriptions which often accompanied them indicating his age and authorship. He was the north European progenitor of self-portraiture as a genre and as such a role model for Rembrandt, that even more prolific self-portraitist of more than a century later. In sixteenth century southern Europe only Titian could be said to have had an 'image' in the modern sense of the word and although he portrayed himself a number of times (sometimes most simply and movingly as in fig.39) other artists painted him more often than he did himself. Titian does not seem to have been as fascinated with his own features as Dürer, for whom the recording of his own likeness became such a habit that he even drew one to show an area of pain to his doctor (Bremen, Kunsthalle). His portraits were created for what one may suppose were different purposes and in different types of medium, from a delicate silverpoint face (1484, Vienna, Albertina) to a bravura example of pen and ink-wash drawing showing himself entirely naked (c.1503 Germany, Weimar Schlossmuseum). The nude self-portrait drawing (later practitioners include Pontormo in the sixteenth century and David Wilkie in the early nineteenth) should be seen in the context of nude figure 'academies' conceived primarily as a studio exercise in which the artist used his own body to study anatomy and foreshortening.[9] Dürer's self-portraits from the age of thirteen onwards, experimented with a wide range of forms and displayed a self-confidence marked by a strong narcissistic element.

Dürer celebrated the staging-posts of his personal life by major painted self-portraits, almost as if he wished to mark such events publicly. Certainly in his case, as with some other artists, the self-portraits drawn on paper were more likely to have been meant for private consumption than his painted ones. In his portrait of 1493 (Paris, Louvre Museum), painted during marriage negotiations, he sought to advertise himself, in the tradition of northern Europe, as the handsome future husband of a wealthy burgher's daughter, holding a flower symbolizing 'luck in love'. The status-conscious self-confident pose of the richly and fashionably dressed dandy who looks out at us from the Prado *Self-portrait* (fig.5), flauntingly celebrated the worldly success he encountered after the publication of his woodcut series of the *Apocalypse* and his first visit to Italy in 1494-6, from where he later wrote to one of his friends that 'Here I am a gentleman, while at home I am a parasite'.[10] The fierce fight to raise the social status of the painter from artisan to artist and gentleman, nowhere more keenly fought than in northern Europe, is implicit in the Prado portrait. The gradual rise in self-portraiture among painters in the sixteenth century cannot, however, be ascribed simplistically to rising social status and increased self-assertion, for there were many other impulses that led artists to paint their own portraits. Some of these motives were the result of cultural, intellectual, economic or technological pressure, others were personal. At the turn of the fifteenth century Dürer portrayed himself in a hieratic, frontal pose with his long hair and beard dressed in a manner which consciously reflected the traditional pose of Christ as Saviour. Far from being blasphemous, Dürer probably intended his pose, as the painted inscription implied, to suggest that the artist's creative gifts separated him from the rest of mankind and ultimately derived their power from divine creativity. This was a precursor of the late eighteenth-century Romantic movement's image of the artist as genius, elevated above the common crowd.

A symbolic image of artistic genius was also created by Dürer in his engraving of the allegorical figure of *Melencolia I* (fig.6), shown as a shadowed, winged figure whose clenched fist supports her head weighed down by brooding thoughts as she sits surrounded by neglected tools and instruments. She embodies both the melancholic humour, which according to contemporaries occasionally afflicted Dürer, and geometry, which in Dürer's mind was inextricably linked to the painter's art. As Panofsky wrote, the print 'is in a sense a spiritual self-portrait'.[11] Her pensive pose distinguished the artist as self-absorbed introspective, divinely inspired and alienated from society. From the writings of Aristotle onwards the melancholic temperament had been associated with artistic genius. In humanist circles of the Renaissance melancholics were also associated with the god Saturn and their supposedly dark, 'saturnine' complexions foreshadowed depression or even madness. Melancholy was thus simultaneously feared as a cause of madness and romanticized as source of creative genius. As expressed in a portrait, melancholy did not necessarily signify a depressive state of mind but a reflective facility which allowed one to contemplate subjects other than mundane preoccupations. Melencolia's pose conjured up the idea of inward-looking

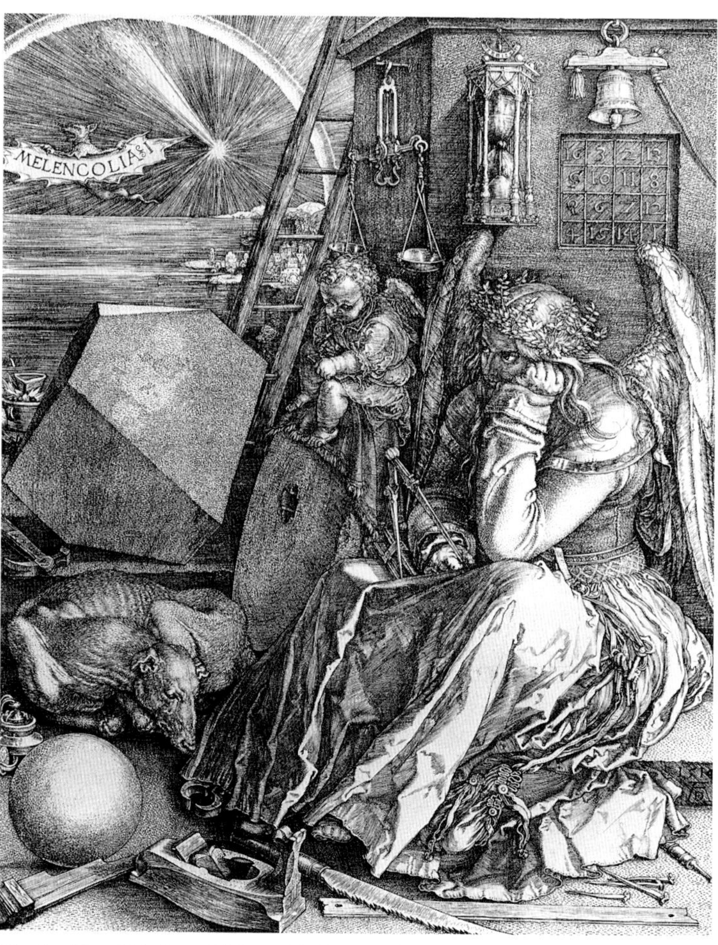

*Fig. 6: Albrecht Dürer, **Melencolia I**, 1514, (Manchester, Whitworth Art Gallery)*

self-absorption and the image came to represent the introspective, contemplative side of an artist's persona, the creative idleness or frustrated inertia that preceded the act. The image of the contemplative artist was contrasted with the active artist at work at an easel represented by the allegorical figure of Pittura (Painting), whose extensive description in Cesare Ripa's emblem book *Iconologia*, first published in 1599 (and often republished throughout the seventeenth and eighteenth centuries), was the source of Artemisia Gentileschi's vivid and vigorous *Self-portrait as an allegory of Painting* (fig.14).

The shadowy brooding visage of Dürer's isolated figure of *Melencolia* had an important effect on the image of the artist in the following centuries. Artists who actually suffered from melancholia, such as Carlo Dolci, adopted the introspective mood and shadowed face for their self-portraits (Cat.no.3). Other seventeenth-century artists such as Salvator Rosa and Luca Giordano (Cat.no.6) used it to recreate themselves as solitary taciturn philosophers or visionaries, and it may also have informed Rembrandt's early shadowed self-portraits (Cat.no.11). In the second half of the eighteenth century the melancholic image merged with that of the eccentrically dressed or behaved young artist as in the self-portrait by Wright of Derby (Cat.no.37) (who suffered from periods of depressed inactivity) and finally emerged as the figure alienated from society, informing the Romantic movement's concept of the artist as a genius, marked out by his superior intellect. In the nineteenth century the pose of Dürer's figure was readapted most famously in Rodin's sculpted figure of *The Thinker*, and was recreated in a more superficial manner in James Sant's image (Cat. no.52) of the artist in his gloomy studio, a clichéd stereotype which still clings to the popular modern-day image of the artist.

The sixteenth century saw a gradual increase in the number of artists' self-portraits, but of equal importance it also saw a widening in the market for portraits of artists, marked especially by the publication in 1568 of the second edition of Vasari's *Lives of the Artists*, illustrated with some 220 engraved portraits of the artists immortalised within. They were added to satisfy the reader's natural curiosity and supposedly to help him understand the artist's work better. Throughout Europe the individualist humanist interest of the Renaissance had encouraged the collection of series of portraits of famous historical and contemporary men and women, but they were usually predominantly rulers, military commanders and clergymen mixed in with a few celebrated faces from literature, fashion and the arts. The most noted collection in Italy was that formed by Paolo Giovio, which had a small section reserved for pictorial artists but which was mainly biased towards the literary arts. In Flanders the humanist writer Domenicus Lampsonius was involved with an illustrated art biography and made a collection of engraved portraits of mainly Netherlandish artists which was published in 1572. In Venice, where the woodcuts illustrating Vasari's *Lives* were made, small collections of artists' portraits could be found in the palaces of one of the leading governing families of the Republic, the Vendramins,

and in the bedroom of the city's leading sculptor, Alessandro Vittoria (1525-1608). These collections were necessarily private ones created in the context of a society which discouraged the public display of portraits and the cult of artistic personality.[12] Gabriel Vendramin's collection was a group of imaginary and real portraits of artists, including famous Venetian painters such as Titian, from whom the Vendramins had commissioned family portraits. Vittoria's was essentially a collection of portraits of himself (several times over in sculpted and painted versions) and his closest friends, some of whom were artists. About seven of them happened to be self-portraits, the most notable being Parmigianino's *Self-portrait in a convex mirror* (fig.1) which was owned by Vittoria when Vasari described it for his *Lives*.

Thus, by the end of the sixteenth century an artist's self-portrait could be treated either as a way to promote his status in society or as a means of celebrating himself to an audience of friends or relations. Vasari's illustrated multiple biographical dictionary, which inspired many derivatives in other languages, must have given a major impetus to the production of self-portraits throughout Europe, and there was already interest among connoisseurs in their acquisition, but it was not until the second half of the following century that a major collection purely of self-portraits began to be formed by the Medici in Florence.

The Seventeenth Century

The seventeenth century was an important one for the development of self-portraiture. It saw the creation of some of the most brilliant and complex self-portraits and there was a boom in their production throughout Europe, which culminated in the formation of the princely collection of the Medici Grand Dukes of Tuscany. The most compulsive and prolific self-portraitist, Rembrandt van Rijn, was also active during the century. Why should the seventeenth century have produced such an increased interest in self-portraiture? The rising social status of artists, indicated by the knighthoods awarded by courts across Europe to Rubens, Van Dyck and Velázquez, certainly stimulated production, often of an increasingly complicated form, but the growth also reflected other intellectual, cultural, religious and economic impulses. The century's fascination with investigating the roots of human personality and specifically the nature of artistic genius was reflected in hundreds of books published on the emotions, memory and physiognomy. Both Catholic and Protestant Europe saw the growth of interest in the inner mind and the nature of the soul.[13] In Catholic Europe such introspection took the form of mental spiritual exercises and devotional practices; in Protestant countries sermons encouraged private self-scrutiny leading to the appearance of autobiography as a literary form. Such developments were evidence of a greater consciousness of self. The seventeenth century was a period of crisis and change that often forced people to reassess themselves and indirectly promoted the growth of self-portraiture. The interest in the creative mind and its links to melancholia was developed further in Robert Burton's *Anatomy of Melancholy* (1621), which ran to five editions in his lifetime. The century's interest in the study of emotions found its classic in the French philosopher Descartes' *Les Passions de l'Ame* (Passions of the Soul) of 1649, and the intellectual concern of the whole century was summed up in his phrase, 'I think therefore I am'.

The growing cult of the artistic personality in the seventeenth century and intellectual society's interest in the nature of artistic creativity was such that even painters for whom portraiture was not a major activity succumbed to the pressures to produce a self-portrait. The French artist Nicholas Poussin (1594-1665) painted himself only twice, on both occasions at the request of friends and patrons, and only (so he claimed) because he could find no portrait painter in Rome who could match his exacting standards. The severe *Self-portrait* (Paris, Louvre) produced for his friend Chantelou in 1650, in which his head is 'framed' by rows of canvases stacked face against a wall, was meant to give an insight into the underlying character of his art through the carefully ordered verticals and horizontals of the frames. It was not intended as a confessional self-portrait, for he has hidden that under an impassive mask of a face, the embodiment of gravitas. In this respect the painting acts as a forerunner of the 'manifesto' self-portrait, a statement about the intellectual nature of the painter's art that was taken up in the eighteenth century by artists like Hogarth (Cat.no.23). Poussin also made a typically cerebral reference to the friendship to which the portrait was dedicated by including on a canvas in the background the allegorical figure of Painting embraced by the disembodied hands of Friendship.

It was not only intensely intellectual artists like Poussin who could produce vivid self-portraits that acted as perceptive commentaries on art, as is evident in the self-portrait by the Spanish artist Bartolomé Esteban Murillo (1616-82). He was known primarily for his religious scenes and sentimental subjects based on the street life of Seville urchins, but his *Self-portrait* (fig.7) created one of the most realistic trompe l'oeil effects, his presence behind and his hand placed over the oval picture frame bringing into focus the disturbing ambiguity of pictorial space. In contrast Hogarth's image of 1745 (Cat.no.23) despite its superficial compositional similarities to Murillo's (which by 1745 was in England in the collection of Frederick, Prince of Wales), was treated purely as a painting within a painting. Murillo's self-portrait was produced at the express wish of his children and dedicated to them on the funerary-like tablet hanging from the ledge below his image. Its manipulation of space, which created a powerful impression of the presence of the artist, might well have encouraged their belief in their father's continued and vivid presence in front of them long after his death.

Other seventeenth-century artists like Salvator Rosa (1615-1673) (fig.22) and Luca Giordano (Cat.no.6)

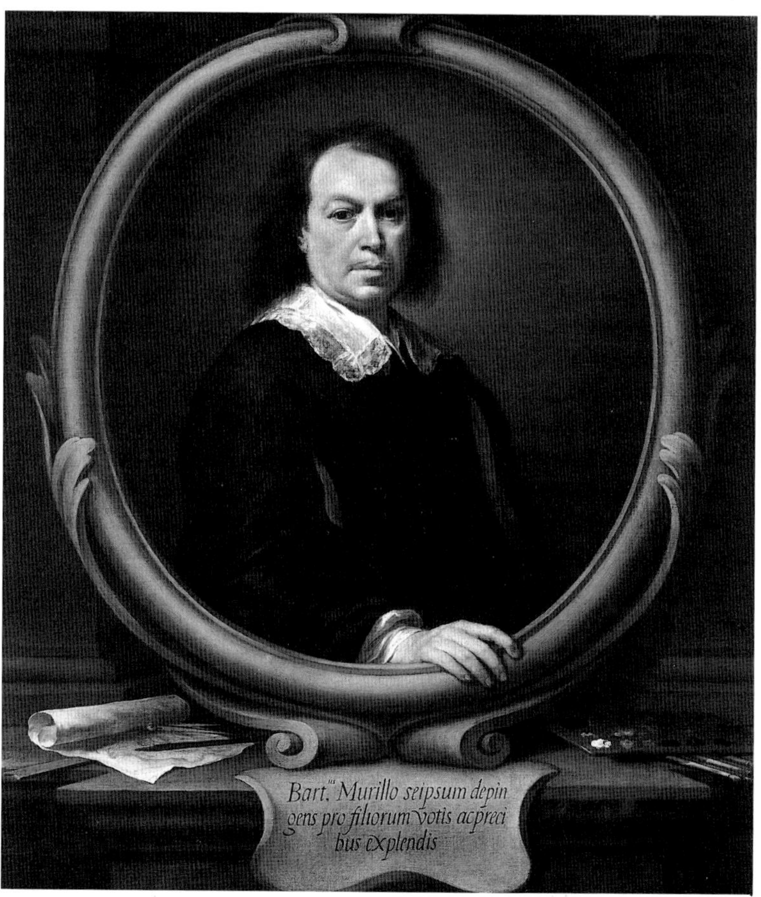

*Fig. 7: Bartolomé Esteban Murillo, **Self-portrait**, about 1670 (London, National Gallery)*

transformed the brooding image of the artist offered by Dürer's figure of *Melencolia* into an image of the artist as a scholar-philosopher, truculent or taciturn, enveloped in dark cloaks with loose unkempt hair, their unconventional dress meant to declare unfettered genius; their scowling or stern faces indicating rebellious and incorruptible isolation from society. Rosa was an original artist as well as a gifted musician, poet, satirist, actor and above all a great self-publicist who always remained something of an outsider, an image of himself that he successfully promoted in his life-style and through his self-portraits. In each self-portrait he projected a distinct persona, sometimes as a soldier or brigand or a fictitious character derived from his alternative career as actor-manager of a Commedia dell'Arte theatrical troupe. It is not surprising that this spirited concept of the artist proved attractive to the Romantic movement and other nineteenth-century artists who adopted a Bohemian life-style.

Rembrandt:

Father of the Self-portrait

The Netherlands, Rembrandt's native country, had a tradition of self-portraiture dating from the fifteenth century or earlier, and promoted by a craft pride expressed through membership of artists' guilds. The guilds' dedication to the patron saint of painters, St. Luke, encouraged some pre Protestant Reformation painters such as Marten van Heemskerck (1498-1574) to paint their portraits into guild chapel altarpieces depicting *St. Luke painting the portrait of the Virgin Mary* (Haarlem, Frans Hals Museum). In Haarlem new guild requirements in the seventeenth century required each artist to present a painting upon admission as Master, and painters such as Judith Leyster (1609-1660) often donated self-portraits (Washington, National Gallery). Still-life and genre painters were often as eager as portrait painters to create self-consciously clever self-portraits which advertised their skills. Evaert Collier's *Still-life* of 1696 (Glasgow, Hunterian Art Gallery) showed a letter-rack, a type of still-life in which he specialised, from which hung a self-portrait medallion. Thus his self-portrait became one small part of his own still-life, a conceit which Hogarth literally enlarged on almost fifty years later (Cat.no.23).

The Netherlands nurtured many other self-portraitists and Rembrandt's student Gerrit Dou (1613-1675) and in turn his pupil Frans van Mieris (1635-1681) painted themselves frequently. Rembrandt was, however, the most prolific, painting himself approximately fifty times and leaving a further thirty etchings and drawings in addition to the occasions when he inserted his face into narrative pictures. In this way he created several of the different forms that self-portraiture took in the seventeenth century. Rarely were Rembrandt's self-portraits the result of narcissism, unlike those of Dürer, although we know by comparing portraits of him by his pupils and his student companion Lievens that he sometimes idealised his pop-eyes and bulbous nose. Rembrandt's self-portraits represented a process of continued self-observation lasting more than forty years. They were produced over the whole of his career, unlike those of Van Gogh three centuries on, whose public image has equally been based on a series of self-portraits. During this period Rembrandt's self-portraits varied in medium and technique, in mood and character, in size and style. An analysis of the different types he developed within the genre also provides an insight into the diverse forms of self-display and self-scrutiny chosen by artists of the seventeenth century and later.

A large proportion of Rembrandt's self-portraits (a third of the paintings and almost half the etchings) date from the beginning of his career, the years spent in his native Leiden to the end of 1631, when he moved to Amsterdam. This is not altogether surprising: student artists often find themselves the best and cheapest material to work on and even established artists could increase their freedom to experiment with pose and expression without the worry of imposing too much on a model. That is precisely what Rembrandt did in his earliest autonomous self-portraits. They form a series of small etchings showing faces pulled in front of the mirror as he acted out exaggerated expressions and extremes of emotion, his uninhibited, scrawled etching technique allowing him to sketch quickly his contorted features and aggressive posturing (Cat.no.10). Once captured in this way the faces were incorporated into his early small-scale history paintings, on the bodies of active participants in religious dramas or bystanders at scenes from classical history (fig.8). For example the bulging-eyed, astonished face of the etched *Self-portrait open mouthed* (Cat.no.10a) reappeared as a witness to the painted *Raising of Lazarus* (Los Angeles County Museum).

Rembrandt's earliest painted self-portraits were traditional in the sense that his face acted as his

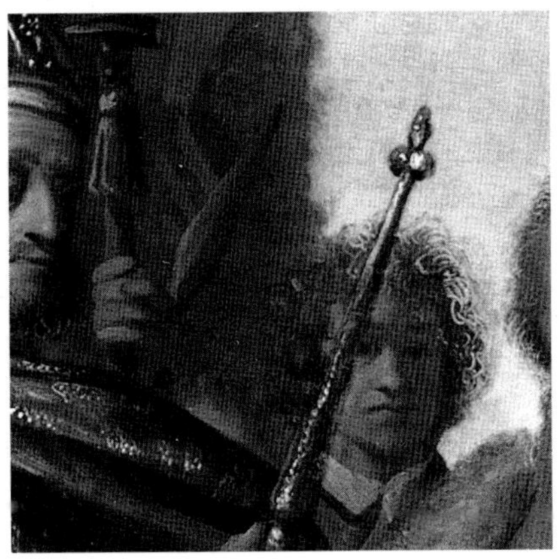

*Fig. 8: Detail from Rembrandt van Rijn's **Historical Composition** about 1626 (Leiden, Stedelijk Museum De Lakenhal) showing Rembrandt's self-portrait in the background.*

'signature' and 'witness' to the event depicted. Towards the end of the 1620s he began to paint independent self-portraits on small wood panels, increasing their size over the next couple of years and culminating in the Liverpool *Portrait of the Artist as a Young Man* (Cat.no.11). Although the painted self-portraits were produced in tandem with some of the etched series they are different, not concerned with acting out emotions and recording the face's subsequent movement, but exploring the fall of light and dark over the face and the effect which different patterns of chiaroscuro had on the overall mood of an image. However wild and unruly he made his hair, however dark the shadows over his face the youthful self-portraits remained tentative products of studio practice rather than attempts to project different persona. The turning point in Rembrandt's self-image came in the period between the Liverpool and the Glasgow portraits (Cat.nos.11,13) representing his geographical and artistic move from Leiden history painter to Amsterdam portraitist in 1632.

Self-portraiture allows artists to experiment without the need to put sitters through endless changes of position or expression. Experimentation was particularly important in portraiture, so dependent on compositional formulas and patterns. A painting like the Glasgow *Self-portrait* enabled an aspiring portrait painter like Rembrandt, wanting to break into a new market, to practice with formulas which could be applied to commissioned portraits. Hence his rejection of the exotic dress of the Liverpool image and the adoption in its place of the conventional dress of Amsterdam's merchant class. Effectively he was using his self-portrait to prime himself for painting the portraits of the burgomasters and regents of Amsterdam. Centuries later the British artist Walter Sickert said that he was using one of his self-portraits as a 'punchball' to train for a major project.[14] By the time Rembrandt came to paint the Glasgow self-portrait in 1632 he knew his face well enough to be able to use the painting to hone his pictorial and technical skills in readiness for launching himself as a portraitist on the Amsterdam market. But, like many of his early self-portraits, the image remains tentative and exploratory in mood. He followed his usual pattern at this time of first experimenting with compositions in an etched form and then transferring to the less spontaneous, more formal medium of paint. Shortly before the Glasgow picture he perfected his etching skills in the same way, working through many states to create the most elaborate and flamboyant piece of self-projection to date, his *Self-portrait wearing an embroidered cloak*. Throughout the next two decades Rembrandt's intense involvement with his own features, studying their changes and moods, also helped clarify his visual perception of other sitters.

After his move to Amsterdam Rembrandt's self-portraits started to show a growing awareness of his own dramatically changed social and artistic status, especially after the celebrated success of *The Anatomy Lesson of Dr Tulp*. There is little doubt that by adopting the everyday dress of the Amsterdam patrician class he was identifying himself with them, and constructing through his self-portraits a status-seeking socially-motivated image of himself. For the next decade all his self-portraits had an element of self-advertisement celebrating his social success. Many involved exuberant and ostentatious role-play in which he dressed up in turbans, armour or other exotic clothing taken from studio stock. The National Gallery self-portrait of 1640 (Cat.no.14) shows both these characteristics, a desire to celebrate worldly success and a willingness to dress up in sixteenth-century costume, but the evident dignity of Rembrandt's pose alluded to another motive for this particular portrait. The pose derived from two portraits by Titian and Raphael which Rembrandt had seen in Amsterdam. His self-portrait was evidently meant to pay tribute to the old masters, but it also staked his claim to rank alongside them.

It was not until his late middle age and after a sharp decline in his economic and social status caused by national economic and personal crises in the 1650s that Rembrandt took a more candid approach to himself. The late self-portraits created in the final decade of his life are the most imposing and seemingly revealing that he ever produced. Some come close to being the meditations on the inner self which post-Freudian sensibilities expect from a self-portrait. However, as Gombrich has rightly said, no painter can truly reveal the character of a sitter although a great portraitist can give us the 'illusion of seeing the face behind the mask'. This is precisely what Rembrandt appears to do in his moving Kenwood self-portrait (Cat.no.16).[15] The deep emotions which lie behind the mask of his late self-portraits seem to intimate a conscious and resigned acceptance of the dying of the light. The symbolic artist's beret so proudly worn by Rembrandt in the Liverpool portrait (Cat.no.11) has changed into something like an old man's night-cap. No longer does he posture to proclaim his social status or celebrate his material wealth. It is perhaps significant that only in this period of his life, living as a bankrupt in rented accommodation, did he choose to acknowledge the tools of his trade and paint himself at the easel with brushes, palette and mahl-stick in hand, when these were almost all that remained to him. Yet these portraits were never purely autobiographical, though much has been read into them in that way. Rather, they are evidence that as commissions for his narrative pictures died away he turned back to self-portraiture to explore human nature. Certainly in what may have been one of his last self-portraits, *Self-portrait laughing* (Cologne, Wallraf-Richartz Museum), he reverted to using his image, as at the beginning of his career, to explore extremes of expression within the format of a history painting. The Cologne portrait is a fragment of a picture which illustrated Pliny's story of the ancient Greek painter Zeuxis, who laughed himself to death as he tried to paint the portrait of a wrinkled old lady. Rembrandt's use of his own features on the cackling old painter was perhaps meant as a final allusive commentary on himself.

Seventeenth-century Netherlands was a country in formation, only recently freed from Spanish domination and undergoing a period of rapid social and economic change. Its resulting instability generated questions about the social order and individual identity. Such a context only partly explains why Rembrandt created the most complex and intense series of self-portraits ever produced. Perhaps Rembrandt, inclined by temperament to see himself as an outsider, was predisposed to the self-definition and self-promotion offered by self-portraiture. But seventeenth-century self-portraits were not necessarily a form of self-analysis. Contemporary autobiographies showed little interest in self-analysis and the fact that Rembrandt, like other internationally famous painters before and since, was happy to have his studio copy his self-portraits suggests that they were treated much like any other forms of portraiture and were not considered any more intimate or revelatory.

Rembrandt's self-portraits pose a complex problem to which the answers are still contrary and elusive. For whom were they intended? And why did he paint so many? The fact that in the 1630s and 1640s Rembrandt allowed his students to copy his self-portraits suggests that there was a market for them as the prime image of a noted artist. Rembrandt's even more celebrated contemporary Rubens (1577-1640) also had his self-portraits copied, particularly his most prestigious one commissioned for Charles I's collection (fig.9). The practice was already known in the studio of the Netherlandish artist Lambert Lombard (1506-1566), who encouraged his pupils to practice their skills by copying his self-portrait and so promote himself and his Liège-based art academy, the first outside Italy. The sketchy, scrawled technique of Rembrandt's earliest etched self-portraits and their use as aids to characterisation in his history paintings may suggest that they were produced for the studio alone and not intended for a market. Yet the number of prints made from them, now found in museum collections around the world, suggest that a large number were printed, perhaps to cater for a market that was as amused by Rembrandt's face-pulling as by Leonardo's grotesque caricatures of the previous century. Certainly the amount of attention Rembrandt lavished on his *Self-portrait in soft hat and embroidered cloak* (1631) and the multiple number of states pulled from it, suggest that it was meant to appeal to the connoisseur collectors who appreciated such demonstrations of skill on the etching plate. They willingly paid handsomely for each new change or addition to the original image. Amongst seventeenth-century collectors and artists Rembrandt was best known as a superbly skilled etcher, and it was primarily through his prints that his fame spread.

The painted self-portraits prove an equally knotty problem, for despite their large number there is little evidence that they were made for a market. Even the portrait of 1640 (Cat.no.14), which would seem to have had the most public and self-promotional intent, does not appear to have been done at a patron's request. It is noticeable that several early self-portraits (Cat.nos.11,13) are on reused supports, an economical procedure which would tend to confirm the idea that they were study works, were it not for the fact that one of them, the Liverpool *Portrait of the Artist as a Young Man* (Cat.no.11) comes closest to being a commissioned self-portrait. Although it is not dated, the Liverpool picture is close in technique and composition to the Boston *Self-portrait wearing a plumed cap*, dated 1629. They made use of a

similar complex and diffuse lighting scheme which lit the head both from behind and in front and made the paint appear to glow. An inventory of Charles I's collection at Whitehall Palace shows that the Liverpool portrait had been presented to the King by Sir Robert Kerr (1578-1654) before June 1633, when he was created Earl of Ancram, and that in 1639 it hung in the 'longe gallorie towards the Orchard' over the door to Ancram's private apartments, to signify perhaps the source of the donation to the King, by one of his most loyal Scots courtiers.[16] Kerr was a man of cultivated tastes, sharing with his close friend Constantijn Huygens, the Secretary to the Dutch Stadholder Frederick-Henry, Prince of Orange, a correspondence with the melancholic poet John Donne. It was probably Huygens, an admirer of Rembrandt and Jan Lievens (Cat.no.8), who alerted Kerr to their work when he visited The Hague in February 1629 on an embassy from Charles I to the Queen of Bohemia. It was presumably at this time that Kerr could have commissioned (or might have been promised through Huygens) the Rembrandt self-portrait along with its companion piece *An Old Woman: the Artist's Mother?* (still in the Royal Collection) and a Lievens genre piece of a *Young Scholar* (now lost), which were presented to King Charles before June 1633. Dutch archival documents reveal that the Lievens picture was said to have been bought by the Prince of Orange and given to the British ambassador, who in turn presented it to the King. According to an entry in the Leiden City Militia journal, Lievens had asked for exemption from military service on 10 April 1629 in order to complete a picture commissioned by the Prince of Orange, needing a further three months uninterrupted work.[17] Once completed, the pictures could have been sent separately to Kerr in London, perhaps accompanying Lievens on his move there in 1632 when he became court artist to the Bohemian Queen in exile. Rembrandt would have been aware of the way that Charles I's ambassadors commissioned works on his behalf and curried favour with him by presenting paintings as gifts, as that had been the way that Rubens' celebrated self-portrait was acquired for Charles in 1623. Rubens' self-portrait was widely publicised through Paulus Pontius's engraving in 1630 (fig.24) and was probably one of the first to enter Charles's small collection of self-portraits. The presence as early as the 1630s of Rembrandt paintings, including his self-portrait, in one of the period's most illustrious collections, which also included self-portraits by Van Dyck, Titian and Dürer (fig.5), attested to Rembrandt's good connections and youthful fame.[18] Rembrandt's probable awareness of his self-portrait's final resting place, in the same collection as that of Rubens, 'Prince of Painters', adds a significance to the golden chain, the long-standing symbol of reward for a court artist, draped over his shoulders in the Liverpool self-portrait.

The Liverpool self-portrait may well be one of the few pieces of evidence for a court phase in Rembrandt's work before he left to seek his fortune with the merchants of Amsterdam. It is also one of only three self-portraits known to be in a private or dealer's collection in Rembrandt's lifetime. The majority of self-portraits would therefore appear to have been painted for himself, to act as advertisements for his skill and style, or derived from studio practice, yet puzzlingly no self-portraits were listed in the 1656 bankruptcy sale of his studio (though they might have been excluded if they had been considered family portraits). The late self-portraits would seem by their nature to be personal and intimate statements, not intended for a wider public but part of a dialogue between the artist and his image, concerned more with the drama of internal reflection than with exterior projection. The whole range of Rembrandt's self-portraiture, whether in etched or painted form, whether the self-conscious tentative early experiments or the magisterial grandeur of his last paintings, had a great impact on the self-portraits of his contemporaries and successors. Several of his own students naturally used formats, motifs, dress and pose culled from his paintings to lay claim to his tradition. In his middle years Dou painted a number of self-portraits based on those of his master, also showing himself in different guises, illustrating his artistic interests and demonstrating his material prosperity and an awareness of his status as the leading painter of Leiden.

Rembrandt also influenced many eighteenth and nineteenth-century artists, particularly British painters, who consciously aped his lighting, costume and style, sometimes with dire effect if they were mediocre artists producing pastiche, derivative images. In Britain Rembrandt's name became so synonymous with self-portraiture as a genre that an artist with a suitably dark palette and tonal range and a similar propensity to paint his own features, such as the nineteenth-century Liverpool artist William Daniels (Cat.no.42), would constantly be compared to his Dutch predecessor. It was perhaps predictable that Rembrandt's firmest hold should have been in England where so many of his paintings had been imported. In the eighteenth century several arrived through the agency of Sir Joshua Reynolds whose numerous own self-portraits emulated (though never directly imitated) Rembrandt in tone, colouring and composition. As a young student in Rome, Reynolds copied Rembrandt's *Self-portrait as St.Paul* (then in the Colonna Palace, now in the Rijksmuseum, Amsterdam) and later was amazed when he came face to face with the audacious brushwork of another (Cat.no.16). He paid tribute to Rembrandt in a number of self-portraits, sometimes overtly and on other occasions more subtly as in his *Self-portrait* shading his eyes (Cat.no.29) and the *Self-portrait as a Doctor of Civil Law* (fig.16) intended as the definitive image of the Royal Academy's President and founding father. During the etching revival of the late nineteenth century Rembrandt's etched portraits made a particular impression, especially his *Self-portrait drawing at a window* (Cat.no.15), which spurred a succession of artists from Whistler (in 1859) onwards to try their hand at recreating themselves in the image of the old master.

The courtly tradition

Compared to the prolific output of Rembrandt that of Peter Paul Rubens (1577-1640) was a model of restraint. When he did paint himself it was either to celebrate or record a friendship, marriage or some other key stage in his personal life, or to fulfil a princely commission, and even then he often did so unwillingly. When in 1623 Lord Danvers relayed the information that Charles, Prince of Wales, was eager to acquire a self-portrait (fig.9) from him, the artist later admitted to a friend that he agreed only because the prince had 'asked so pressingly' and could hardly be refused despite Rubens' feelings of modesty and his belief that it was not fitting to present such a work to a prince of such degree.[19] It was the first self-portrait by a living artist to enter Charles's collection. His reticence to portray himself was not the only way in which Rubens, the most renowned artist in seventeenth-century Europe, differed from his Dutch contemporary. Compared to the sometimes ravaged features of Rembrandt's late self-portraits Rubens always showed himself as a handsome man (covering his middle-aged baldness with a boldly-angled hat); a man of impeccable breeding and taste and above all one who never refered in paint to his artistic profession, the source of his fame and wealth. Unlike Rembrandt or Titian in their late paintings (Cat.no.16, fig.39) he never showed himself brush in hand or, like other north European artists, at work in the studio surrounded by family or friends. Even when he painted himself amongst friends (fig.31) he placed himself in a scholar's study rather than the artist's studio and surrounded himself with philosophers, literary humanists and intellectuals who shared his interest in antiquity. Rubens' was the epitome of the courtly image, the artist as the court gentleman and professional diplomat. Sometimes he showed himself aristocratically holding a fine leather glove and resting his hand on the sword that his rank entitled him to wear, the outward sign of his nobility (Vienna, Kunsthistorisches Museum); on other occasions he wore the gold chain of royal favour discreetly around his neck (fig.9), to suggest the status at court which success as an artist had earned him and which enabled him to buy a palatial residence in Antwerp and a manorial estate in the country.

In the seventeenth century the question of an artist's social status was a key issue. It had as much to do with the artist's behaviour as his art. No one was more aware of that than Rubens' Flemish compatriot and one time assistant, the precociously skilled Anthony van Dyck (Cat.no.4), son of a wealthy Antwerp silk merchant. Van Dyck had his own studio by the age of sixteen, by when he had probably also produced his first painted self-portrait. Rubens' self-image, however courtly, was always discreet and straightforward and certainly displayed less of the narcissistic flamboyance that was striking in Van Dyck's more numerous self-portraits. Van Dyck's behaviour was the epitome of a courtier, as the description of the confident young artist in Italy in the 1620s made clear: 'He behaved more like a noble than an ordinary person; and he shone in rich garments; since he was accustomed in the circle of Rubens to noblemen, ... and anxious to make himself distinguished, he therefore wore - as well as silks - a hat with feathers and brooches, gold chains across his chest, and was accompanied by servants.'[20] Such affected airs irritated his northern compatriots in the artistic colony in Rome but his cultivated manner obviously increased his success with his Genoese portrait sitters. His aristocratic style of living continued when he moved to the English court of Charles I in 1632 and immediately received a knighthood.

That Van Dyck was aware of the need to promote the status of artists through their image is evident in his major series of eighty engraved portraits of famous contemporaries, *Iconography*, the majority of whom (some 52) were artists or connoisseurs. Many were his friends and colleagues from the Flemish art world, including Lievens, whom Van Dyck knew at the English court, but not Rembrandt. In Van Dyck's portraits the artists rarely hold palettes. Instead the emphasis is on a suavely vivacious pose and the silk sheen of their cloaks. The artists were characterized as people of consequence, as full of bravura and animation as the princes, military commanders and statesmen they accompanied in the series; none reflected the mundane reality of working at the easel. The frontispiece to the *Iconography* was Van Dyck's self-portrait shown as a work of art, a sculpted bust on a pedestal, but retaining his favourite elegantly twisted pose looking at the viewer over his shoulder. His self-portraits suggest that Van Dyck was acutely conscious of the image he presented to the world. The air of monumentality added by columns and baroque drapery to even his earliest coyly dandyish self-portraits emulated that found in his portraits of the nobility. The typical elongation of the body, used to give his aristocratic sitters an air of social aloofness and authority, he also practised on himself, particularly on his hands which were always the most eloquent part of his work, acting as an expression of refinement. His strong sense of pride in his social achievements was evident in the gesture of display with his gold chain in his *Self-portrait with a sunflower* (Cat.no.4).

The difference in concept between the elegant courtier developed by Van Dyck and even the most courtly image produced by Rembrandt can be seen in the changing portrayal of Jan Lievens. Lievens' early self-portrait of about 1627, in fancy dress (Copenhagen, Statens Museum), shows him in deeply shadowed profile, dressed exotically in a manner reminiscent of Rembrandt's theatrical style, whereas the National Gallery *Self-portrait* (Cat.no.8) filtered his image through Van Dyck's style. Lievens came under the spell of Van Dyck during his stay at Charles I's court and he continued to model his own style on that of the Flemish artist after his return to Antwerp in the mid 1630s. By the middle of the century Van Dyck and Rembrandt were considered stylistic polar opposites, the Dutchman the example of the rough manner of painting and the Flemish artist the model of the smoothness, that was considered appropriate for court art. Van Dyck's courtly life-style also provided a role-model for other artists, for the essence of the courtier-artist lay as much in his behaviour as in his art. As the eighteenth-century diarist George Vertue wrote of Godfried Schalken's works (Cat.no.17), 'he always sold at a considerable price and do still keep or increase their value besides his art his graceful behaviour and courtesy gained him the respect and esteem among people of quality and distinction'.[21]

Painters' images of themselves soon reflected the social success at court of artists like Rubens and Van Dyck. Both artists provided an alternative self-portrait model to that produced by Rembrandt which had an impact on the future of the genre. Peter Lely (Cat.no.7) modelled his style of portraiture and living on that of Van Dyck and succeeded him as court painter once the post had been revived after the Restoration. Some of

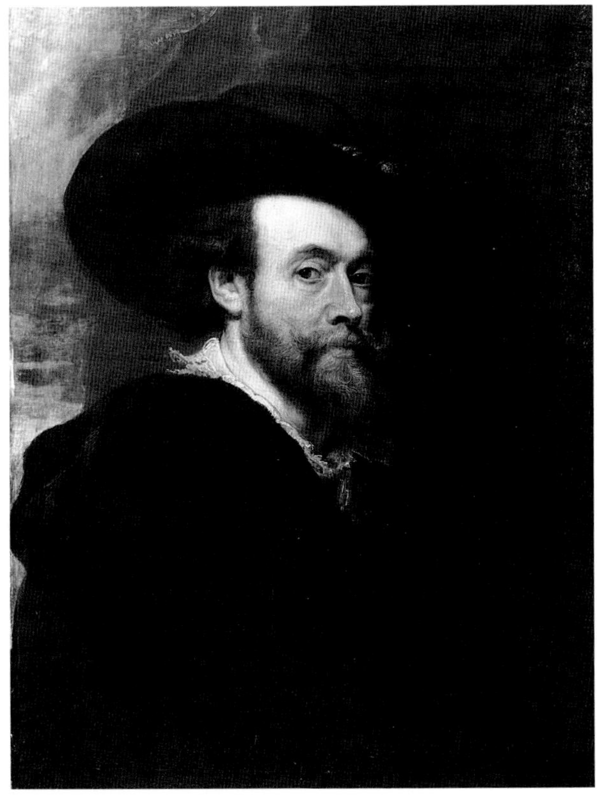

*Fig. 9. Peter Paul Rubens, **Self-portrait**, 1623 (The Royal Collection ©, Her Majesty The Queen)*

Lely's self-portraits also have Vandyckian overtones. Lely's self-portrait painted as a tribute to his friendship with the court architect Hugh May evoked in character that of Van Dyck's with his friend the courtier Endymion Porter (Madrid, Prado Museum), the only occasion on which Van Dyck painted himself with another person. The National Portrait Gallery's self-portrait by Lely (fig.23), in which he showed himself as a connoisseur holding a terracotta statuette, reflected Van Dyck in its pose. Lely's noted art collection also included 37 of the grisailles sketches Van Dyck produced for his *Iconography*. As a court portrait painter Lely was known for treating people of high rank as his equals and never fawning on them, even before he received his knighthood in 1680. Charles II enjoyed an easy relationship with Lely of whom it was said 'it would be hard to determine whether he was a better painter or a more accomplished gentleman'.[22]

Across Europe even painters who were not court artists adopted similar attitudes with their aristocratic patrons. Carlo Maratta (Cat.no.9) treated even his most highly-placed patron as an equal. In one self-portrait he painted himself at the easel but splendidly dressed and completely at ease with his patron the Marchese Pallavicini (Stourhead, Wiltshire). The emphasis on social status was equally well indicated by Maratta's high fees. Although such presumption sometimes amazed visiting British gentlemen on the Grand Tour it only added to Maratta's appeal. He added further to his fame by producing self-portrait drawings (Cat.no.9) to be engraved or given to his Grand Tour patrons as a souvenir of their meeting with him.

Most of these artists were aided in their claims to status by being knighted, as indeed eventually was the creator of that supreme and most original example of the court artist's self-portrait, Diego Velázquez's *Las Meninas (The Maids of Honour)* (fig.10). With unprecedented boldness Velázquez inserted himself into the picture and thus transformed and merged the established genres of royal group portrait and the artist in his studio. It was in some ways a self-portrait of the court itself, an informal scene which nevertheless portrayed court formality and hierarchy in practice, for all figures whether human or animal play the roles established for them at court: whilst the young Infanta Margarita turns to look at her parents King Philip IV and Queen Mariana (seen by us in the mirrored reflection in the centre of the picture), her maids attend to her needs, the dwarves entertain, the dog acts as a calm guardian, the chaperones remain in the background and a palace official stands at the open doorway awaiting the passage of their majesties. For painters, critics and spectators this painting has always been a masterpiece of pictorial illusion, in which the gazes of the royal couple, the princess and her attendants, and above all the artist combine artfully to draw the observer into the artist's world, the pictorial space. To Velázquez the importance of this painting as both a declaration of his personal noble status and a statement about the nobility of art was emphasised when, three years later, he received the noble Order of Santiago and returned to the picture to add the Order's distinctive red cross to his clothes. The story that Philip IV himself painted in the cross, thus endowing the art of painting with royal status, although probably apocryphal, is nevertheless symbolically significant. It mirrored the famous incident in which Emperor Charles V (Philip IV's predecessor as King of Spain) had retrieved one of Titian's fallen brushes

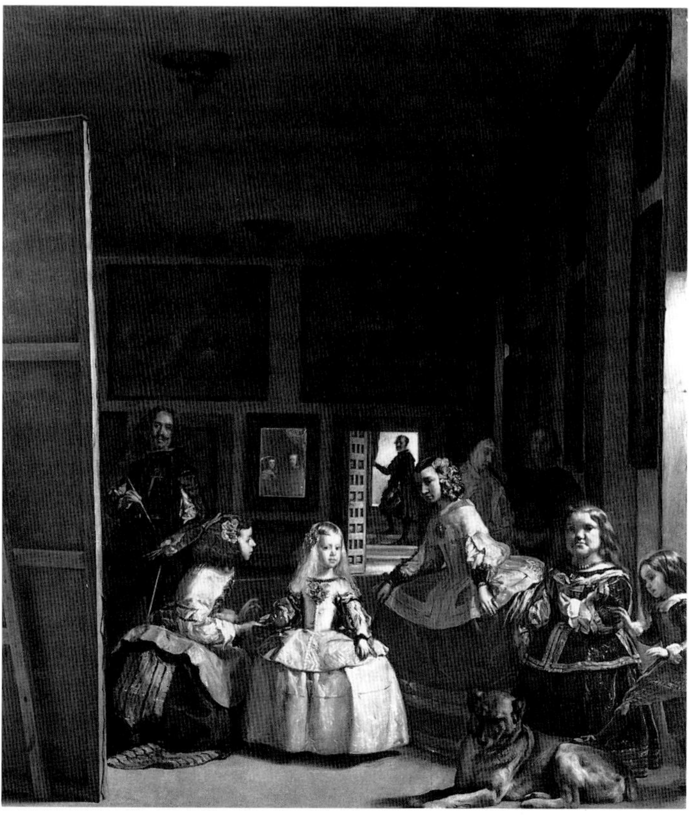

*Fig. 10. Diego Velázquez, **Las Meninas**, 1656 (Madrid, Prado Museum)*

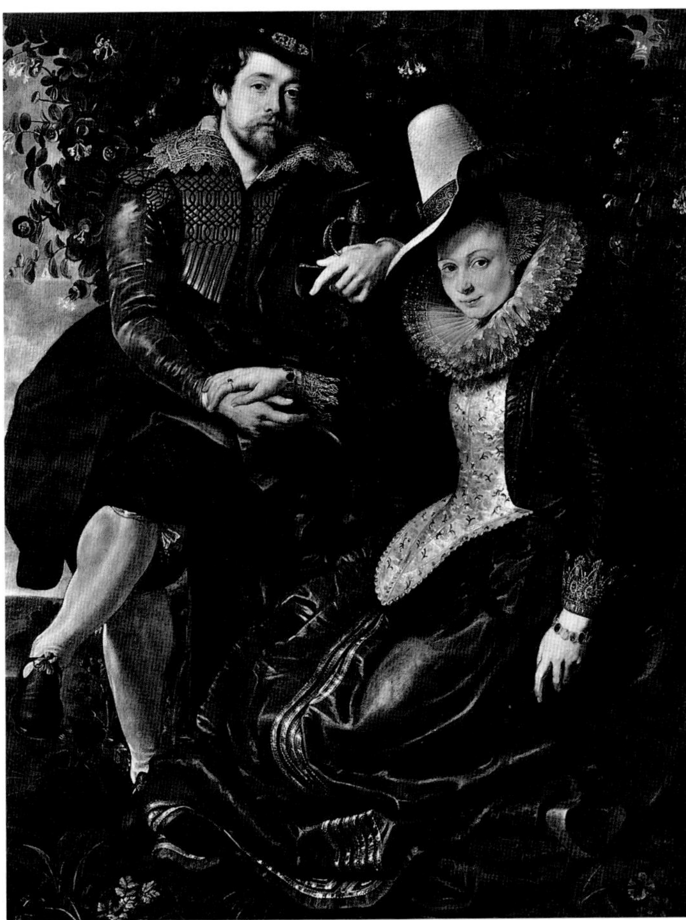

Fig.11. Peter Paul Rubens, *Self-portrait with Isabella Brant: The Honeysuckle Bower*, 1609-10 (Munich, Alte Pinakothek)

from the floor whilst having his portrait painted, a legend which itself was a distant echo of the close relationship between Alexander the Great and his court painter Apelles.

The low social status of the artist in Spanish society had been a long-standing grievance with intellectual and economic consequences. When Velázquez painted *Las Meninas* in 1656 the picture also had a personal significance, as he had just begun the procedure for attaining membership of the Order of Santiago. The importance of the painting as the most powerful statement about the status of the artist and of art is stressed further by the fact that although Van Dyck received a knighthood as soon as he was appointed to King Charles's court (whereas Velázquez had to wait until the close of his career), he never presumed to include himself in any of his royal portraits, let alone in such a dominant position.[23] Van Dyck marked his allegiance to his king in a more allusive manner in his *Self-portrait with a Sunflower*, where the status of the artist as loyal subject symbolised by the chain and the sunflower was very much the reflected glory of his king. That was not the impression given to the viewer by *Las Meninas*. It is their majesties who are the reflections of themselves, while the artist stands, literally overseeing all other figures, royal or servant. He is dressed in the clothes of a courtier and with the key of his office as Palace Chamberlain, but at work in his studio in the royal palace on yet another court portrait; whether a portrait of their majesties or of their only daughter and her entourage one will never know for Velázquez has resolutely shown us only the back of the huge canvas dominating the foreground of the picture. As the artist stands back contemplating the scene in front of him during that all important creative pause between imagining what to paint and painting it, *Las Meninas* becomes as much a 'portrait' about art and its creation as about the artist and his court or the princess and her entourage. Velázquez's remarkable and seemingly egalitarian inclusion of the artist in a group portrait of a royal family continued to have an impact in the group portraits produced for the Spanish court (one of the most hierarchical in Europe) in the late eighteenth and early nineteenth centuries by the court artist Francisco Goya (1746-1828). He repeatedly introduced himself into such portraits, partly in emulation of Velázquez, notably in his *Charles IV and his family* of 1800 (Madrid, Prado Museum), *The Infante Don Luis and his family* of 1783 (Parma, Magnani-Rocca Foundation) and also of 1783 the portrait of Charles IV's prime minister *Count Floridablanca* (Madrid, Bank of Spain).

Love as the inspirer of Art

As Rubens knew, behind the surface of the artist's courtly image the reality was still that the painter was not a gentleman but a craftsman. When Rubens came to choose his second wife he wrote that although some would have had him marry a court lady he chose a middle-class wife (the daughter of a silk merchant) 'one who would not blush to see me take my brushes in my hand'.[24] Second to displaying his role as a courtier Rubens painted his portrait most often as part of personal and tender celebrations of marriage and family life. His double portrait of himself seated beside his first wife Isabella Brant, *The Honeysuckle Bower* (fig.11), was probably painted either at the request of Isabella's father or as a present to him from the couple, showing both their prosperity and domestic contentment. *The Walk in the Garden* (Munich, Alte Pinakothek), the first of several pictures to honour his family life with his second wife Hélène Fourment, was painted shortly after their marriage. The garden settings of both were intended as symbolic and actual visualizations of the medieval imagery of the garden of love, the couples' poses and dress conveying both mutual affection and social position.

Other artists were equally inspired by the informal Rubensian approach to this traditional imagery, none more so than Jacob Jordaens (1593-1678). His large *Self-portrait with his family* of 1621-22 (fig.12) posed his wife and daughter seated in a garden with the artist proudly holding his favourite lute, the instrument symbolising both domestic harmony and music, a sister art to painting. The maidservant included in the family group ensured that the portrait combined a display of family devotion with the artist's social advancement. Jordaens' self-portrait was one of a series in which he grouped himself first with his parents, brothers and sisters c.1615-16 (St. Petersburg, Hermitage Museum) and in the same year with the family of his painting master Adam van Noort (Kassel, Gemäldegalerie), whose daughter Katharina he married in 1616. The three portraits may have been intended to mark both professional and personal celebrations, the artist's engagement and his entry into the Antwerp Guild of artists in 1615-16 and his appointment as the Guild's Dean in 1621. All convey a convivial sense of how much his domestic and artistic families meant to him.

Artists' self-portraits with their wives and families had a strong tradition in the Netherlands which continued to flourish in different forms throughout the seventeenth century and into the eighteenth. From the end of the fifteenth century examples of double portraits of an artist and his wife can be found, such as that produced by the Master of Frankfurt in 1496 (Antwerp, Koninklijk Museum) probably to commemorate his marriage, which also showed the arms of the Antwerp painters' guild. Other popular forms included the artist at his easel with his wife and family, or painting his wife's portrait. The growth of publications in the Netherlands by humanist and religious writers and moralists emphasising familial love, which had begun in the 1560s and had become a flood by the seventeenth century, stimulated the more informal double portrait format produced by Rubens. By the end of the century Adriaen van der Werff (1659-1722) painted himself

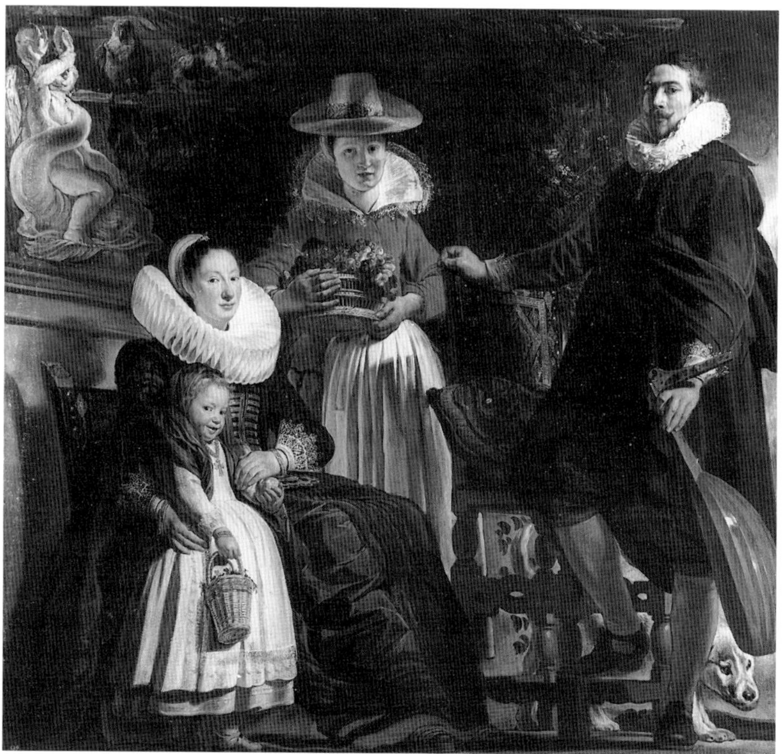

*Fig.12. Jacob Jordaens, **Self-portrait with his Family**, 1621-22,*
(Madrid, Prado Museum)

holding, as an example of his work, a portrait of his wife and child (Amsterdam, Rijksmuseum). The popularity of this self-portrait type was probably bolstered by the humanist theme of the creative power of love, which was derived from the legend related by the classical author Pliny the Elder of the young Corinthian woman who drew the outline of the shadow of her lover's head and so discovered the art of painting.[25] The theme of love as the ultimate inspirer of the arts was strongly promoted in sixteenth- and seventeenth-century Netherlands and Flanders both in humanist circles and as a suitable subject for festival decorations by painters' guilds and staging by rhetoricians' clubs during city celebrations such as those held in Antwerp.[26]

The artist inspired by his domestic milieu remained a specifically Netherlandish-based topos throughout the seventeenth, eighteenth and nineteenth centuries, unlike the type of self-portrait which declared an artist's status or showed him or her with the instruments of their craft, which was found Europe-wide. Even those countries such as Britain which had absorbed many painters from the Netherlands and Flanders and whose artistic practice derived much from their example seem to have ignored this as a theme worthy of development. The few British examples of artists portraying themselves with their wives include: Allan Ramsay's unfinished painting (Cat.no.28), begun whilst on honeymoon, which showed him in the process of capturing his wife's features on canvas; and Richard Cosway's etched *Self-portrait with his wife Maria* (Cat.no.20), a talented artist in her own right (although she spent most of her married life acting as hostess at her husband's fashionable parties). Both these artists sought inspiration from Rubens' *Honeysuckle Bower* self-portrait (fig.11), Cosway blatantly and Ramsay obliquely. Ramsay is known to have sketched it on his honeymoon.[27] The rare British artist who painted himself with his wife in his studio, such as the Scottish artist William Kidd (1790-1863), did so as a parody, turning the artist and his muse into a merry tippling painter in a shambles of a studio (fig.13). The indifference to the theme perhaps emerged from the negative attitude of the British artistic establishment to the effect of marriage and domestic life on an artist's creative abilities. Reynolds was supposed to have caustically exclaimed to a young painter seeking advice, 'Married then you are ruined as an artist'.[28] Whilst Millais once told a patron, 'People had better buy my pictures now, when I am working for fame, than a few years later, when I shall be married for a wife and children'.[29] The same sentiment was more movingly and perceptively echoed by the wife of George Kelly (Cat.no.48) in a letter to her son: 'Dear old Father had to work for bread and butter, not for fame or for important exhibition pictures'. The attitude was perhaps less due to misogyny than to a realistic assessment of the effect on an artist's reputation of the need to produce potboilers for money. It was a particularly acute problem for those artists in the eighteenth and nineteenth centuries who worked for a living without the certain support of court or gentry patronage. Without the backing of a court post enjoyed by both Ramsay and Cosway or a successful and lucrative studio a spouse and family might seem less like an artist's muse and inspiration. Significantly, perhaps, successful women artists like Kauffmann and Vigée Le Brun often remained partnerless for major periods of their career.

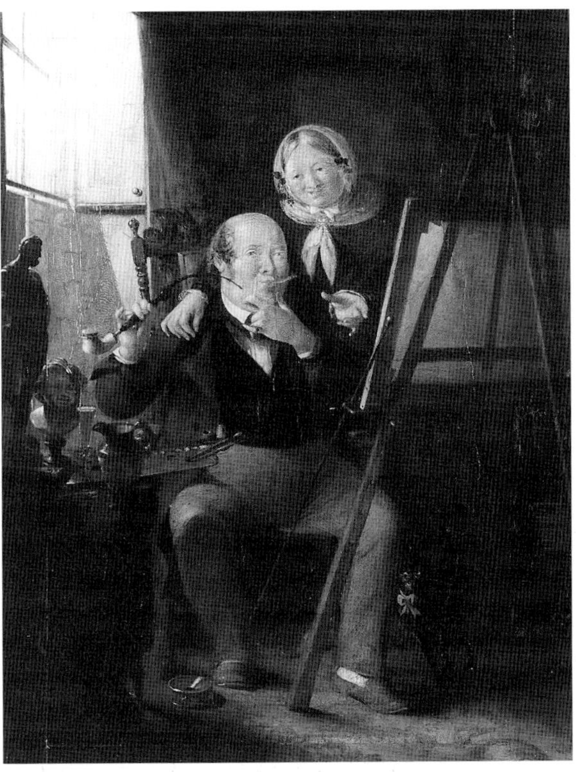

*Fig.13. William Kidd, **Self-portrait with his Wife**, 1850s*
(Arbroath, The Patrick Allan-Fraser of Hospitalfield Trust)

The Institutional Impetus

In the sixteenth century the genre of self-portraiture had been given a stimulus by the publication of Vasari's revised edition of *Lives of the Artists* (1568), which spawned a number of equivalents across northern Europe in the following century. But it was only when Cardinal Leopoldo de' Medici (1617-1675) established in the Uffizi in Florence between 1664 and 1675 a collection exclusively of painted self-portraits that a major institutional impetus for the genre was created. There were precedents for the Cardinal's collection in the small groups of self-portraits found in the collections of artists' academies and princely rulers. Leopoldo's was itself assembled in a methodical and systematic manner around a core of about fifteen self-portraits that had been gathered haphazardly by his predecessors. The Accademia del Disegno in Florence also had some self-portraits and its example was followed by the artists' academy in Rome, but neither of them held only self-portraits, they collected portraits or copies of portraits of illustrious artists as well. In northern Europe the painters' craft guilds had played a similar though less planned role in stimulating some artists to portray themselves in order to commemorate their acceptance into the guild.

Perhaps the most notable precedent for the Uffizi collection was the self-portraits owned by Charles I, which numbered at least twelve by the time of his death and included the work of Rubens (fig.9), Van Dyck, Daniel Mytens (acquired in 1630) and Rembrandt (Cat.no.11). The self-portrait by Artemisia Gentileschi (fig.14) may have been presented after she had joined her father at court in 1638. With the exception of Rembrandt all of these artists had worked for Charles I, but the King also owned historic self-portraits including a Dürer (fig.5) presented to him by the city of Nuremberg, a Titian and a Joos van Cleve (bought by the king from a Dutch merchant). Although the King hung his court artists Rubens, Van Dyck and Mytens together in the Breakfast Chamber outside the King's Withdrawing Room the rest were scattered about the Palace of Whitehall.[30] Charles I's collection was not hung as a coherent whole as were the self-portraits acquired by Cardinal Leopoldo de' Medici.

The Cardinal's collection was originally kept together in the private Medici family picture gallery in the Pitti Palace. After Leopoldo's death (when they numbered some 80 paintings) they were transferred by his nephew Cosimo III to a single room, specially created and decorated in his honour, in the more public Uffizi. Leopoldo was the last great patron in the Medici tradition, a poet, a dilettante artist and collector. He had been educated in the Galilean culture of scientific and philosophical enquiry and his large and varied collections reflected his many interests, which ran from the performing and visual arts to theology and the natural sciences. His collection was in the tradition of the seventeenth-century intellectual world, encyclopaedic and all-encompassing. In addition to 697 pictures it embraced some 4,000 medals and coins, 500 miniatures, 700 pieces of porcelain and miriads of statues, arms, gems, and minerals as well as a magnificent library.[31] His interest in portraits of artists may have stemmed from his involvement in the scheme for the frescoes on the ceiling of the west corridor in the Uffizi (1658-79), meant to illustrate the achievement of Florence's most famous citizens. However, his decision to collect only self-portraits, rather than portraits of artists painted by others, also reflected the seventeenth-century's changing concept of portraiture in which a portrait was no longer merely a record of someone's features but an expression of their innermost character and soul.

Leopoldo's collecting proceeded in a methodical manner once the first self-portraits had been commissioned from Guercino and Pietro da Cortona in 1664. By 1666 he had distributed lists of portraits already acquired and soon had agents all over Europe commissioning works (Cat.no.17, fig.26) and searching out suitable purchases. His agents included not only diplomats and other collectors but also artists such as Cortona and Ciro Ferri. The Cardinal also kept close contact with Florentine artists, particularly admiring the meticulous but painfully slow painter of portraits and devotional religious pictures Carlo Dolci. He probably commissioned from him the arresting self-portrait (Florence, Uffizi, see Cat.no.3) which was completed one year before the Cardinal's death. The commission was in line with a gradually adopted policy of ordering self-portraits directly from the artists and rewarding them with a chain and medal showing the portrait of the grand duke. Although by Leopoldo's death the collection included works by foreigners such as Rembrandt and Dürer the bulk of the pictures were by Italians, and almost half were by Tuscan, Bolognese and Venetian painters. It was left to his nephew Grand Duke Cosimo III and the first custodian of the collection, the artist biographer Baldinucci, to expand the foreign representation through Cosimo's extensive travels in Germany, Holland, Spain, Portugal, England and France. Though Cosimo's interest in art was limited he had a particular regard for Dutch art of the detailed smoothly-finished fijnschilder school, and he acquired several small-format self-portraits by its masters for the Medici collection. Under Cosimo and Baldinucci a form of standardization was also introduced and some artists were requested to produce self-portraits that would conform to particular types, either showing themselves in the act of painting or with an example of their work.[32] The collection continued to grow steadily to 1710, by which time it had more than 180 paintings arranged by schools in a single room whose walls were lined with red velvet to imitate the famous Uffizi Tribuna, which housed the Medici's most precious works of art. It was hung from skirting to ceiling with self-portraits apart from a niche opposite the entrance in which was placed a statue of Leopoldo. Growth was more sporadic from 1710 onwards due to worsening economic conditions in the Grand Duchy, but by then the collection was considered unrivalled and was famous across Europe.

The establishment of Leopoldo's collection was influential in promoting other such assemblages, initially in Florence. That of Antonio Pazzi, a pupil and collaborator of Giovanni Campiglia (Cat.no.19) who had been custodian of the Uffizi collection, included some 120 paintings, particularly representative of seventeenth- and eighteenth-century Florentine artists. In the 1760s it was acquired and merged with the Uffizi's necessitating the use of a second room. The Florentine diplomat, collector and writer at the court of Cosimo III, Niccolò Gabburri (1676-1742), another curator of the Uffizi collection, amassed a large number of drawn self-portraits originally brought together to illustrate his collected biographies of Tuscan artists *Vite dei Pittori*, begun about 1719 but never published.[33] Gabburri may have seen his collection as matching on paper the painted series in the Uffizi. It included drawings by contemporaries and friends in Florence and elsewhere, including Campiglia and Maratta, which were often remarkable for their vitality. The most prized works with the most elaborate mounts, however, were those by artists who were long dead and whose rarity value was greater. Gabburri may have promised artists that their drawings would be engraved in return for their donation, thus encouraging production. Like the Grand-ducal collection Gabburri also reserved one room in his palace to display his collection. A similar series of portrait drawings formed in Rome by the biographer Nicola Pio was almost certainly assembled between 1714 and 1719 as an adjunct to his manuscript anthology of artists' lives. Such collections of self-portraits on paper were particularly attractive to artists and to a wider social range of collectors with smaller financial resources, as they committed both parties to much less expenditure: of time, effort and materials on the part of the artist, and money and storage space on the part of the collector.

Women Artists

For women painters the need to establish their status as artists was always paramount. The proud desire to declare themselves artists and claim for themselves a place alongside their male colleagues continued to act as a spur for women's self-portraits from the sixteenth century through to the dawn of the twentieth. In the sixteenth century artists such as Lavinia Fontana (1552-1614) often included written inscriptions on their paintings to stress that they were both female and painters, so that their image could not be mistaken for a male artist's wife or model. England's first professional woman painter, Mary Beale (Cat.no.1), stares steadily out at us and insistently points to herself as the artist and main breadwinner for her family standing next to her.

Beale, like several of the most prolific women artists of the eighteenth century such as Angelica Kauffmann and Vigée Le Brun, had begun work early in life with paternal backing in order to support family and relatives. For all of them painting was never the amateur pursuit recommended for leisured women in the seventeenth and eighteenth centuries, but a way of making a living. In the late eighteenth century Adélaïde Labille-Guiard made clear her claim to equal status with male artists by showing herself seated at an easel in a studio with two female pupils watching her (New York, Metropolitan Museum). The portrait was painted in 1785 to celebrate her entry to the Académie as one of only four women allowed this honour. Labille-Guiard's more celebrated compatriot and rival Elisabeth Vigée Le Brun was another such woman. Her acceptance by the Académie two years earlier was almost entirely the result of the popular success of her *Self-portrait* (Cat.no.35), in which she successfully emulated Rubens by modelling her pose, dress and fluid technique on those used by the Flemish artist in his coquettish portrait of his future sister-in-law Susanna Lunden (fig.32). The *Self-portrait* was part of a process of selling her skills as a colourist and portrait painter by 'selling' herself; with her ever-present gentle smile, loose trailing hair and large eyes Vigée Le Brun's self-portraits were very much concerned with self-advertisement. Unlike Labille-Guiard there was nothing discreet or sedate about her self-image. She was willing to use her femininity and charm to promote her career and social position. Her many self-portraits (twenty or so) were frequently exhibited publicly and engraved and some were painted for admirers. Vigée Le Brun's self-portraits were not intended to be contemplative or reflective in nature; whether they showed her as an artist with palette and easel, or as a loving mother hugging her daughter they were always about self-projection, as indeed was her life-style at the court of Queen Marie-Antoinette. She was a fashionable society lady as well as an artist and combined the two roles when she created a new dress style, wearing simply-draped white muslin or lawn gowns with shawls and loose unpowdered hair. The emphasis of her self-portraits on her looks, clothing and maternal instincts have led in the recent past to feminist disapproval of her work.[34] Unfavourable contrasts have been drawn with the self-portrait by one of her predecessors, the leading female artist of the seventeenth century, Artemisia Gentileschi (1593-1652) (fig.14), despite the fact that they were equally technically skilled and as successful in manipulating their image, and both were ambitious for professional recognition, social status and financial success. Vigée Le Brun succeeded to a remarkable degree. At the height of her career she was acknowledged as one of the foremost painters of her time and had been made a member of many of Europe's most distinguished academies and institutes of art. Her memoirs, written as a diary but not published until near the end of her career, reveal that she was also aware of and concerned for her future reputation. Her self-portraits not only celebrated her status as one of France's most renowned artists of her generation, (despite her post French Revolution exile from her native land), but also provided a stylish role model for female sitters and sister artists, like her pupil Marie Victoire Lemoine, who in 1796 painted herself at work in Vigée Le Brun's studio with her mentor standing beside her (fig.15).

The boldness of Vigée Le Brun's self-imaging was comparable, though in dramatic contrast, to that of Artemisia Gentileschi's *Self-portrait as the Allegory of Painting* of a century and a half earlier (fig.14). Instead of the manicured charming presence, all too aware of the spectator's gaze, Gentileschi presents us with a vigorously active artist, so totally absorbed in her work that she seems as heedless of the image presented by her

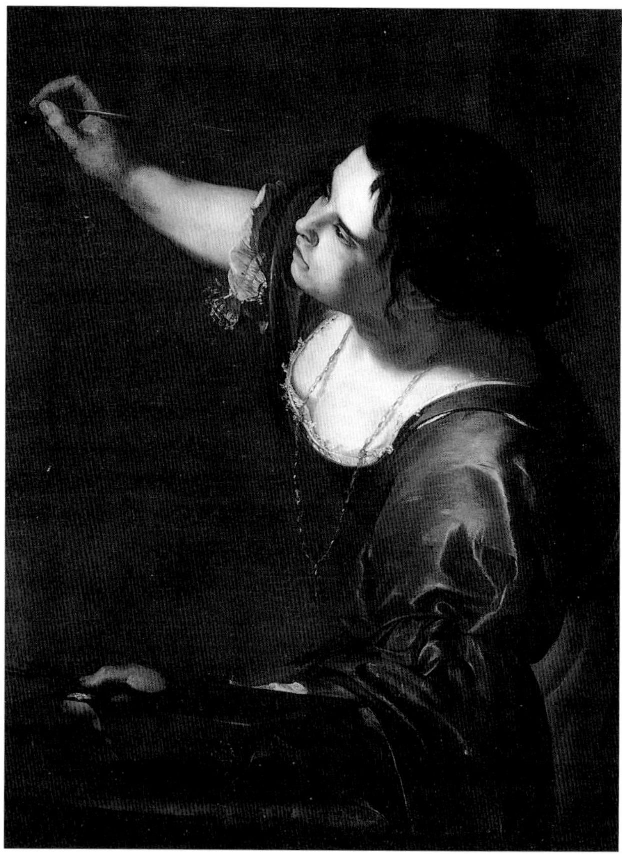

Fig.14. Artemisia Gentileschi, **Self-portrait as La Pittura,** *about 1630 (The Royal Collection ©, Her Majesty The Queen)*

unkempt locks of hair and ungainly pose as she is of us the viewers. The self-portrait was probably originally meant for her main patron in Rome, the scholar and collector Cassiano dal Pozzo, but never reached him and was instead presented to Charles I. One can well imagine that her comment might have been of this painting as it was of another 'And I will show your Most Illustrious Lordship what a woman can do, hoping to give you the greatest pleasure'.[35] Artemisia's self-portrait is the only one by either male or female artist that gives any impression of the sheer physicality and hard work of a painter, yet paradoxically she showed herself in the guise of an abstract personification, the allegorical figure of Painting (Pittura) as described in Cesare Ripa's best-selling emblem book *Iconologia*, first published in 1593.[36] The loose hair denoting inspired imagination, the mask on a chain swinging from her neck representing imitation and the dress of changing hues which demonstrated an artist's skill in handling colour had all been vividly brought to life in a naturalistic snapshot of a painter at work, about to turn her artistic concept into actuality on a blank canvas. Gentileschi showed herself as the living embodiment of Painting, in her the person and the concept were one.

Women artists had this one advantage over their male colleagues in their self-imaging, for only they could directly and personally identify themselves with the allegorical representation of La Pittura, traditionally personified as a woman. Seventeenth-century male artists who tried to show themselves as personifications of the art of painting were forced to do so by indirect methods through awkward conjunctions of attributes and figures. The seventeenth-century Italian artist G.-D. Cerrini rather incongruously showed himself as a painted self-portrait held by a half-naked woman representing Painting (Bologna, Pinacoteca Nazionale), whilst Poussin more plausibly placed himself in front of a painted image of La Peinture (Paris, Louvre Museum), but in both cases the figure of the painter and the figure of Painting remained separate. The most direct, naturalistic and witty means of combining the painter's person with the personification of Painting was available only to women. The opportunity offered to women in their self-portraits meant that they could slip in an out of symbolic roles without undermining their individuality, and could create multiple levels on which their character could be read by the viewer. Allegorised self-portraits often failed to work on multiple levels for men as the symbolic figures were just tacked on to the composition and when they were female could create unwanted salacious overtones. Men usually preferred, therefore, to suggest the artistic inspirational muse through art objects as in Michael Dahl's *Self-portrait* (Cat.no.2), where his finger pointing to a classical bust pays tribute both to the artist's source of inspiration in general and the specific importance for an artist's education of the study of classical sculpture.

In the eighteenth century women artists continued to experiment ingeniously with their ability to combine the allegorical, role-playing and portrait traditions in self-portraiture. Angelica Kauffmann became part of her own history painting in her *Portrait of the Artist Hestitating between the Arts of Music and Painting* (Cat.no.25) and produced what is probably one of the

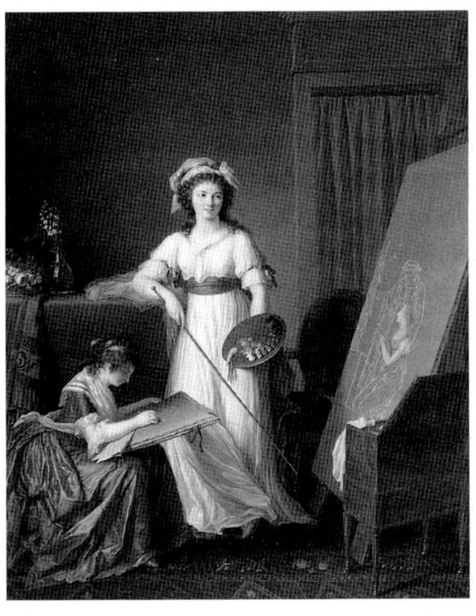

Fig.15. Marie Victoire Lemoine, **The Atelier of a Woman Painter**, *1796, (New York, The Metropolitan Museum of Art)*

largest self-portraits. She took as the theme for her history painting a private autobiographical event in which as a young girl she was made to choose between her passion for music and a profession as a painter, which was considered intellectually and physically more arduous, requiring lengthier training but ultimately leading to higher rewards. She turned this real dilemma into a metaphorical statement about the status of women artists and the choices they had to make, which was as bold in concept as it was in scale. Her self-portrait acted as a clear declaration of the sense of achievement that followed her decision to abandon music and choose a path traditionally reserved for men. Since the Renaissance proficiency in music had always been considered a more suitable accomplishment for young women, as was implied by Lavinia Fontana's self-portrait (Florence, Pitti Palace), which showed her seated at a clavichord rather than an easel, thus masking her unfeminine artistic talent behind her more decorous skill as a musician. The sisterly rivalry between painting and other Liberal Arts, especially poetry and music, featured in other Kauffmann self-portraits and was part of the long-standing battle to raise painting to the ranks of arts which were considered intellectually superior. Music also occasionally surfaced in self-portraits by men, where it helped to symbolise the breadth of an artist's creativity. The difficulty of creating compositions which combined naturally with abstract female personification ensured that their self-portraits were usually more prosaic, such as that of the nineteenth-century painter William Huggins, who indicated his love of music by inserting a favourite guitar into his *Self-portrait* (Cat.no.47).

Angelica Kauffmann's self-portraits, like those of her French counterpart, were much in demand among her friends and patrons. Two of the several versions of Angelica's *Hesitating between the Arts* appear to have been produced on commission, one for another woman artist, Franziska Schöpfer, and the other possibly for the French ambassador in Rome.[37] From Gentileschi onwards there has probably always been a large market for women's self-portraits. Their curiosity value makes them more likely to have been commissioned and it is still the

case that they receive more public attention than those by men. As a general rule of thumb the more visually complex self-portraits were usually produced by artists such as Angelica Kauffmann and James Barry (Cat.no.38), who saw themselves as history painters and consequently conceived their images in that light. This is particularly evident in Kauffmann's complex role-playing and allegorical self-portraits such as her *Zeuxis choosing his models for his Helen of Troy* (Providence, Rhode Island, Brown University), which used classical themes to explore the role of women artists in a male-dominated artistic community. In the latter she inserted her self-portrait as one of the five models from whom Zeuxis chose the most perfect parts to paint the portrait of the legendary Helen of Troy, but she placed herself behind the artist's back, usurping his position by picking up his brushes and standing ready to paint in front of the canvas, bare except for Kauffmann's signature.[38] Portraits of Kauffmann by other artists such as Nathaniel Dance (Stamford, Burghley House), show her in modern dress (not neo-classical), as a hard-working no-nonsense painter rather than a muse of painting. Such a strong element of self-identification with the artistic muses brought problems in its wake as was made clear by Henry Fuseli's comment that Kauffmann's 'heroines are herself' and the scandalous suggestion that when she painted classical subjects she was her own nude model, which she vigorously denied as it pandered to male fantasies about women artists.

The Eighteenth Century

By the end of the 1730s a market for self-portraits had been created across Europe. Furthermore, between 1731 and 1762 the fame of the Uffizi collection was extended with the publication in ten deluxe illustrated volumes of its picture collection, the *Musaeum Florentinum*. These volumes, some of which were illustrated by Campiglia (Cat.no.19), prompted competition between rivals. Artists such as Angelica Kauffmann in 1763 and 1787, Mengs in 1773, Reynolds in 1775 and Vigée Le Brun all donated their portraits to the Uffizi to hang alongside the illustrious faces of Titian and Veronese. By 1779 the artist Giuseppe Macpherson had reproduced in miniature form the whole self-portrait collection which was subsequently presented by Earl Cowper to George III instead of a Mengs self-portrait (Cat.no.26) originally offered. The Uffizi collection gained the summit of its influence in the eighteenth century. By the end of the nineteenth century entry had become an honour seldom sought and rarely productive of innovative or dramatic compositions.

In addition to the impetus provided for self-portraiture by motives of prestige, artistic rivalry, and money, demand was further stimulated by artists' academies across Europe. Several of Vigée Le Brun's many self-portraits were produced for academies as geographically diverse as those of Rome and St. Petersburg. The regulations of the Académie in Paris encouraged a confident pride in the status of French artists, which was reflected in the magnificent portraits of artists submitted on entry by French engravers and by self-portraits such as Nicolas de Largillierre's *Artist in his Studio* (Norfolk, Virginia, Chrysler Museum), painted around 1686. The artists were usually shown in casual dress, but the grand impression given by the size and quality of the engraved portraits was increased after 1704 when it was stipulated that they should be presented in elaborate three-dimensionally conceived surrounds. Such institutional support helped create in France an artistic community that had a much better developed sense of its self-image, a higher social profile and a greater pride in its status than was the case for artist colleagues across the Channel, as someone like Hogarth (Cat.no.23), sensitively attuned to such matters, must have realised when he visited Paris in 1743.

In England the Royal Academy from its foundation in 1769 had wanted to raise the quality of art education as much as the social standing of the artist. It wished to drag the English profession away from its dependance on 'imitative' portraiture by encouraging an indigenous school of the higher, more intellectual genre of history painting, and so evolved a haphazard and arbitrary set of rules that implicitly and, after 1816 (when it rejected Raeburn's *Self-portrait*, fig.30), explicitly discouraged artists from submitting self-portraits as diploma works.[39] The restriction had no adverse effect as it came too late in the day, for the eighteenth century proved to be the age of the self-portrait in Britain. The Academy itself had in its founder Sir Joshua Reynolds' own portrait (fig.16) one of the most imposing self-portraits of the age, a confident statement of the artist's pride in his profession and his predecessors. For any self-respecting British artist the production of a self-portrait became so obligatory that even a provincial English artist such as Hamlet Winstanley (Cat.no.36), with only one trip to Rome under the belt, felt the need to celebrate his professional status by painting one. In the first half of the eighteenth century, for provincial and less well known male artists such as Winstanley and Peter Tillemans (Cat.no.34), the self-portrait was still a means to establish their status or role in society, but as self-portraiture became a more routine task other male artists sought to explore more thoroughly other aspects of self-portraiture and diversify into new forms.

Whereas seventeenth-century portraits can be characterized as either manifesting status or revealing inner thought, those of the eighteenth century sought to explore the sitter's character and their social relationships. As artists' concerns moved away from a simple advertisement of their skills and social advancement their self-portraits also diversified, and in reaction to the overt gesticulation of a seventeenth-century self-portrait they sought restraint. The conventional format showing the artist in his studio was the first to be revised to create a refined commentary on

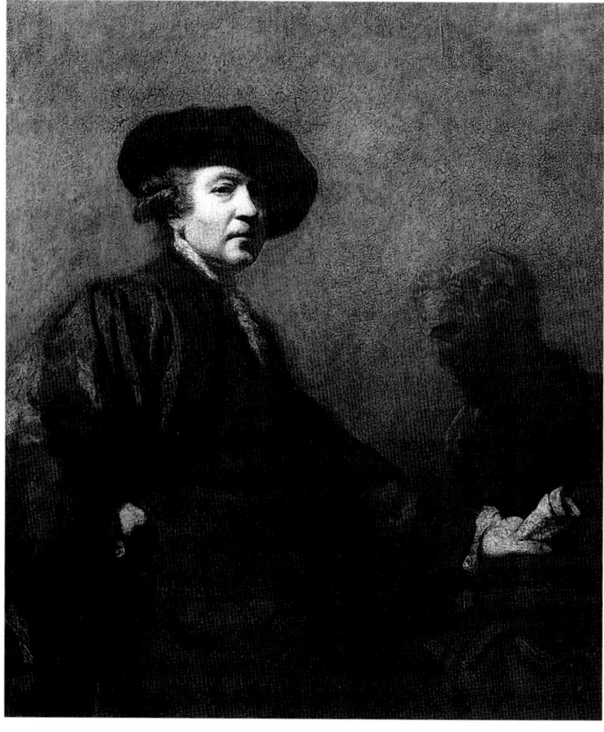

Fig.16. Sir Joshua Reynolds,
Self-portrait as a Doctor of
Civil Law, *about 1780, (London,*
Royal Academy of Arts)

the changing relationship between artist and patron. As portraiture developed toward the greater informality of the conversation piece so the artist was increasingly seen alongside his patron in the studio. Nor was it any longer the case that the artist used the artist-patron relationship purely to highlight his own rising status. As the self-portrait of a relatively unknown aspiring painter-craftsman like Tillemans suggests (Cat.no.34). A patron might gain as much kudos by association with an artist as the artist with the patron. Tillemans' patron Cox Macro was obviously proud of his connection, ordering on the painter's death a terracotta bust of him from Rysbrack and recording the death with an inscription on the last painting on which the artist had worked. The self-portrait had now become a commentary on the artist's social experience.

The polished sophistication of Hayman's studio-cum-fashionable salon provided an appropriate setting to cultivate his self-assured somewhat self-satisfied patron. Though Hayman (Cat.no.22) is suitably deferential towards his patron Grosvenor Bedford, the discussion between them is obviously that of near equals. The artist's studio as shown in self-portraits was rarely a realistic depiction of the artist's own workplace, and Hayman's was derived from a French engraving. The studio was primarily a means to demonstrate the visual education and training required to produce an artist. The artistic education provided by the Italian Grand Tour and the inspiration derived from classical and baroque Rome also supplied a subject for self-portraiture in the eighteenth century. David Allan made his only excursion into the grand manner when he was studying in Italy producing a self-portrait as a souvenir of his formal academic training for his patron at home (Cat.no.18). Allan's self-portrait was nevertheless in a long standing tradition harking back at least to Heemskerck's *Self-portrait in front of the Colisseum* (Cambridge, Fitzwilliam Museum) of 1553.

By the late eighteenth century the hierarchically charged artist-patron relationships had subtly developed into seemingly more egalitarian friendships, as reflected by Romney's self-portrait with his patron, son and friend, significantly entitled *The Four Friends*. The title consciously aped that of Rubens' *The Four Philosophers* (fig.31), which may have been its pictorial inspiration, but the picture also reflected the important role played by friendship in eighteenth century British politics and society. Cicero's *On Friendship*, a book prominently placed in Romney's picture, was a key text for Georgian society because its views accorded with those of his eighteenth century readers. Georgian England was Cicero's great age, a successful and eulogistic biography was produced, translations of his speeches and letters were published and his discourse on friends and friendship along with other treatises on duty formed the basis of a Georgian gentleman's moral outlook. His view of society as a network of friendship ties and connections which men must use to progress, particularly those (like artists) without the benefits of high birth, also had strong affinities with that of Georgian England. A self-portrait helped to increase an artist's prospects, particularly one as neurotically shy and diffident about himself as Romney. Self-portraits which confirmed and reaffirmed artistic friendships and patronage ties also allowed the artist to introduce a greater informality, an element of relaxed playfulness or even raucous laughter in the case of Alexander Runciman's self-portrait with his friend John Brown (Cat.no.31).

The English art establishment's concern to provide an institutional structure for the development of the profession and a theoretical basis for art education in the form of an academy also encouraged a particular type of self-portrait, which publicized the artist's theories and acted as a statement of an artistic creed. The most complex and didactic, as well as the wittiest and earliest of these manifesto self-portraits was Hogarth's *Self-portrait with his Pug* (Cat.no.23), in which his belief that the artist should be guided by nature not artistic rules was set out. Hogarth's portrait is shown as a painting within a painting, flanked by his palette, signifying art, and representing nature as his dog, an alter ego after whom his detractors would referred to Hogarth as Painter Pug.[40] Hogarth felt greatly the need for English artists, led by himself, to create a type of art which was distinctive from the example provided by Continental practice and particularly the old master art of the Italian schools. His desire to popularise his own work and his ambition to create a market for modern British art, independent of the demands of individual patrons, led him to use a number of publicity techniques to advertise his paintings to a larger market across Europe. Some techniques were novel, such as raffling his pictures, others tried and tested, like the consistent engraving of his pictures. His self-portrait of 1745 (Cat.no.23), was itself engraved as the frontispiece to volumes of his collected prints, and was yet another subtle way to publicise himself and promote his views on art to a wider audience than could be achieved through the painted canvas alone. Hogarth's background, as a self-taught artist who had progressed from an apprenticeship as an engraver of satirical prints through theatrical scene painting to creating portraits, satirically didactic conversation pieces and ambitious history paintings, may have increased his desire to develop academic theories on art and popularise them through a practical example of his work, a self-portrait. The inclusion on the palette of his self-portrait of the serpentine 'Line of Beauty and Grace' an abstract concept which he did not discuss publicly until his treatise *The Analysis of Beauty* was published in 1753, successfully aroused curiosity and speculation as to its meaning among artists, connoisseurs and the public, and showed Hogarth's eye for self-publicity. He even had the 'Line of Beauty' painted as a crest on his coach, rather like an advertising gimmick.[41] Other Hogarth self-portraits such as the *Self-portrait painting the Comic Muse* (fig.27) also show that he was concerned to use this type of portrait to say something about his relationship to his work and its relationship to society.

Other English artists also sought to assert their role within mainstream European art through their self-portraits, but unlike Hogarth, Joshua Reynolds sought to emulate the old masters and Continental practice, as a succession of his self-portraits makes clear. Several of Reynolds' earliest self-portraits, including the *Self-portrait* aged about 24 (Cat.no.29), reflected a dependence on Rembrandt's technique and style and a fascination with the hallmark of his youthful self-portraits, the shadow cast over the eyes. Reynolds, as always, never borrowed motifs directly but hid his source in an everyday gesture. Rembrandt was enormously popular with mid eighteenth-century British painters and collectors and the legends surrounding his life and character also influenced artists. Hogarth identified himself with Rembrandt, particularly in the last ten years of his life. He rarely sought to imitate Rembrandt's style but rather what he took to be his principles as a painter of everyday life, guided by nature not rules and the art of the past, commenting: 'My portraitures met with the fate somewhat similar to those of Rembrandt. By some they were said to be nature itself by others declared most execrable'.[42] Contemporaries also saw similarities of character between Reynolds and Rembrandt; like Rembrandt Reynolds was not a 'courtier', his knighthood bestowed in the year after his election as President of the Royal Academy, rather than for any activities at court.[43] Like Rembrandt he lacked good looks and was described in the mid 1770s as having coarse features, a slovenly outward appearance, a broad plain face and a blunt nose, which in his Academy self-portrait (fig.16) were all carefully disguised beneath shadows and a dignified stance. He was, however, much more candid and brutal with his own features than were contemporaries, as the bland and idealised features in John Francis Rigaud's *Sir William Chambers, Joseph Wilton & Sir Joshua Reynolds* (National Portrait Gallery) of 1782 demonstrate.[44]

The casual pose Reynolds adopted in his youthful self-portraits was later replaced by more dignified displays that stressed his role as leader of the artistic profession in England, its representative on the Continent, and an intellectual man of letters. His Royal Academy self-portrait (fig.16) presented in 1780, was intended as a public image of the Academy's founding president, hung high in the Assembly Room of its newly-built premises in Somerset House, where Reynolds could preside over the assembled group of Academicians even when he was not present. He wears no artist's clothing: instead of a painter's beret and smock there was an academic's bonnet and scarlet robes, and in place of a palette he held the honorary doctorate of civil law awarded to him in 1773 by Oxford University. He exuded the air of self-confident authority bestowed upon him by his office, and conveyed the high seriousness which befitted a portrait intended for a seat of learning like the Academy. The portrait also proclaimed his artistic creed. It explicitly paid homage to Michelangelo, another of Reynolds' great artist heroes and a constant source of inspiration whose genius and imagination he repeatedly extolled, through the presiding bust of Michelangelo (which Reynolds owned), but it did so by emulating Rembrandt in its colouring, painting technique and lighting. Its composition showed intriguing links to Rembrandt's *Aristotle contemplating the Bust of Homer* (New York, Metropolitan Museum), in which one

philosopher honoured his allegiance to another and which by 1815 belonged to a friend of Reynolds, Sir Abraham Hume. Reynolds described to his students at the Academy how Rembrandt often depicted 'little more than one spot of light in the midst of a large quantity of shadow' and similarities of execution between the artists were noted by contemporaries.[45] The bust and the composition placed Reynolds within the great artistic tradition, whilst the academic robes and papers emphasised the intellectual qualities which he thought indispensable to a professional artist. The high seriousness of this self-portrait is particularly exposed when compared with Angelica Kauffmann's informal and affectionate representation of Reynolds in fanciful seventeenth-century dress (Plympton, Saltram House), in which the same bust of Michelangelo looks benignly from the background. Reynolds' self-image as an academic man of letters became his standard public likeness: when he could not attend the reception for his inauguration as Mayor of his native town of Plympton in 1773, he sent a portrait to hang in the dining room instead.

Reynolds' eagerness to show his admiration for Rembrandt through his self-portraits was not surprising, as he was the greatest proponent and theorist of imitation in art. In the fifteen *Discourses* delivered to Academicians and students between 1769 and 1790 he expounded at length on the subject and advised that imitation should not be merely a procedure reserved for students but a standard exercise for artists throughout their career: 'by imitation only variety and even originality of invention is produced'.[46] The *Discourses* repeatedly stressed the importance for all artists, no matter how lowly the type of painting they made, of studying ancient sculpture and the Old Masters, naming a pantheon who could provide inspiration and models, including Raphael, Titian, Rembrandt and Michelangelo. Reynolds' Academy self-portrait represented the more intellectual form of one artist paying tribute to others through the manipulation of his own image. A more superficial form of emulation can be seen in Richard Cosway's *Self-portrait in fancy dress* (Cat.no.20), in which by painting himself in Vandyckian dress he proclaimed his allegiance to the Van Dyck style and placed himself within the courtly school of English portraiture. Reynolds, in his turn, became a portrait painter to be imitated. In the nineteenth century an aspiring Devonian artist, Philip Steer, was advised that if he wanted to make an artistic mark on the London scene he should copy a Reynolds self-portrait.[47]

Reynolds, like Rembrandt, was also a prolific self-portraitist producing many to mark key stages of his life: his start as a portrait-painter after returning to Plymouth from London; his visit to Rome; his election to the Society of Dilettanti; his early years at the Royal Academy; his mayoralty of Plympton; European recognition of his reputation; and his retirement from active work. In the intimate portraits which Reynolds produced of himself in old age, some of which were intended for an audience of friends (London, National Gallery), he seemed to confront his approaching death and showed himself having suffered two strokes, frail, deaf and short-sighted (Royal Collection). But apart from the image which he produced at the start of his career (Cat.no.29), in which he holds a palette, he shied away from showing his practical involvement in art. Even when he portrayed himself with a portfolio of drawings, as in his Dilettanti Society self-portrait of 1766, he did not hold a porte-crayon and the portrait could easily be that of a collector at the Society, unlike that of his rival Anton Mengs, whose juxtaposition of chalk and drawings in his Uffizi self-portrait suggested that they were the artist's own work. The willingness of Mengs to be seen alongside an easel advertising his wares (Cat.no.26) was not the only way in which he and Reynolds were regarded as opposites. The German's smooth and highly finished technique contrasted with that of the Englishman, as was noted on several occasions when their respective self-portraits for the Uffizi, painted within a year of each other, were compared. As they hung side by side their different techniques clashed spectacularly.[48] Despite their differences they pursued similar objectives and saw eye to eye on the need to follow the models created by artists of the past. Mengs, as the leading Continental artist of the neo-classical style, subscribed to the German antiquarian scholar Winkelmann's belief that 'There is but one way for the moderns to become great, and perhaps unequalled; ... by imitating the ancients. ... especially the Greek arts. But then we must be as familiar with them as with a friend'.[49] Mengs' Liverpool *Self-portrait* (Cat.no.26) was his attempt to show himself as the modern artist of his mentor Winckelmann, creating works of art which emulated the perfection and beauty he saw in the sculpture of Ancient Greece and Rome.

The Romantic Genius

By the end of the eighteenth century artists had begun to question the models of the classical and renaissance past and indeed to question the need for models at all. The younger generation of artists that formed around the British-based Swiss artist Henry Fuseli (1741-1825), including Alexander and John Runciman, James Barry and George Romney, had a different concept of creativity. Their vision of the artist as an inspired creator derived from William Blake's belief that taste and genius were not teachable or acquirable 'but are born within us', the complete antithesis of the beliefs expounded by Reynolds and Mengs respectively in their *Discourses* and *Gedanken über die Schonheit* (*Thoughts on Beauty*). Members of the new generation wished to show the individuality of their response to their predecessors' work rather than to mirror it. The new approach to art experimented with the possibilities of the artist's own pictorial imagination. This proto-Romantic ironic questioning of tradition can be seen informing John Runciman's response to Michelangelo (Cat.no.32). Compared to that of Reynolds, where the bust acted as a physical embodiment of a much admired artist, Runciman's self-portrait is concerned more with the sculptor's impact on the imagination, the hazy ill-defined sculpture in the background representing a subconscious influence. Furthermore, Fuseli's circle despised the desire to please a wide audience, and took as hero the artist ignored by

the mass and isolated from society. Their attitude was summed up by Fuseli's words, 'It is the lot of genius to be opposed and to be invigorated by opposition', and encapsulated visually in its most dramatic form in James Barry's *Self-portrait as Timanthes* (Cat.no.38), the archetypal manifesto self-portrait of the isolated, despised genius who was inspired to excel by the envy of others.[50]

Barry was thoroughly committed to the artist's role as prophet and teacher. For him art was a didactic instrument to castigate vice and uphold virtue, and to this end the artist must be his own master, free from the restrictions and compromises enforced by a patron. He believed that there was no higher calling than that of history painter, with its traditionally defined subject matter drawn from the standard repertoire of literary sources - the Bible, classical history and mythology and epic poetry. Both his Dublin self-portrait (Cat.no.38) and his complex image within a painting within a painting of his *Self-portrait with Paine and Lefèvre* (London, National Portrait Gallery) have the qualities of a history painting, although of a more abstruse type than the straightforwardly allegorizing self-portraits of Angelica Kauffmann. Although Barry was an antagonist of Reynolds he shared with him a fascination with the image and role of the artist in society. It is not surprising, therefore, that no British artist other than Reynolds engaged in such extensive self-scrutiny as Barry. From 1767 to the end of his life he produced a wide range of self-portraits in paint, pencil and ink providing a personal record of his mental and physical condition through varying states of mind, from the exuberance of youth and contemplative self-absorbtion to the demonic gaze and disillusionment of his final images. His moving portrayals of the despondent, solitary genius became part of the Romantic image of the artist, as much as they were a reincarnation of that familiar type, the brooding, melancholy artist.

It was increasingly the case, on the brink of the nineteenth century, that the nature of an artist's work was thought to be a direct result of personal character which could be read in the faces rather than as before in clothes, gestures or symbolic accompaniments. After the publication of *Physiognomische Fragmente* by Fuseli's friend Johan Lavater, and its translation into English (1793) and French, the science of physiognomy, which sought to read character in a person's features, was revived and it stimulated artists to try to show all by the face alone. It lead to the characteristic Romantic self-portrait which focussed on the head and expressed the artist's character through brushwork and by dramatic lighting of the face, particularly the forehead which signified the artist's inner mind, as Henry Raeburn did in his self-portrait of 1816 (fig.30). Compositionally the portraits were often less complex but visually more intense, as the close-up focus enhanced their emotional impact and the brushwork added a mood of nervous excitement, and often an underlying feeling of instability.

The progression of self-portraiture in Europe from the age of Enlightenment to the Romantic era, from the last third of the eighteenth century through the first third of the nineteenth, was peerlessly reflected in the

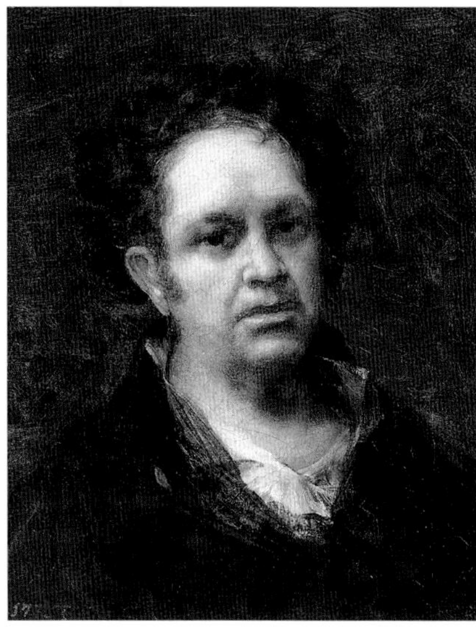

*Fig.17. Francisco Goya, **Self-portrait**, 1815, (Madrid, Prado Museum)*

self-portraits of the Spanish court artist Francisco Goya (1746-1828). His first, painted for his parents in 1769-70 before setting out for Italy to extend his artistic education and seek his fortune, presented the epitome of the young eighteenth-century man. His later portraits were more self-revelatory. That painted in his seventieth year (fig.17), in which his tilted head, set against an engulfing dark background, reveals a face wearied by the political, personal and medical troubles of the intervening years. Goya was as preoccupied by the challenge of self-representation as had been his artistic mentor and guide, Rembrandt. Although he produced only about a third as many self-portraits as the Dutch painter, Goya's images displayed similar qualities of insight and mood and the same searching scrutiny of his face. Rembrandt was the deep-seated model for Goya's repeated self-analysis. His self-portraits moved from emulating his great Spanish predecessor Velázquez's *Las Meninas* (fig.10) in his *Family of Charles IV* (Madrid, Prado Museum) to the intense single image of 1815 (fig.17) via the autobiographical narrative of the picture painted to celebrate his recovery from an apparently mortal illness, his *Self-portrait with Doctor Arrieta* (Minneapolis Institute of Arts). The latter's psychic turbulence prefigured the mood of many of Van Gogh's self-portraits a century later. Goya's work spanned a period of progression from the last vestiges of the rococo to the dawn of the photographic era.

The Nineteenth Century:

Self-portraiture in the age of photography

The Romantic era was an age of portraiture with an overpowering emphasis on the character of the sitter, but the invention of photography with its apparently objective realism did much to complicate matters for portrait painters. Photography had a particularly marked effect on self-portraiture because for the first time artists could see themselves as others saw them; to see themselves as they 'really' were, or so it appeared, without the complicating intervention of the mirrored image. Some British artists such as Frith and Sant (fig.37) embraced photography, using photographic 'visiting cards' to publicise themselves. Watts thought the science of photography was a wonderful invention and was 'of the opinion ... that it ought to help artists considerably in seeing nature truly'.[51] From a practical point of view some artists, freed from the need to scrutinise themselves closely in a mirror, accepted the camera in their working practice and used photographs to help portray themselves in ways impossible before, like the closed eyes of Watts' moving final self-portrait (Cat.no.55), in which his lowered eyelids seem to signify the close of his life.

Painters reacted in two diverse ways to survive the challenge of the portrait photograph, both of which attempted to subjectivise the portrait, to capture a more complex, multi-faceted nature of human personality and so to differentiate their product from a photograph which could capture only a momentary likeness. The first of these reactions was to create an autobiographical narrative around the artist, a narrative that might cover many years of the artist's life. In Britain this resulted in portraits like those produced 'in character' by the artist-friends of the Scottish landowner, philanthropist and former painter Patrick Allan-Fraser, in which the artist became an actor in a play about his own life. John Phillip, nicknamed Spanish Phillip because of his penchant for Spanish scenes, naturally produced a self-portrait in character which was set in Spain and indirectly commented on the image-making power of the artist (Cat.no.51). Augustus Egg (Cat.no.44) showed himself in an acting role playing the part of a writer in another's play, but in a role which also reflected on the position of the destitute patronless artist left at the mercy of the fickle taste of the market, a symbol of genius neglected by society's philistinism. Egg's concern for the fate of contemporaries who despite their abilities had fallen from favour was shared by Patrick Allan-Fraser. Egg's self-portrait both mirrored this concern and acted as a coded message of support for Allan-Fraser's attempt to create on his estate near Arbroath a foundation for the

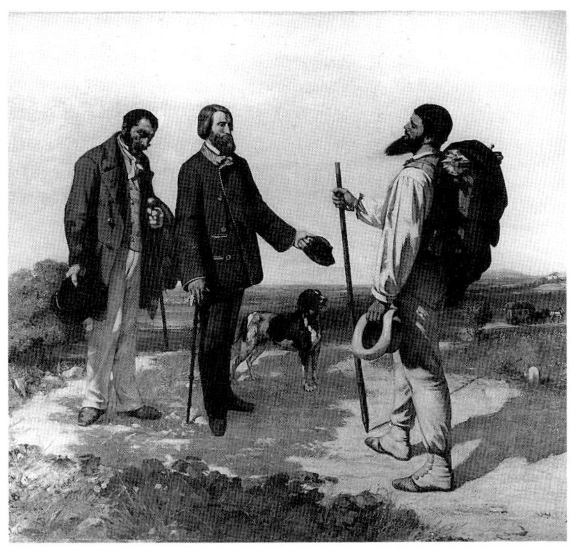

Fig.18 Gustave
Courbet, **Bonjour
M. Courbet**, 1854,
(Montpellier,
Musée Fabre,
©Photo R.M.N.)

arts that 'could be the cause of painting in others', a centre for the education of artists and artisans and the promotion of their careers.[52] Allan-Fraser decorated his house with a collection of contemporary art, including many commissioned self-portraits. These narrative self-portraits were not just the result of his philanthropic patronage, for they chimed well with the mid-Victorian liking for entertaining story-pictures, anecdotal and humorous scenes drawn from daily life, like Frith's self-portrait *The SleepingModel* (Cat.no.46).

On the Continent the narrative spirit was epitomised by the work of an artist like Gustave Courbet (1819-1877), whose self-portraits are notable for their self-dramatisation. He was the most prolific self-portraitist of the mid nineteenth century and between 1842 and 1872 he produced pictures in which he constantly play-acted or assumed a role, sometimes as victim, at other times a handsome lover, madman or noble prisoner. His *Bonjour M. Courbet* (fig.18) of 1854 and another painted in the following year, *The Artist's Studio* (Paris, Musée d'Orsay), were complex statements about the artist's role in society. The first related to the relationship between the artist and his patron, the former shown as the dominant figure, staff in hand, accepting the greetings of the more deferential patron, a reversal of the relationship shown in the eighteenth century by Hayman in his *Self-portrait with Grosvenor Bedford* (Cat.no.22). The intentions of the *Artist's Studio* were encapsulated in its subtitle, *A real allegory summing up seven years of my life as an artist*. It was a grand history painting, updated to the nineteenth century, in which the figures crowding into his studio, representing people from all walks of life, served a symbolic purpose, since they were the friends who had sustained and assisted him since the Revolution of 1848.

The Artist in the Studio

As is evident in Courbet's work, the narrative self-portrait lent itself to the theme of the artist in the studio. In some cases the result was an anecdotal scene such as Frith's *The Sleeping Model*, which revealed more about the artist's ambivalent position in society than might at first be thought. However, it also produced the archetypal image of the destitute, bohemian artist absorbed in his own inner world brooding over his work in a garret or basement studio, exemplified by the self-images produced by Sant and Egg (Cat.nos.52,44). The disillusioned, struggling artist became a motif among Romantic artists at the beginning of the nineteenth century. The image was the culmination of several sources which stretched back to the sixteenth- and seventeenth-century view of solitary and self-absorbed Melancholy, and included material drawn from the eighteenth-century working studio filled with plaster casts and models, and the early nineteenth-century Romantic imagery of the artist as the young, thwarted genius poverty-stricken and ignored.

Paradoxically the origins of the Romantic bohemian artist lay partly in the behaviour and dandyism of artists like Richard Cosway (Cat.nos.20,21). He consciously created a reputation as a connoisseur which helped to attract, reassure and flatter the clients for his fashionable portrait miniatures. His antiquarian and artistic collection, modelled partly on those of Rubens and Rembrandt, was kept in his house which was itself furnished distinctively as an 'artist's house'.[53] Here lay the origins of the cult of the artist's studio that emerged among fashionable artists in the second half of the nineteenth century. Cosway's house was, however, a rare example, closer to reality probably was the studio in Rome visited in 1845 by Ford Madox Brown which was 'a waste, as painting-rooms were in those days, when bric-à-brac, Oriental rugs, or armour were not much thought of.'[54]

The liking for historical and unconventional dress was adopted by a young artist like James Jefferys (Cat.no.24), whose own self-portrait reflected other elements of the image of the romantic artistic genius. Such an artist was preferably young and untrained, unfettered by years of study or copying old masters. It also helped if one died young, preferably mad or consumptive, although one probably still qualified if like Jefferys one died of a cold, aged thirty-two. Jefferys showed himself caught up in the world of his own imagination struggling to create his work and disillusioned with the art establishment. It had been this type of Romantic image that Morland in typical fashion both parodied and doused under a cold shower of realism in *The artist in his studio with his man Gibbs* (Cat.no.50), in which the artist sat glumly at his easel in a garret whilst his man engaged in the equally important activity of cooking the sausages. The image of the thwarted struggling artist became more sentimental in the paintings by Egg and Sant (44,52). Egg's picture was a complex theatrical self-portrait complete with spotlit illumination from the garret's skylight. The stereotype of the unconventional, poverty-stricken artist was embedded in people's minds by the mid nineteenth century, as several anecdotes related in Frith's *Reminiscences* reveal. A wealthy but parvenu artist like Frith (Cat.no.46), who lived in a large house with servants and a tradesman's entrance for his models, had little instinctive sympathy for the image and was irritated to find it dominated the mind of his aristocratic sitters. On one occasion the mother of a bridesmaid at the Prince of Wales's wedding came to check the suitability of Frith's studio for her daughter's visit. She asked bewilderedly 'This is where you live?' and the artist had continued the conversation in his own mind, 'and not in the garret where you had evidently been taught that most artist's reside; and as I have a coal-cellar I am not forced to keep fuel in a corner of the garret, and I am not always dining on the traditional red herring'.[55] The question of social status, his own and that of artists in general, was a constant preoccupation of Frith's memoirs and, as his obituary in *The Times* noted, the memoirs were those of a man who regarded 'art as a profession like any other' and believed that people should 'clear their minds of any mysterious and sacramental ideas in connection with it'.[56] Paradoxically it was precisely such a concept of the artist that formed the basis of the second way in which artists reacted to the problems posed by photography.

The Artist Alone

The end of the nineteenth century saw a revival of portraiture in general and with it a move away from the anecdotal narrative genre of self-portraiture. Artists reverted to portraying themselves as inspired solitary geniuses, conveying this image with dramatic lighting and brush-technique and focussing on the head once again in a revived and adapted form of the Romantic era self-portrait. Watts (Cat.no.55) was a leading light of the revival. His distinctive portraits, which aimed to convey the spiritual likeness of a person rather than a mere record of physical characteristics, were often at odds with conventional notions of society portraiture. Watts conceived the idea of producing a 'Hall of Fame' to be left to the nation, and requested sittings from eminent members of society rather than expecting the sitters to commission him, as was traditional.

Artists who had few or no patrons to satisfy often experimented through self-portraits, although for some, such as the Impressionists and the Pre-Raphaelite Brotherhood, self-portraiture was marginal. The latter preferred to confirm their close-knit friendships by exchanging drawn or painted portraits of each other, unlike the later artistic friendships of the Post-Impressionists in France. Van Gogh, Gauguin and Emile Bernard frequently reaffirmed their friendships and swapped ideas by exchanging self-portraits. The self-portraits that Gauguin (1848-1903) and Vincent Van Gogh (1853-90) exchanged in 1888 attempted not only to capture their own likeness and spirit but also to symbolise 'an Impressionist in general' as Vincent wrote

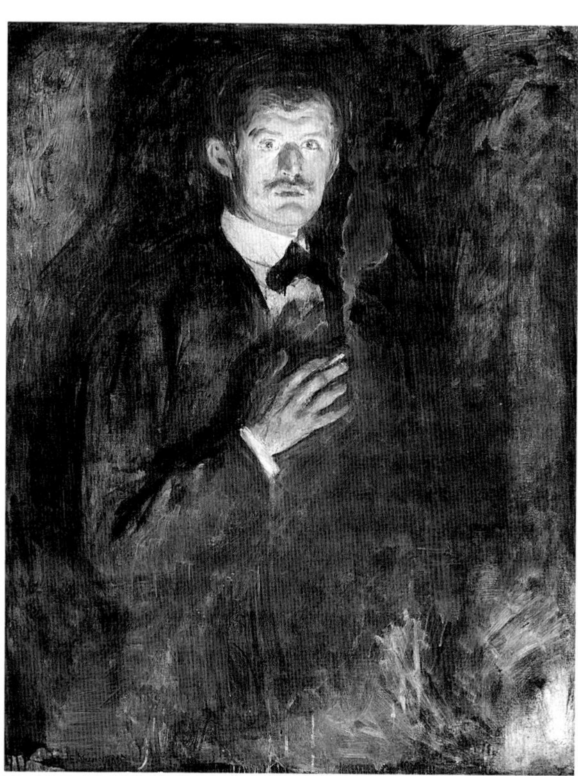

*Fig.19 Edvard Munch, **Self-portrait with Cigarette**, 1895, (Oslo, Nasjonalgalleriet)*

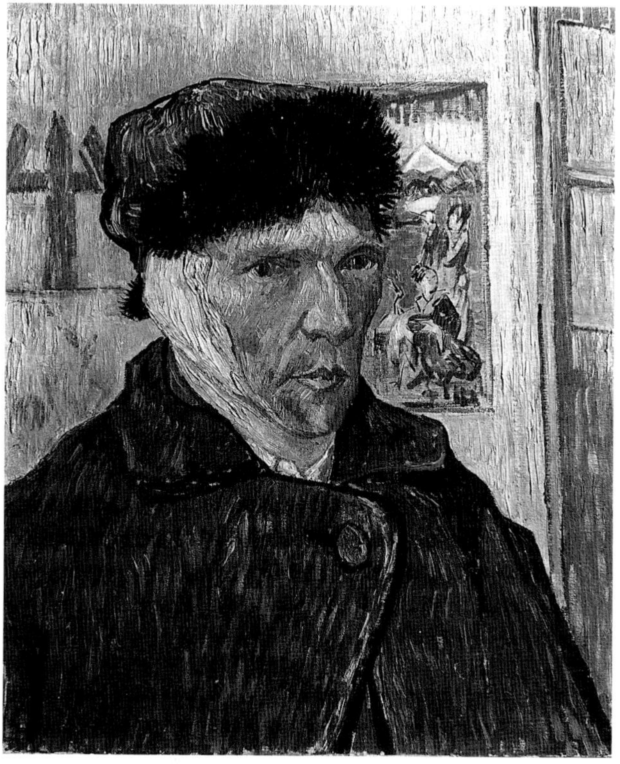

*Fig.20 Vincent Van Gogh, **Self-portrait with bandaged ear**, 1889 (London, Courtauld Institute Galleries)*

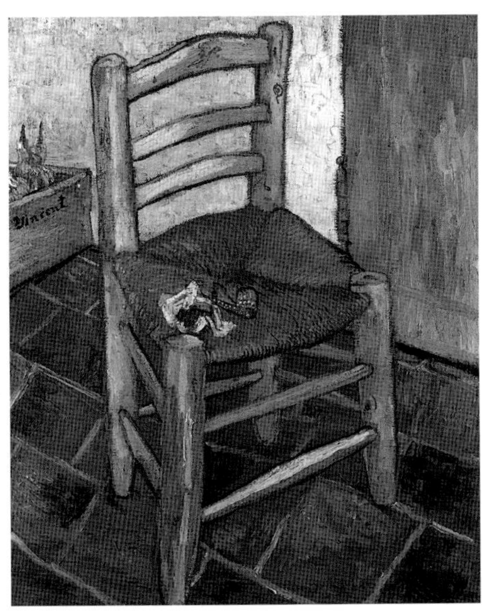

Fig.21 Vincent Van Gogh, **The Chair and the Pipe***, 1889, (London, National Gallery)*

to his brother, his self-portrait being conceived as that of a Buddhist monk (Cambridge, USA, Fogg Art Museum) whereas Gauguin's (Amsterdam, Rijksmuseum) was visualised as the anti-hero brigand Jean Valjean from Hugo's *Les Misérables*. Such friendships were broken as well as cemented via self-portraits, perhaps most famously with the series of self-portraits which included Van Gogh's *Self-portrait with bandaged ear* (fig.20), painted after he had mutilated his ear in a frenzy of despair.

It was Van Gogh who began to use the self-portrait as a form of self-analysis. For an expressionist artist like the Norwegian Edvard Munch (1863-1944) this type of self-portrait also became a way of displaying his own subjectivity, projecting his interior state of mind. Munch's self-portraits often had a psychological intensity heightened by theatrical lighting and elements of play-acting evident in his Mephistophelian *Self-portrait with burning cigarette* (fig.19). Post-Impressionists like Expressionists were preoccupied by the relationship between external and internal reality, which could best be explored through self-portraiture. The disquieting, rather sinister images favoured by them were adopted at the end of the century by British-based artists such as Conder and Sickert (Cat.nos.41,53) both of whom had direct contact with the Post-Impressionists in France.

The best known Post-Impressionist self-portraitist was Van Gogh, an artist who has become as closely associated with self-portraiture as Rembrandt, and who over a far shorter period was almost as prolific. Between 1886 and 1888 he painted 22 self-portraits, invariably concentrating on the head and shoulders, conveying expression through paint and colour handling alone. He continued to produce them during his mental breakdown and hospitalization in Arles, including the two which show him with bandaged ear (fig.20). As with Rembrandt, Van Gogh's self-portraits did much to create the myth of Van Gogh the painter. Through them he came to personify the artist as tormented genius and grew into the epitome of the Artist - misunderstood, neglected, mad and self-destructive. The myth became so compelling that since then it has often been assumed that all self-portraits were created for the reasons which stimulated Van Gogh, as an outcry against society's alienation of the artist - but, as this essay has shown, many other factors produce the impulse to portray oneself.

On occasions Van Gogh's portraits of himself were meant as a reaction to photography. In the summer of 1888 Van Gogh wrote to his sister Willemina about his *Self-portrait with easel* (Amsterdam, Van Gogh Museum) 'You will say that this is rather like a death's head ... well, yes that's the sort of face it is and it isn't easy to paint oneself - at any rate, it's something quite different from a photograph. And you see, this, in my opinion, is the great advantage of impressionism - it is not banal, and one seeks a deeper resemblance than the photographer's'.[57] The self-portrait's conventional composition had been partly inspired by Rembrandt's self-portrait in the Louvre, which had attracted his attention earlier that year, yet in style it looked forward to the expressionist and symbolic self-portraits of the twentieth century. By the dawn of the twentieth century art had reached a stage where all of an artist's work was considered self-referential and every work, whatever its ostensible theme, could become a metaphorical self-portrait. Van Gogh's *The Chair and the Pipe* (fig.21) was one of a pair of emblematic portraits of himself and Gauguin (Amsterdam, Van Gogh Museum). The straw chair lit by daylight with his pipe on its seat and spring bulbs sprouting in the background captured Van Gogh's relatively optimistic mood in 1888, though one threatened by the underlying message of death symbolised by the smoking pipe with its reference to the biblical phrase 'and my days shall be consumed like smoke'. Van Gogh had painted objects as metaphors for himself on other occasions (*A Pair of Boots*, Amsterdam, Rijksmuseum). Indirectly the birth of photography not only ensured that artists no longer needed to contemplate themselves face to face in a mirror in order to create a self-portrait, but that they no longer needed a face at all.

Footnotes

1. Quoted in Manchester City Art Gallery, *A Century of Collecting*, 1983, p.129.
2. W.P. Frith, *My Autobiography and Reminiscences*, 1888, pp.462-3.
3. Elizabeth Croft 'Recollections of Sir Thomas Lawrence PRA' in *Sir Thomas Lawrence's Letter-bag*, G.S.Layard ed., 1906, p.265 quoted by Helen Valentine, *From Reynolds to Lawrence: the first sixty years of the Royal Academy of Arts and its Collections*, 1991, p.25.
4. Giorgio Vasari, *Lives of the Artists*, trans. G.Bull, 1987, vol.II, pp.187-189.
5. Leon Battista Alberti, *Della Pittura*, 1972 edn., Bk.II, p.89.
6. *Advice on the Painting of Portraits* in *The Memoirs of Elisabeth Vigée Le Brun*, (1835-7), trans. Siân Evans, 1989, p.354.
7. Alberti, *Della Pittura*, Bk.II p.83
8. Karl van Mander, *Den grondt der edel vrij schilder-const*, (1604), trans. and ed. H. Miedema, 1973, vol.1, p.166.
9. Pontormo red chalk drawing c.1525, London, British Museum. I. Bignamini & M. Postle, *The Artist's Model Its Role in British Art from Lely to Etty*, Nottingham University Art Gallery, 1991, p.21 ill.5, quoting Benjamin Haydon's description of finding Wilkie at breakfast time drawing himself, seated naked 'on his bed claiming that 'It's jest copital practice [sic]'.
10. Letter to Wilibald Pircheimer October 1506 quoted in William M. Conway, *The Writings of Albrecht Dürer*, 1958, p.58.
11. Erwin Panofsky, *Albrecht Dürer*, 1948, vol.I, p.154.
12. Jennifer Fletcher, '"Fatto al Specchio": Venetian Renaissance Attitudes to Self-portraiture', *Imaging the Self in Renaissance Italy, Fenway Court: Isabella Stewart Gardner Museum Bulletin*, 1990-91, p.47.
13. Psychology was a term first coined in the sixteenth century from the ancient Greek for study of the soul. F.H. Lapointe 'Who originated the term 'Psychology"', *Journal of History of Behavioural Science*, 1972, vol.8, pp.328-35 quoted by H. Perry Chapman 'Expression, Temperament and Imagination in Rembrandt's earliest Self-portraits', *Art History*, 1989, vol.12, p.166 n.48.
14. Walter Sickert in a letter prior to starting his Mornington Town series of nudes in 1907, as quoted by Wendy Baron, *Sickert Paintings*, Royal Academy, 1992, cat.no.62, p.194.
15. Ernst Gombrich 'Ritualized gesture and expression in art', *The Image and the Eye*, 1982, p.134-5.
16. Oliver Millar, 'Abraham van der Doort's Catalogue of the Collections of Charles I', *Walpole Society*, 1960, vol.37, pp.41, 57 no.87.

17. Christopher White, 'Did Rembrandt ever visit England', *Apollo* May 1962, pp.178, 180, quoting the burgomaster of Leiden, J. Orlers, *Beschrijvinghe der Stadt Leyden*, 1641 and the journal of the Leiden City Militia for 10 April 1629. Lievens also mentioned that having completed the Prince's commission he hoped to set out for England.
18. O. Millar *The Queen's Pictures*, 1984, p.38, 49 and Millar, 'Collections of Charles I', as above, p.16.
19. Letter of January 10 1625 in *Letters of Peter Paul Rubens*, trans. and ed. Ruth S. Magurn, 1955, p.101-102.
20. G.P. Bellori, *Le Vite de Pittori*, 1672, pp.255-6, as quoted by Michael Levey *Painting at Court*, 1971, p.124.
21. George Vertue, *Notebooks Volume II, Walpole Society*, 1931-2, vol.XX, p.139.
22. Vertue, as above, p.148.
23. Another painter, the Portuguese Felix da Costa, first remarked in his *The Antiquity of the Art of Painting*, 1696, that the picture seemed more like a portrait of Velázquez than of the Princess, quoted by Enriqueta Harris, *Velázquez*, 1982, p.170.
24. Letter of 18 December 1634 to Peiresc, *Letters*, ed. Magurn, as above, p.393.
25. Pliny the Elder's, *Natural History*, quoted in Robert Rosenblum, 'The Origin of Painting: A Problem in the Iconography of Romantic Classicism', *Art Bulletin*, 1957, vol.XXXIX, p.279.
26. Joanna Woodall, 'A case of coupled identity. Marriage and social status in portraits by Antonis Mor', paper given at Whitworth Art Gallery, Manchester, *Portraiture and the Problematics of Representation* conference held September 1993.
27. Alistair Smart, *Allan Ramsay: Painter Essayist and Man of Enlightenment*, 1992, p.294, n.87.
28. William Hayley, *Life of George Romney*, 1809, p.24.
29. G.B. Hill, *Letters of Dante Gabriel Rossetti to William Allingham 1854-70*, 1897, p.133.
30. O. Millar, 'The Inventories and Valuations of the King's Goods 1649-51', *The Walpole Society*, 1972, vol.43, p.186 no.5; Millar, 'Abraham van der Doort's Catalogue', as above, pp.37-8 nos.2, 4, 5, (in the long gallery) Rembrandt p.57, Titian p.16 no.11, (and in the privy gallery) Dürer p.68 no.30 and Joos van Cleve p.64 no.13; Millar, *The Queen's Pictures*, 1984, p.35. The inventory also listed among others supposed self-portraits by Bronzino, Pordenone, Guilio Romano and Giorgione some of which hung in the Long Gallery at Whitehall along with the Rembrandt.

31. Wolfram Prinz, 'La Collezione degli Autoritratti' in the general catalogue of *Gli Uffizi*, 1979, pp.766ff; *Painters by Painters* exhibition catalogue National Academy of Design, New York, 1988, p.11ff.

32. *Painters by Painters,* as above, cat.no.19.

33. Nicholas Turner, 'The Gabburri/Rogers series of drawn self-portraits and portraits of artists', *Journal of the History of Collections*, 1993, vol.5, pp.179-216.

34. Simone de Beauvoir, *Le deuxième sexe*, 1977, vol.II, p.70 as quoted in Joseph Baillio, *Elisabeth Louise Vigée Le Brun*, 1982, cat.no.11, p.45.

35. Letter of 7 August 1649 to her Sicilian patron Don Antonio Ruffo to whom she also promised a self-portrait that was never delivered, in Mary D. Garrard, *Artemisia Gentileschi*, 1989, p.357, Appendix A 21, p.86 n.138.

36. Cesare Ripa, *Iconologia*, 1610 edn., p.429. From its first publication in 1593 it became a best-seller and re-editions continued into the second half of the eighteenth century. The personification of Pittura was not illustrated until a French edition of 1644.

37. Angela Rosenthal, 'Angelica Kauffmann Ma(s)king Claims', *Art History*, March 1992, vol.15 no.1, p.42 n.16.

38. Rosenthal, as above, p.49 pl.14.

39. Helen Valentine, *From Reynolds to Lawrence*, 1991, p.11.

40. Ronald Paulson, *Hogarth his life, art and times*, 1971, vol.II, p.3.

41. Frederick Antal, *Hogarth and his place in European Art*, 1962, p.12.

42. Antal, as above, p.44.

43. Henry Angelo, *Reminiscences*, 1828, vol.I, p.359 as quoted in David Mannings, *Sir Joshua Reynolds: The Self Portraits*, Plymouth City Museums, 1992, p.6.

44. Though the features were themselves criticised by a reviewer of the day for copying 'so exactly the vulgarity of the President's countenance' such was the idealisation expected of a portrait at that time. William Whitley, *Artists and their friends in England 1700-1799*, 1928, vol.I, p.300 as quoted in Mannings, as above, cat.no.32, p.44.

45. *Reynolds Discourses on Art VIII*, ed. R. Wark, 1975, p.147 as quoted by H. Valentine, as above, p.25.

46. *Discourses VI*, as above, p.96, as quoted in Joseph Baillio, 'Vigée Le Brun and the Classical Practice of Imitation', *Papers in Art History from Pennsylvania State University*, 1988, vol.IV, p.102.

47. Bruce Laughton, *Philip Wilson Steer*, 1971, p.1.

48. James Northcote, Reynolds' pupil, wrote to his brother Samuel on 11 August 1778: 'Unfortunately for him [Mengs] they have hung Sir Joshua's close to it, which makes it look like a devil, for they ought not to come together, for Mengs' is finished so that you can almost tell the hairs of his beard and Sir Joshua's appears as if it was painted with his fingers.', quoted by Steffi Roettgen, *Anton Raphael Mengs and his British Patrons*, Kenwood, 1993, p.18 n.53.

49. J.J. Winckelmann's *Reflections on the Painting and Sculpture of the Greeks*, 1755, (trans. H.Fuseli 1765) quoted by David Irwin *Winckelmann: Wrtings on Art*, 1972, p.61.

50. Quoted by Desmond Shawe-Taylor, *Genial Company: The theme of genius in Eighteenth-Century British Portraiture*, 1987, p.67.

51. Mrs. Russell Barrington, *G.F. Watts*, 1905, p.95

52. William Payne, *Hospitalfield: Patrick Allan-Fraser and his art collection*, National Gallery of Scotland, 1990, pp.3-14; W.P. Frith *Reminiscences*, 1887, vol.1, p.299.

53. It was referred to as such by Sir Thomas Lawrence. For other detailed descriptions of Cosway's house see Stephen Lloyd, 'Richard Cosway, RA: The artist as collector, connoisseur and virtuoso', *Apollo*, June 1991, pp.398-405.

54. Describing his visit to Peter Cornelius's studio in the 'Universal Review' of May 1888 as quoted in Ford M. Hueffer, *Ford Madox Brown: A Record of his Life and Work*, 1896, p.45.

55. Frith, as above, vol.1, p.238; On another occasion he had been secretly amused at the embarrassment caused by young Prince Leopold's comment, 'I didn't know artists lived in such big houses', whilst accompanying his mother Queen Victoria for a sitting in the artist's studio, quoted in Paula Gillett, *The Victorian Painter's World*, 1990, p.93.

56. Gillett, as above, p.72.

57. Letter of late June-July 1888 from Van Gogh to Willemina (no.4), quoted in *Van Gogh à Paris*, Musée d'Orsay, 1988, cat.68, pp.174-75.

1 **Mary Beale** 1633-1699

Self-portrait with her Husband Charles and their Son Bartholomew about 1663-4
Oil on canvas, 63.5 x 76.2cm.
(Geffrye Museum, London, no.49/1978)

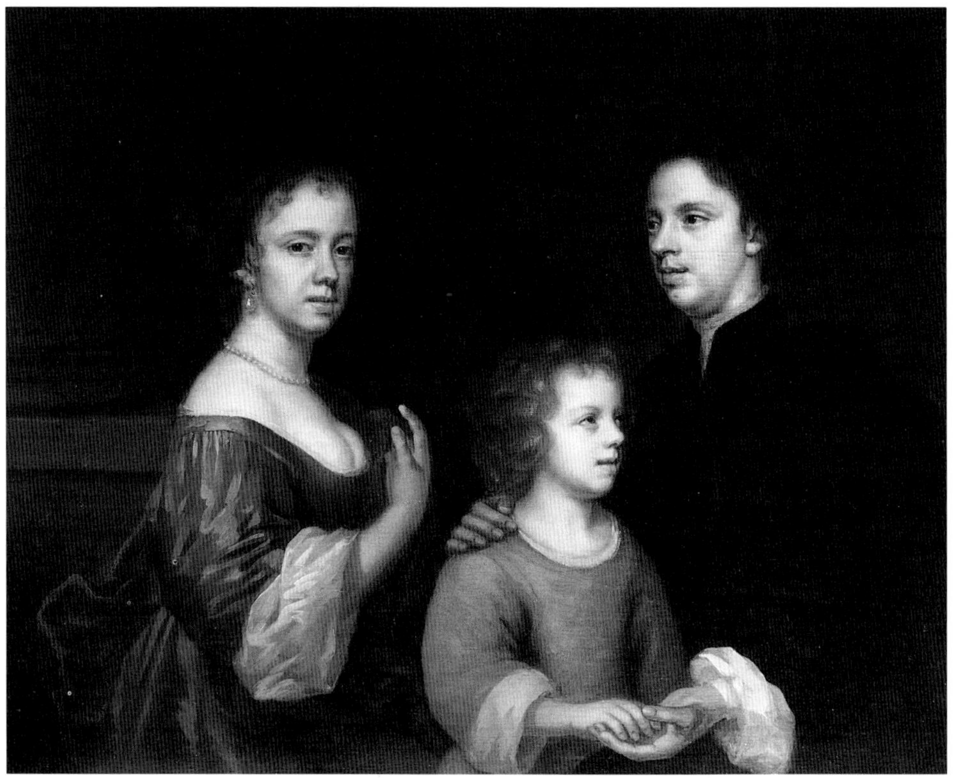

This is the earliest known self-portrait of Mary Beale one of the first professional woman artists in England to paint on a major scale. It shows her with her husband, Charles and eldest son both of whom were to play a role in the running of her prolific studio and is the only group portrait of them she painted. The picture looks like a conventional portrait of a mid-seventeenth century professional family in London, which was what they were when Mary Beale painted the picture in the 'paintinge room' set aside in the spacious lodgings above the Patent Office, off Fleet Street, where Charles was a civil servant. Although there is no direct indication that Mary Beale is an artist the emphatic pointing gesture to herself marks her out as the centre of attention and distinguishes it from the usual portrait which would have given this position to the husband, as head of the family. Her determined look out of the picture also suggests Mary Beale's self-confident nature, which supported her throughout her painting career, especially after her husband was made redundant in 1665. She then took on the unusual role of breadwinner for the family whilst her husband happily acted as studio assistant, grinding up her colours, preparing her canvases, dealing with clients and keeping the accounts as well as a detailed note from 1671-81 of all the work of his "dearest heart", as he always referred to her. The need to support her family spurred her to work hard. She produced a stream of rather formulaic portraits of middle-class and noble sitters in the style made fashionable by Sir Peter Lely, alongside a small group of sensitive more relaxed portraits of family and friends, drawn from the Anglican Church and the legal, scientific, and civil service professions. Her exclusion from formal artistic training as a woman meant Beale relied heavily on learning and copying from other male artists, in particular Lely who paid her the singular compliment of allowing her to watch him at work and copy from his collection and portraits. According to her husband's notebooks the self-portraits, which she produced throughout her career, were often painted for 'study and improvement', sometimes using novel canvas types such as onion-sacks, or to advertise her portrait formats to prospective sitters.[1] It is possible that this self-portrait, the only one in which she is part of a family group, was an example of a group format intended to show to patrons at the beginning of her career. If so she was perhaps not happy with the awkward positioning of her husband and son whose blank stares create a lack of interaction with her and the viewer. In later self-portraits, like the more accomplished one of about 1666 (National Portrait Gallery), she showed herself as an artist with a palette hanging on a wall, her two sons represented by the portrait heads painted on the canvas she held in her hand, whilst her husband was painted separately in a companion portrait. As well as depicting herself as an artist and with her family Beale also took advantage of the opportunities offerred by her sex to paint herself as an allegorical figure; in 1664 in the guise of Pallas Athene, the classical goddess of the arts and learning. It is now lost and known only through its description in Samuel Woodforde's poem *To Belisa* dedicated to 'The Excellent Mrs. Beale'.[2]

1. Christopher Reeve, *Mrs. Mary Beale, Paintress*, Manor House Museum, Bury St. Edmunds, 1994, p.16 cat.no.3; Elizabeth Walsh & Richard Jeffree, *'The Excellent Mrs Mary Beale*, Geffrye Museum, 1975, pp.14, 68-69.

2. Walsh & Jeffree, as above, p.2.

2 **Michael Dahl** ?1659-1743
Self-portrait signed and dated 1691
Oil on canvas, 125.5 x 101cm (National Portrait Gallery, London, inv.NPG3822)

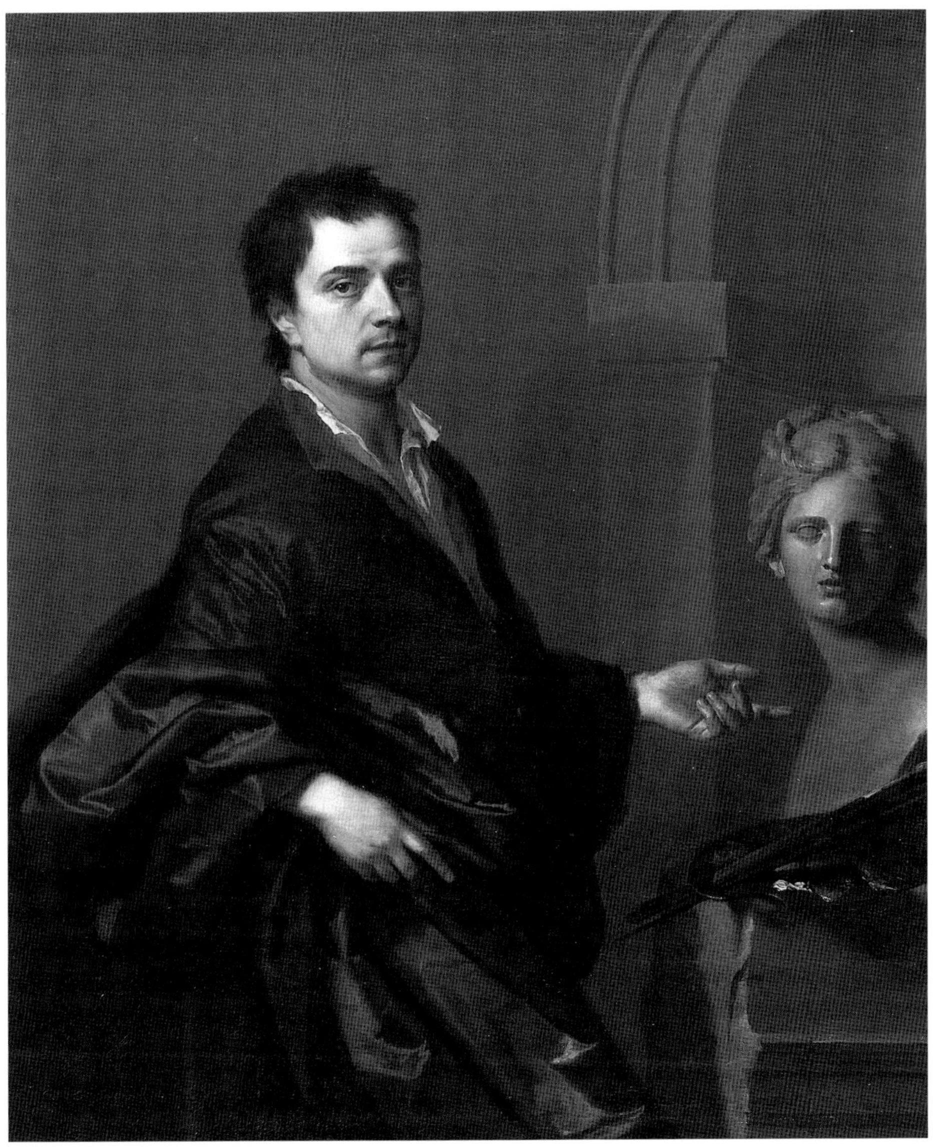

Dahl was a Swedish artist who made his name in Rome by painting the portrait of Queen Christina of Sweden. He settled for the rest of his long life in England in 1689. By 1700 he had become a leading portrait painter at the court of Princess (later Queen) Anne, modelling himself on and rivalling Godfrey Kneller. The self-portrait was painted when Dahl was still relatively unkown but keen to establish himself as a portrait painter, successful enough to support his aged, widowed mother back in Sweden. He shows himself as a painter, his used palette and brushes have been carefully balanced, almost as if in tribute, before a classical female bust to which Dahl points. The formality of the pose and architecture is belied by the informality of his open-necked shirt and his bare-head with its uncropped ruffled hair suggestive of distracted artistic creativity. Unlike Tillemans (Cat.no.34) he does not wear a wig, symbolic of a gentleman's non-manual status and the sign of a public image, nor does he wear a cap or turban, the acknowledged symbol of the artistic or literary man by 1709 when Dahl was shown with a turban in a portrait miniature portrait by Christian Richter. In all other respects Dahl is dressed smartly, as befitted the bachelor about town he was

known to have been in the 1690s.[1] The antique bust, on a suitably cracked plinth, was probably included as a testament to the classical basis of art and to Dahl's connoisseurship, the foundation for which he laid in his study of the antique in Rome. The sculpture may also refer to the importance of history painting, a genre which Dahl at the beginning of his career in England had originally hoped to follow, producing for example a *Holy Family* in 1691 (National Museum, Stockholm). Some five years later in the long art gallery above his studio he would display examples of his mythological scenes alongside works by Rembrandt and Maratta and his collection of portrait medals, including several of himself and his friends, in which he took great pride.[2] Dahl's modest and unassuming nature, commented on by contemporaries, is reflected in the understated ambitions revealed by the self-portrait.[3]

1. Wilhelm Nisser, *Michael Dahl and the Contemporary Swedish School of Painting in England,* 1927, p.14.
2. Nisser, as above, pp.16, 65-66
3. Nisser, as above, p28.

3 **Carlo Dolci** 1616-1686
Self-portrait signed and dated 1674
Inscribed: A[nn]o S[alu]tis 1674 di Annj 58 Per Sua Alteza Re[verendissimo] Jo, Carlo Dolci
Oil on canvas, 95.6 x 82.5cm
(Private Collection)

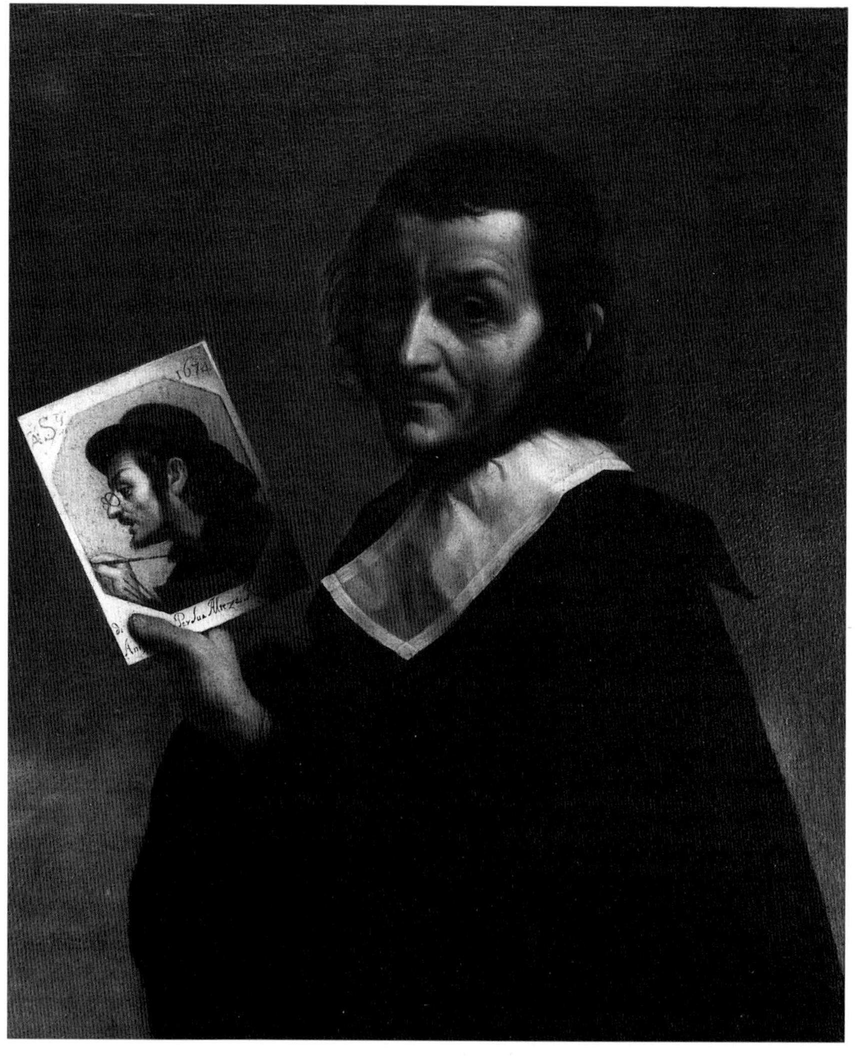

This *Self-portrait* by Dolci is a copy by the Florentine artist of his *Self-portrait* dedicated to and probably commissioned by Cardinal Leopoldo de' Medici the founder of the self-portrait collection in the Uffizi Gallery, Florence. The Cardinal was one of the many influential admirers across Europe of Dolci's talents as a portrait painter, particularly his ability to render details of dress and features and infuse them with emotional power, as is evident in his self-portrait's disturbing presence. Dolci has painted himself holding a drawing in coloured chalks of himself, fine brushes in hand, mouth half-open in concentration, at work on what is probably a miniature at which he stares intently through his pince-nez spectacles. The drawing signed, dated and inscribed with the dedication to His Most Reverend Highness still exists in the Uffizi's collection and was probably also commissioned by the Cardinal. But the painted self-portrait is more than just a clever example of the artist portraying himself in a naturalistic manner both face on to the viewer and in profile. It reveals more to its dedicatee than an artist showing off his multiple skill in the arts of painting, drawing and, by extension, work in miniature, an art which Dolci also practised. The listless look in his eyes as Dolci glances out at the viewer and the shadows lying across his face are a reminder of the allegorical figure of Melancholy (fig.6) a state of mind inextricably linked to that of the introspective, divinely inspired yet frustrated artist, and a condition from which Dolci suffered severely in the 1670s. According to his biographer Baldinucci Dolci, a naturally withdrawn and timorous man who painstakingly produced his portraits and emotionally intense religious works, fell into a deep depression in the first half of the 1670s, losing all belief in his abilities: 'because of a pernicious melancholic humour ... it was not possible for him to utter a single word; but only sighs'.[1] As Dolci holds out the drawing for our inspection and admiration he also contrasts the active inspired artist at work with the passive brooding thinker moodily awaiting inspiration (concerned perhaps that it may not come at all); a contrast between the representative figures of Pittura and Melancholia.

1. Filippo Baldinucci, *Notizie riguardanti la vita di Carlo Dolci*, edn.1886, pp.32-33.

Lit: C. Caneva & A. Natali, *Painters by Painters* exhibition catalogue, National Academy of Design, New York, 1988, cat.no.15

4 Sir Anthony van Dyck 1599-1641
Self-portrait with a Sunflower about 1633
Oil on canvas, 60.3 x 73cm
(By kind permission of his Grace the Duke of Westminster)
(colour plate 1)

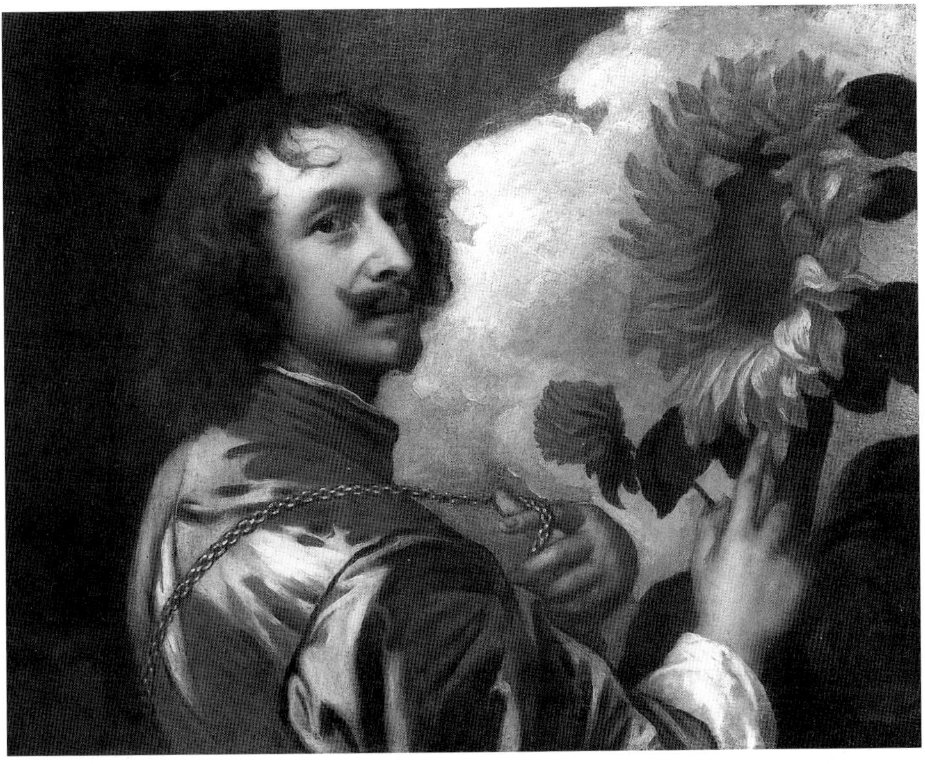

Of all Van Dyck's self-portraits this is the most complex in its composition and ostentatious symbolic content. Seventeenth-century English emblem books commonly represented the sunflower as a symbol of the appropriate relationship between subject and monarch. Just as the sunflower always turned towards the sun for strength and sustenance, so should dutiful subjects devotedly follow their prince. Courtiers in particular were likened to sunflowers 'waiting upon the sonne of Majestie' and the flower was used to denote specifically the dependence of the subject on the goodwill of the monarch.[1] Van Dyck with his demonstrative gestures pointing towards the towering sunflower with one hand, and with the other lifting up the chain around his chest, equates himself the courtier-artist devoted and dependent on King Charles I, with the courtly sunflower. Van Dyck was more dependent than most on royal favour as it was thanks to the King that his palatial lodgings were outside the jurisdiction of London's painters' guild, which constantly petitioned against the presence of foreign artists in London. Within a few months of his arrival at Charles I's court in April 1632 Van Dyck had been knighted by the king, who made him his 'principal painter', and less than a year later gave him in recognition of his position a gold chain and medal. Although the portrait medal of the King is hidden from view in Van Dyck's *Self-portrait* the chain he proudly displays must celebrate his recognition as the leading painter of one of Europe's most artistically inclined monarchs. An earlier gift of a gold chain from the Duke of Mantua in 1622 had led Van Dyck to paint himself wearing it (Munich, Bayerische Staatsgemäldesammlungen).[2]   A sunflower also featured symbolically in the background of Van Dyck's portrait of one of Charles I's courtiers, Sir Kenelm Digby, whose portrait was possibly commissioned between his retirement from courtly life in 1633 and his return to Catholicism in 1635.[3] In some ways Van Dyck's self-portrait may be seen as a response to this portrait of one of the first courtiers with whom he became closely acquainted. Both chain and sunflower were also emblematic symbols of art. The chain featured in the allegorical representation of Painting as described in Cesare Ripa's *Iconologia* (1599). In Dutch seventeenth-century poetry and emblematic literature the sunflower represented the art of painting, devoted to following the beauty of nature.[4] The latter interpretation of the sunflower was how it was understood by the eighteenth-century writer on art, George Vertue, when he described the *Self-portrait* as 'having a Sun Flower alluding to his imitation of the beautys of nature and flower, is said to follow the light of the sun'.[5] Van Dyck may well have thought of this self-portait as both a declaration of his devotion as courtier to the King, and a celebration of an act of royal generosity and of himself as the courtier-artist par excellence.

1. George Withers *A Collection of Emblemes Ancient and Moderne*, 1635, as quoted in R.R. Wark, 'Note on Van Dyck's *Self-portrait with a Sunflower*', *Burlington Magazine*, 1956, p.53.
2. Walter Liedtke, 'Anthony van Dyck', *The Metropolitan Museum of Art Bulletin*, Winter 1984/5, p.20.
3. A. Wheelock, S. Barnes & J. Held, *Van Dyck Paintings*, National Gallery, Washington, 1991, pp.70-71.
4. J. Bruyn & J.A. Emmens, 'The Sunflower Again', *Burlington Magazine*, 1957, p.96.
5. G. Vertue, *Notebooks Vol. II, Walpole Society*, vol.XX, 1931-32, p.107.
Lit: Christopher Brown, *Van Dyck*, 1982.

Self-portrait about 1670
Oil on canvas, 125.7 x 100.3cm
(National Portrait Gallery, London inv.NPG2104)

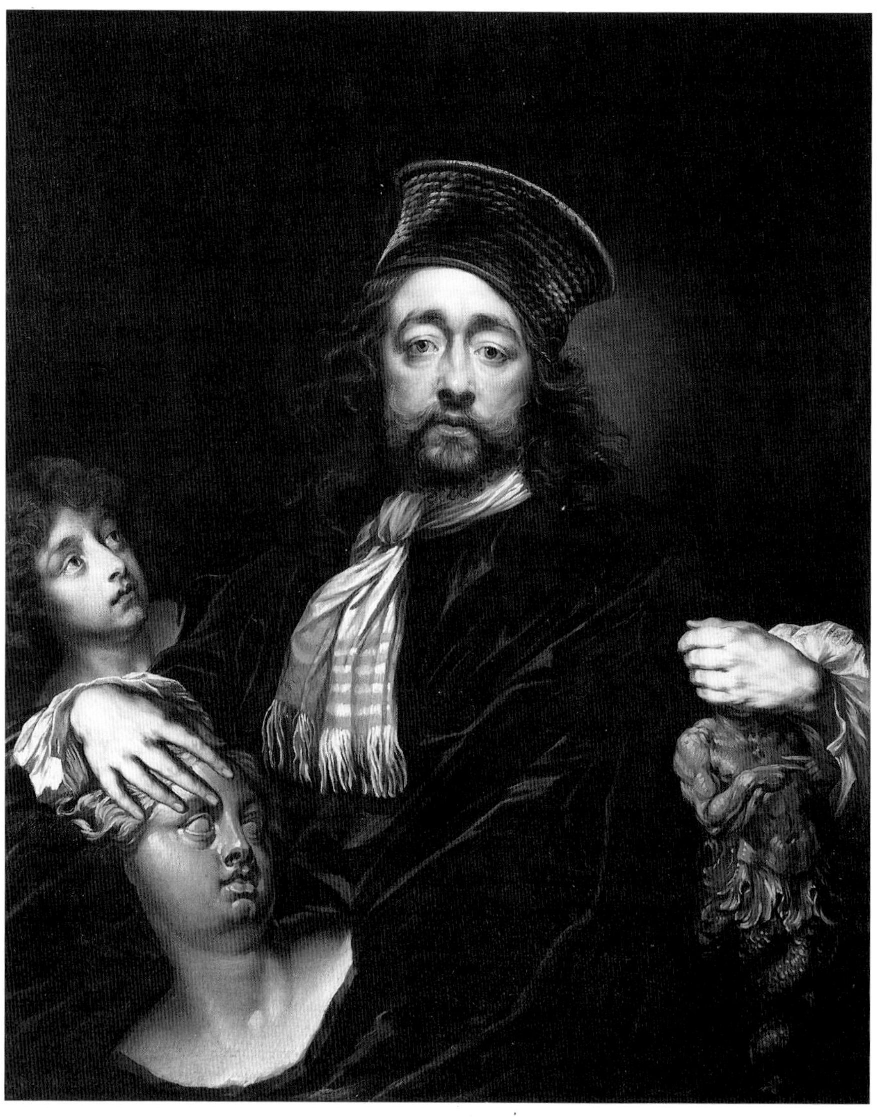

Little is known about Isaac Fuller's artistic career but what is known confirms the larger than life bravura of the self-portrait, whose quirky disordered clothes and ruddy face suggests a bohemian bon-viveur. His face and hands reflect the effect of his dissolute bibulous lifestyle and exhibit the vigorous raw painting style which shocked some later commentators. Vertue, who collected material from one of Fuller's pupils, complained that he was apt to 'make the muscelling too strong and prominent'.[1] The most substantial examples of his work are the five large canvases representing the escape of Charles II from the battle of Worcester (National Portrait Gallery, London). Fuller appears to have divided his time between Oxford, where he painted altarpieces for college chapels, and London where he painted for the theatre and worked on decorative schemes for inns, inspired by classical mythologies. Another self-portrait dated 1670 in which he holds a drawing (Bodleian Library, Oxford) was commissioned by the inn-keeper of the Mitre Tavern in Fenchurch Street, London, for which he had painted a whole series of Bacchic scenes. In the National Portrait Gallery self-portrait Fuller seems to present himself as an artist-connoisseur holding a bust in one hand and a bronze of a marine triton, (half man half god) in the other. But the alarmed glance which the female bust appears to cast across at the triton smothered by the artist's firm hand suggests that the artist may be intending a joke at the expense of portraits like Dahl's (Cat.no.2) or Lely's (fig.23) in which the artist is shown carefully handling or reverently pointing to classical busts and other objets d'art. The look of concern-cum-wonder on the face of the young boy (thought to be Fuller's son), seems to confirm the underlying humour of the self-portrait, although the portrait's pensive quality and its tinge of despondency may show Fuller's awareness, towards the end of his life, of what his admirer Lely had lamented: 'that so great a genius should so beset or neglect so great a talent'.[2]

1. George Vertue, *Notebooks Volume II, Walpole Society*, vol.XX, 1931-32, p.128.
2. As reported by George Vertue and quoted in H. Collins Baker, *Lely and the Stuart Portrait Painters*, 1912, p.124.
Lit: Malcolm Rogers, 'Isaac Fuller and Charles II's escape from the Battle of Worcester', *The Connoisseur*, July 1979, pp.164-169.

6 **Luca Giordano** 1634-1705
Self-portrait in the guise of a Philosopher about 1650-53
Inscribed: MEGLIO E' MORIR CON LI AMICI, CHE VIVER FRA' LI INIMICI
Oil on canvas, 103 x 87cm
(Private collection, Capesthorne Hall)

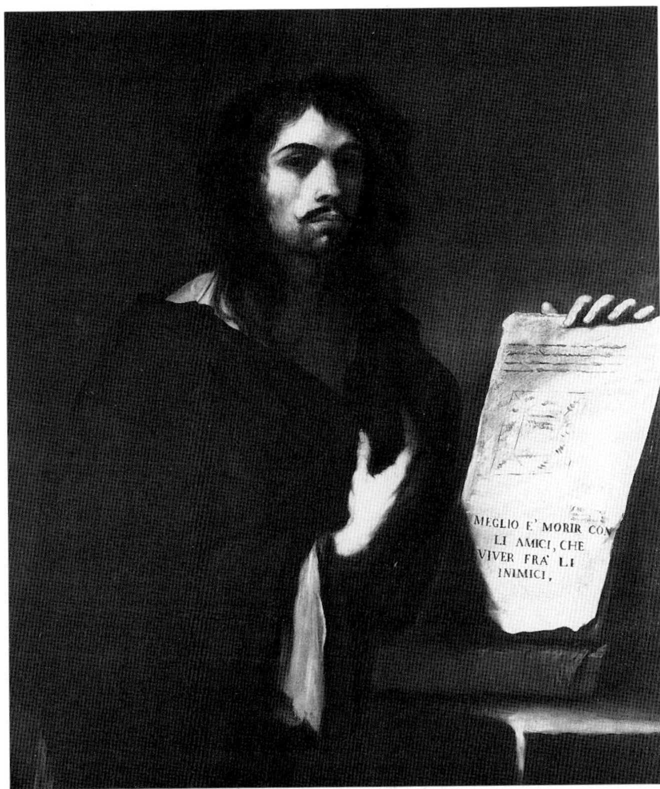

The Neapolitan artist has cast himself as an astrologer-philosopher. His enveloping dark cloak and the long straggling unkempt hair and unshaven face identify the figure as a recluse. In one hand he holds a piece of paper with a curious geometrical motif on it under which is written in Italian the motto: Better to die with friends than live amongst enemies. The geometrical shape is part of an astrological chart (presumably intended as Giordano's own horoscope) showing a central rectangle surrounded by the 12 triangular segments representing the 12 'houses' of the zodiac. The self-portrait was painted early in Giordano's prodigious career, but it was not the first time that he had portrayed himself in the character of a philosopher. By tradition the pair of portraits in Munich (Alte Pinakothek) show both Luca and his father Antonio, also an artist, as philosophers. Imaginary 'portraits' of named Greek philosophers or of philosopher types such as the 'scientist' and 'beggar' philosopher had been a popular pictorial theme within the Neapolitan workshop of the Spanish artist Jusepe de Ribera under whom Giordano had trained until Ribera's death in 1652, and whose style is evident in the flesh painting of Giordano's self-portrait. It is difficult to tell whether it is meant to portray a specific philosopher, although a copy of the painting was inscribed *Carthesius*.[1] It was traditional to decorate studies and libraries with portraits of philosophers and writers. In the first half of the seventeenth century intellectual circles in Naples combined an interest in science, which in their age would have included astrological investigations, with neo-Stoic beliefs derived from the teachings of philosophers, such as Diogenes or Seneca, which valued meditating on death. Giordano had close links with these circles through his contact with the Accademia degli Investiganti and may have shared many of their ideals, as the sombre motto suggests. The spur to painting himself in the guise of a philosopher in the early 1650s may have come from Giordano's visit in 1652 to Florence, where he could have seen the Neapolitan artist Salvator Rosa's self-portrait as an aggressively taciturn scholar-philosopher demanding of viewers that they should 'Be silent unless what you have to say is better than silence' (fig.22).[2] Later, when Giordano was an extremely successful internationally famed artist and had less need of striking a dramatic pose to make his mark, he preferred to concentrate on a simple head and shoulders image, allowing his aspirations as an intellectual to be symbolised only by his wearing of his trade-mark spectacles.

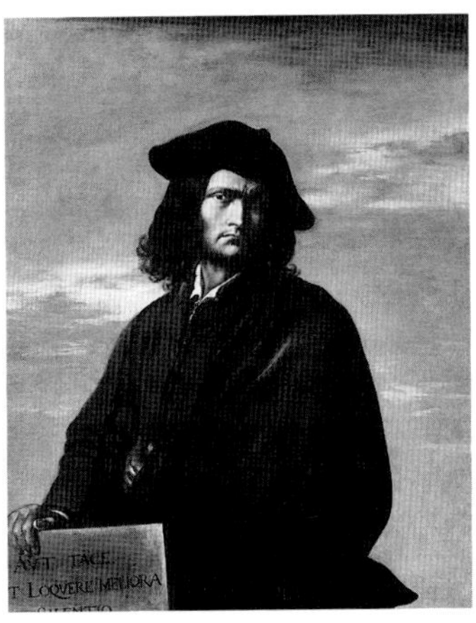

Fig.22 Salvator Rosa, **Self-portrait***, about 1641, (London, National Gallery)*

1. O. Ferrari & G. Scavizzi, *Luca Giordano L'opera completa*, 1992, vol.I, p.255, A30. A supposed 'portrait' of *Democritus* (Hamburg, Kunsthalle) shows him holding an astrological chart amongst other diagrams.

2. In the early 1650s Rosa also painted himself as a philosopher in retreat in his *Self-portrait with a skull* (New York, Metropolitan Museum) and as an alchemist (Milan, Brera Gallery), as above, A31.

7 **Sir Peter Lely** 1618-1680
Self-portrait with Hugh May about 1675
Oil on canvas, 144 x 183cm
(Owned by the Braybrooke Trust on long loan to Engish Heritage at Audley End House)
(colour plate 2)

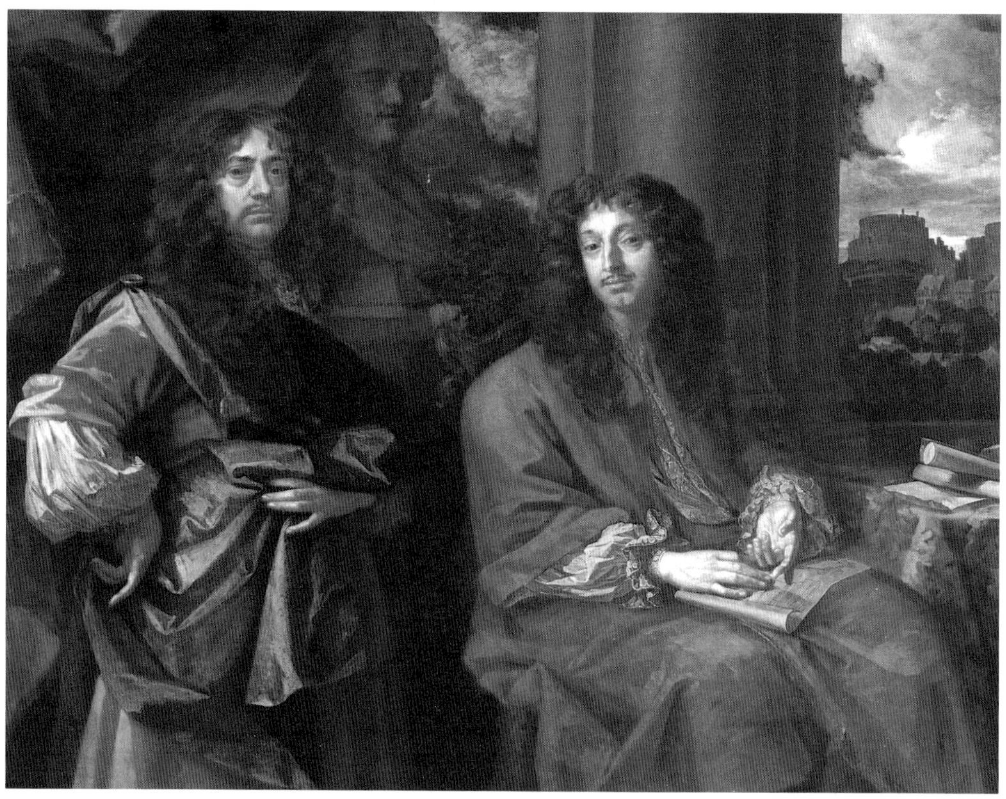

This self-portrait of the proud standing figure of Peter Lely the principal portrait painter to Charles II is also a group portrait commemorating the work of three friends and artist colleagues on the most important commission of their careers, their work for Charles II at Windsor Castle, which can be seen rising above the landscape in the background. Hugh May, the seated figure for whom the portrait may have been painted, was appointed Comptroller of the architectural works at the Castle in November 1673, while the pudgy features of the 'antique Roman' bust set between Lely and May bear a resemblance to those of the King's master carver Grinling Gibbons, who carved the wooden friezes in the newly built grand state rooms and chapel of the Castle. The artistic careers of these three men were all interwoven. Lely and May had been friends since the 1650s when they had left England together to join the exiled court of the future Charles II in Holland. While Gibbons (like Lely of Dutch extraction and training) was brought to the attention of the Court in 1671 through Lely, and was provided with his first major commissions at Windsor by May. As well as being identified as an architect by the architectural drawings he holds on his lap May's finger on fore-finger pose was a recognized rhetorical gesture sometimes used by artists to symbolise arithmetic and perhaps by extension its application to architecture.[1] Lely's aristocratic pose stresses his social position at court rather than his status as artist or connoisseur as in his earlier self-portrait (fig.23), which may have been painted for his artist friend Mary Beale (Cat.no.1). Pepys' description of the

'pomp of his table' and of Lely as, 'a mighty proud man and full of state', hints at his surprise that a painter should adopt such an aristocratic way of life.[2] Lely's stately lifestyle obviously aped that of his predecessor at Charles I's court Sir Anthony van Dyck, and is evident in the dress and demeanour of his self-portrait. His hand on hip with the hand turned outwards was a recognized sign of pride and ostentation[3], often used in seventeenth-century portraits of noble landowners showing off their estates, here used by an artist to portray himself several years before receiving his knighthood in January 1680. What adds irony to modern eyes is that although Lely was a major landowner in his own right, the only landed estate visible is that of his royal master Charles II, with whom he enjoyed an amicable relationship.

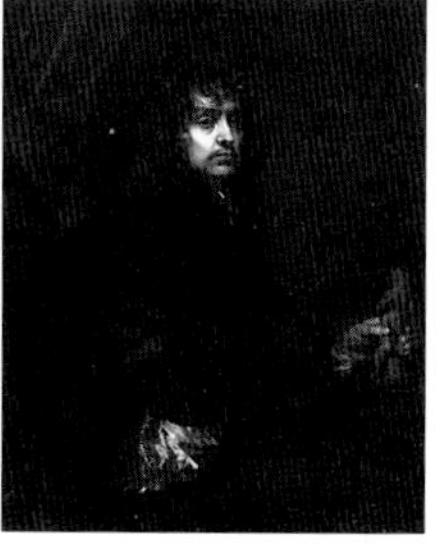

*Fig.23 Peter Lely, **Self-portrait**, about 1660, (London, National Portrait Gallery)*

1. John Bulwer, *Chironomia: or the Art of Manual Rhetoricke*, 1644, p.85.
2. Quoted in O. Millar, *Sir Peter Lely*, National Portrait Gallery, 1978, p.15.
3. Bulwer, as above, p.104.

8 **Jan Lievens** 1607-74
Self-portrait about 1638
Oil on canvas, 96.2 x 77cm
(Trustees of the National Gallery, London, NG2864)
(colour plate 3)

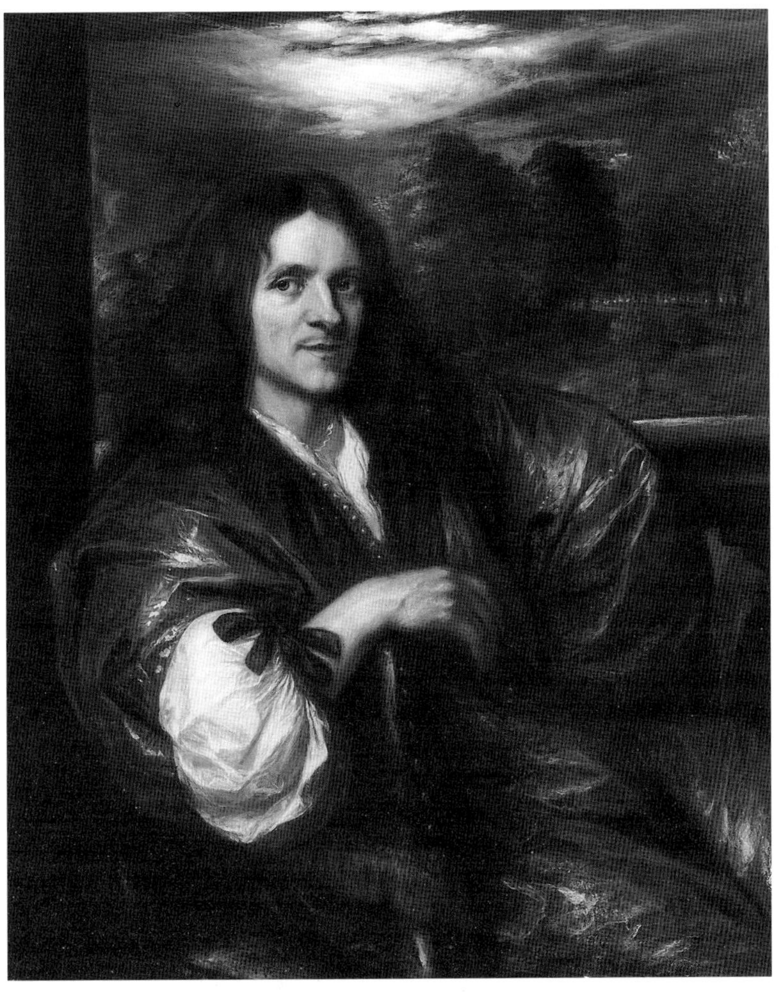

Lievens' flamboyant pose, hand on hip with his other arm draped elegantly over the back of his chair, displays much of the self-confidence that Earl Ancram commented on after sitting for his portrait in Antwerp in 1654: 'He is the better because he hath so high a conceit of himself that he thinks there is none to be compared with him in all Germany, Holland nor the rest of the 17 Provinces'.[1] It was probably earlier commissions from the Earl of Ancram in 1629 which persuaded Lievens in 1632 to leave his home town of Leiden, where he had shared his technique, subjects and possibly his studio with Rembrandt, and seek to further his career in Britain at the court of Charles I. The visit had a dramatic impact on Lievens style as his self-portraits show. An early self-portrait (Copenhagen) shows Lievens in fancy dress, his features dramatically lit against the dark, shadowed backgrounds that we now refer to as 'Rembrandtesque'. Although posterity has placed Lievens very much in the shadow of Rembrandt, at the time connoisseurs, such as Constantijn Huygens, rated Lievens' work as highly as that of Rembrandt, his friend and rival, particularly commending Lievens for his 'inventiveness and audacious themes'.[2] Although he only stayed at Charles I's court for a brief time (by 1635 he had moved to Antwerp) it was long enough for his style to be greatly affected by that of the court's outstanding artist, Sir Anthony Van Dyck. For one of his self-portraits (London, Dulwich Picture Gallery) Lievens even borrowed the over-the-shoulder pose of Van Dyck's *Self-portrait with sunflower* (Cat.no.4). The nonchalant pose and bravura handling of the shimmering, golden silk of the National Gallery's *Self-portrait* also owed much to his artistic mentor Van Dyck. The silvery moonlit, wooded landscape which dominates the background and adds to the rich baroque effect of the whole portrait is typical of Lievens' distinctive landscape style which he developed from the late 1630s, basing it on that of Rubens. The picture gives no intimation that the man portrayed is an artist, indeed his manner of dress and attitude have the air of a courtier. In particular his hand on hip pose was an assertively commanding attitude which often featured in seventeenth-century portraits of aristocratic men. Perhaps the whole portrait betrays too extravagant an insistence on the courtly pose and rich clothing, by a proud artist who hankered after the role of courtier artist but who never gained a title nor found a court to settle at, unlike Van Dyck the artist he emulated and admired.

1. *Correspondence of Sir Robert Kerr, First Earl of Ancram, and his son William, Third Earl of Lothian*, ed. D. Laing, 1875, vol.2, p.383.
2. *Rembrandt & Lievens in Leiden*, Stedelijk Museum De Lakenhal, 1991, pp.17-18, 23.

9 **Carlo Maratta** 1625-1713
Self-portrait dated 1684
Inscribed: Ritratto di Carlo Maratti di Sua mano fatto il secondo d' Settembre 1684
Red chalk on paper, 38 x 28.8cm
(Trustees of the British Museum, London, inv.1902-8-22-11)

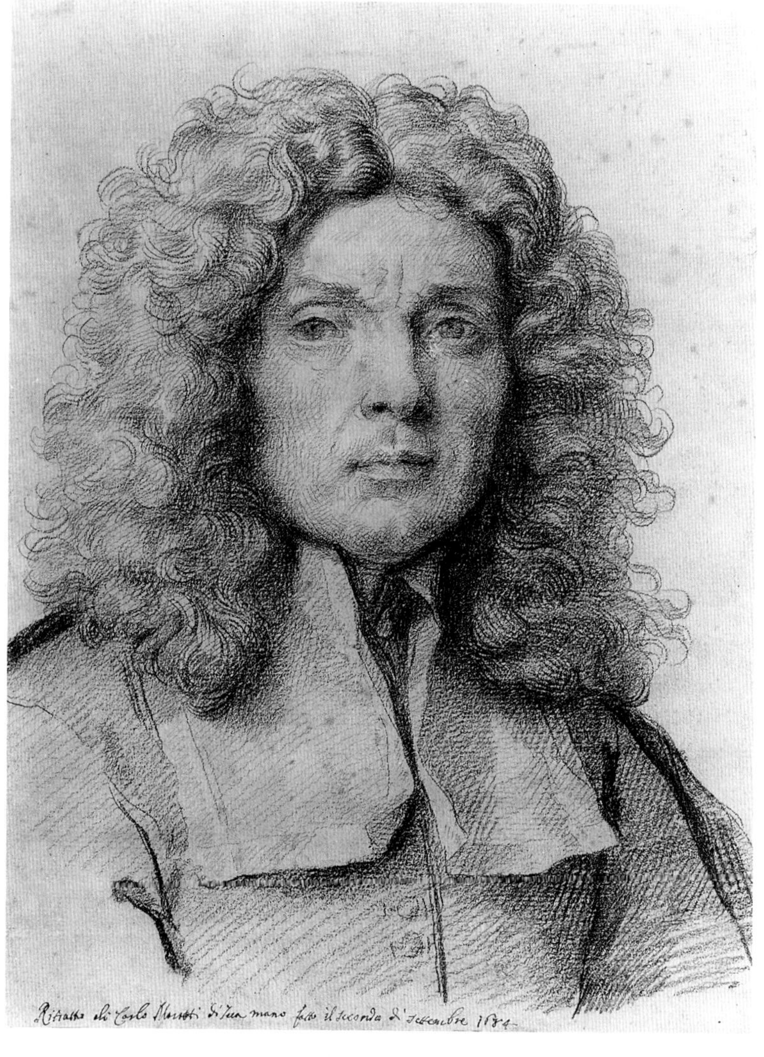

By the time of Bernini's death in 1680 Maratta was one of Rome's pre-eminent and most sought after painters, patronised by the Pope, president of the Accademia di San Luca, curator of the Vatican apartments and master to a generation of artists. British artists trained under him and his fame and skill as a portrait painter, despite his high prices, also attracted many English travellers to his studio near the Palazzo Barberini, where his extensive art collection was made accessible to students and patrons. One such visitor was Sir Andrew Fountaine who, according to an inscription pencilled in English underneath the frame-mount, was given the drawing by Maratta in Rome in 1692. A further ink inscription in Italian dates it precisely to the second of September 1684. The drawing may originally have been intended as a study for the painted self-portrait in the Uffizi collection to which it is related. The disparity in dates suggests that Maratta may have kept drawings of himself in his studio, ready perhaps to offer to selected patrons. The stated date of the gift, when Andrew Fountaine (1676-1753) was sixteen and had yet to receive his knighthood, may have been mistaken as the first known visit by Sir Andrew to Rome was in June 1702. Nevertheless the presentation of the drawing illustrates the patronage link between the baroque Roman painter and the Norfolk connoisseur, at a formative period in the development of Fountaine's taste for Italian art, and in particular the work of Maratta and his pupils. Maratta reaffirmed this link with a red chalk portrait of Sir Andrew which emphasised the fresh-face of a young man whose wit and handsome features won him favour in courts around Europe.[1] Both artist and patron were interested in self-portraits. On his second tour of Italy in 1714-15 Fountaine became a personal friend of Cosimo III de Medici and was instrumental in encouraging several Italian artists, particularly portrait painters, to present their self-portraits to the Grand Duke's collection in the Uffizi. Maratta produced several self-portraits in drawn and painted form throughout his career. A drawn self-portrait allowed Maratta greater vitality and freedom of handling than his painted equivalents, as is visible in this drawing's soft free handling of hair and the sensitive capturing of the strained expression as the artist gazed intently into the mirror, and out at the viewer.

1. Andrew Moore, *Norfolk & the Grand Tour*, Norfolk Museums, 1985, pp.26-31, Cat.no.15.

10 **Rembrandt van Rijn** 1606-1669
a) *Self-portrait open mouthed* 1630
b) *Self-portrait open mouthed shouting* 1630
c) *Self-portrait frowning* 1630
Etchings
(Trustees of the British Museum, London, invs.1973.V.769, 1973.U. 767, 1973.U.765)

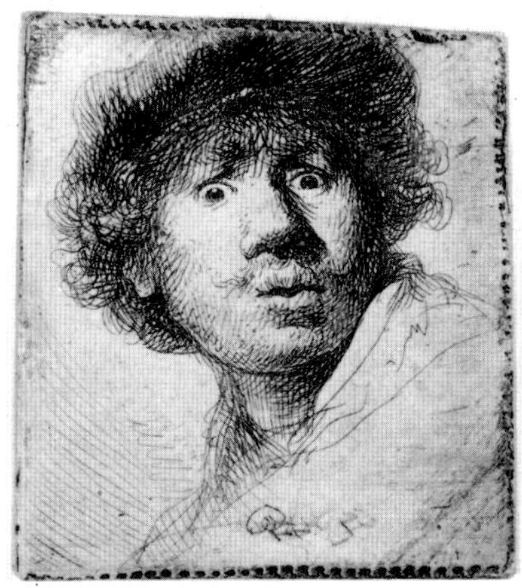

10a

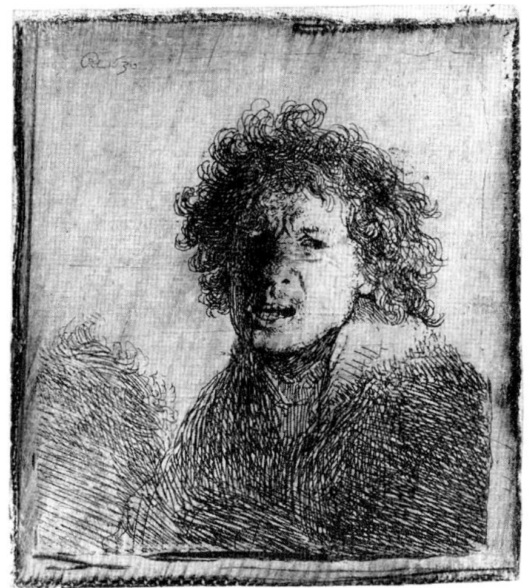

10b

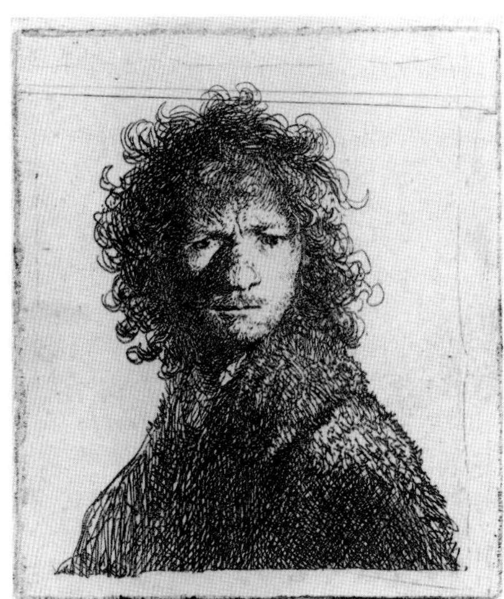

10c

A great number of Rembrandt's self-portraits (a third of his paintings and almost a half of the etchings) date from the years spent in his native Leiden up to the end of 1631. Once he had set up a studio in about 1625 Rembrandt primarily produced small history paintings relating biblical, mythological and historical themes. History paintings required the artist to create figures that showed a wide range of emotions and like many artists at the beginning of his career Rembrandt found the cheapest and best model to be himself. He often inserted himself into his own pictures, his features imposed on a figure in a crowd witnessing some scene from classical history (fig.8) or even taking part in a biblical event, such as *The Raising of the Cross* (Munich, Alte Pinakothek). The 'participant' form of self-portraiture had a long artistic tradition dating from the mid fifteenth century or earlier. The face functioned both as a pictorial signature, expressing the artist's pride in his work and as a present-day mediator between the viewer and the event witnessed. It is clear from the stream of etchings that Rembrandt produced at this stage that he used his own face to act out the expressions he wanted to use in his history paintings, literally recreating the faces he pulled in the mirror with the scrawled spontaneity of his etching needle. The anguished mouth snarling in pain of the *Self-portrait open-mouthed shouting* reappeared the following year in painted

form on the face of the crucified saviour in *Christ on the Cross*, suggesting that Rembrandt used the etching to study the facial gesture he wanted for that altarpiece.[1] The theatrically raised brows widened eyes and pursed lips of *Self-portrait open mouthed* appear on the amazed faces in his *Raising of Lazarus* (Los Angeles, County Museum of Art) of about 1630, whilst a similar expression to that of the *Self-portrait frowning* is found on a figure in Rembrandt's *Descent from the Cross* (Munich, Alte Pinakothek) of about 1633. But, in the 1630 etching the tense glare was further emphasised by wild leonine hair and a furred cloak. Further evidence for Rembrandt's studio practice of acting out emotions in front of a mirror is found in a statement by Samuel van Hoogstraten, his pupil in the 1640s, who wrote 'benefit can be derived from the depiction of your own passions, at best in front of a mirror, where you are simultaneously the performer and the beholder'.[2]

1. Parish church of Le Mas d'Agenais (Lot et Garonne), illus. H. Perry Chapman 'Expression, Temperament and Imagination in Rembrandt's Earliest Self-portraits' *Art History*, 1989, vol.12 no.2, p.121.
2. Samuel van Hoogstraten, *Inleyding tot de hooge schoole der schilderkonst*, 1678, p.110 as quoted by Chapman, as above, p.163 n.31.

11 **Rembrandt van Rijn** 1606-1669
Portrait of the Artist as a Young Man about 1630
Oil on wood, 69.7 x 57 cm
(Board of Trustees of the National Museums & Galleries on Merseyside, Walker Art Gallery, inv.WAG1011)
(colour plate 4)

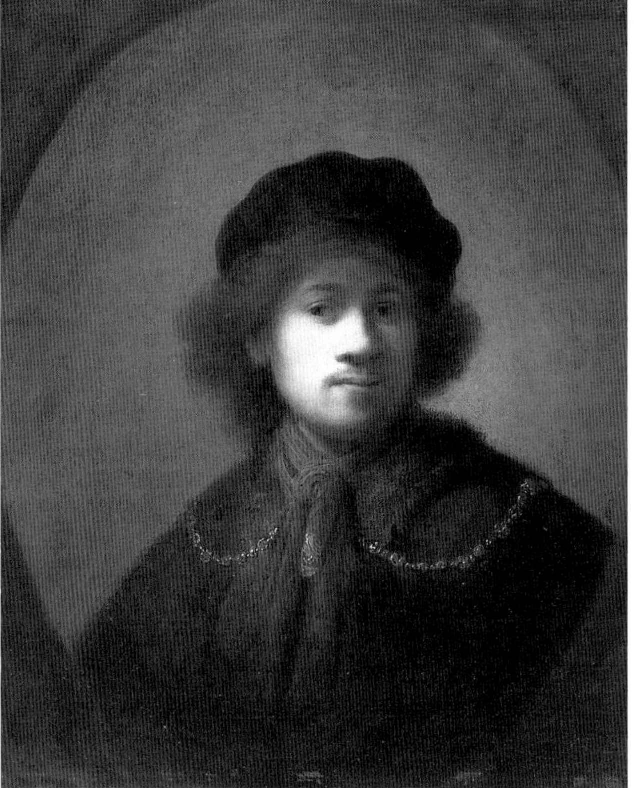

The self-portrait is one of the best documented from Rembrandt's lifetime and one of the first works by him to enter an English collection. It was described in the 1639 inventory of Charles I's collection as: 'above my Lo: Ankroms doore the picture done by Rembrant. being his owne picture & done by himself in a Black capp and furrd habbitt with a litle goulden chaine uppon both his Shouldrs In an Ovall and a square black frame'.[1] Compared to his earliest painted self-portraits with their wild abandoned hair and faces cast in deep shadow this is a tamer, more formal and larger composition, but it retains their evocative handling of light and shade. The fictive oval 'frame' painted onto the rectangular panel and the golden halo of light, against which his head is silhouetted, focus our attention on to Rembrandt's face, reinforcing the 'shape' of our gaze as we stare at the artist. The effect of the concentrated gaze was to give an impression of the intense scrutiny Rembrandt gave himself in the mirror, but more practically it allowed the young artist to avoid painting that difficult piece of anatomy, particularly in a self-portrait, the hands. Rembrandt, however, denies us the expected result of our focus by covering with shadow his eyes, the 'mirrors of the soul', by which we are accustomed to gauge somebody's character.[2] Instead he highlights only the tip of his bulbous nose leaving the rest in shadow, thus idealising a face which we know from portraits by pupils and students to have been pop-eyed and coarse-featured. The shaded eyes have become unreadable, and indicative of the introspective creative mind of the melancholy artist. Despite the assertive frontal pose the portrait's mood is reserved almost guarded and gives little away, by shadowing his eyes Rembrandt effectively concealed rather than revealed his character to the viewer. Neither is it obvious that the person portrayed is an artist, although to any of Rembrandt's contemporaries the unconventional clothes and especially his beret, already considered an archetypal item of artistic dress, would have marked him as different. The beret featured frequently in the self-portraits he inserted into his history paintings and became a recurring motif in the self-portraits of several of his pupils. Another element of his dress that hinted that he might be an artist was the golden chain draped over his shoulders and glinting in the half-shadow. Differences of opinion have been expressed as to the interpretation placed on the chain.[3] As it appears in fifteen out of the fifty or so painted self-portraits it could be merely a studio prop used to enrich the picture. But since antiquity golden chains have been a sought after sign of a ruler's favour, and a symbol of the court artist, often displayed by them in their self-portraits (Van Dyck Cat.no.4, Titian fig.39). Rembrandt, however, was not a court artist, but this did not make his use of a chain a presumptuous attempt to award himself what others had been given, nor was it necessarily evidence of his social ambition, but perhaps a symbolic attribute, honouring art and artists in general. The chain is placed in a more symbolic light by the fact that the Liverpool self-portrait is the closest any of Rembrandt's self-portraits came to being a commissioned work (see p.17-18), destined for the collection of Charles I which already included Rubens' *Self-portrait* (fig.9), much publicized by Paulus Pontius's engraving of 1630, which was known to Rembrandt (see fig.24). Rembrandt's awareness of the Rubens self-portrait may have spurred him to pay tribute to a renowned contemporary, and celebrate his entry into such a prestigious collection by combining in his image the chain wearing court-artist with the shadowed-face of the introspective melancholic artist.[4]

1. O. Millar, ed. 'Abraham van der Doort's Catalogue of the Collection of Charles I', *Walpole Society* 1960, vol.37, p.57 no.87.
2. K. van Mander, *Den grondt der edel vrij schilderconst*, ed. H. Miedema, 1973 vol.1, pp.174-5. Van Mander the Dutch art-theorist also observed that the forehead and brows 'reveal the thoughts' and in them 'one can read the mind'.
3. Svetlana Alpers, *Rembrandt's Enterprise: The Studio and the Market*, 1988, p.67-68
4. As suggested by H. Perry Chapman in *Rembrandt's Self-portraits: A Study in Seventeenth Century Identity*, 1990 p.54 and her essay 'Rembrandt's Fashioning of the Self', in *Rembrandt by Himself*, Glasgow Museums & Art Galleries, 1990, p.17

Plate 1
Sir Anthony van Dyck
Self-portrait with a Sunflower (Cat.no.4)
(By kind permission of his Grace the Duke of Westminster)

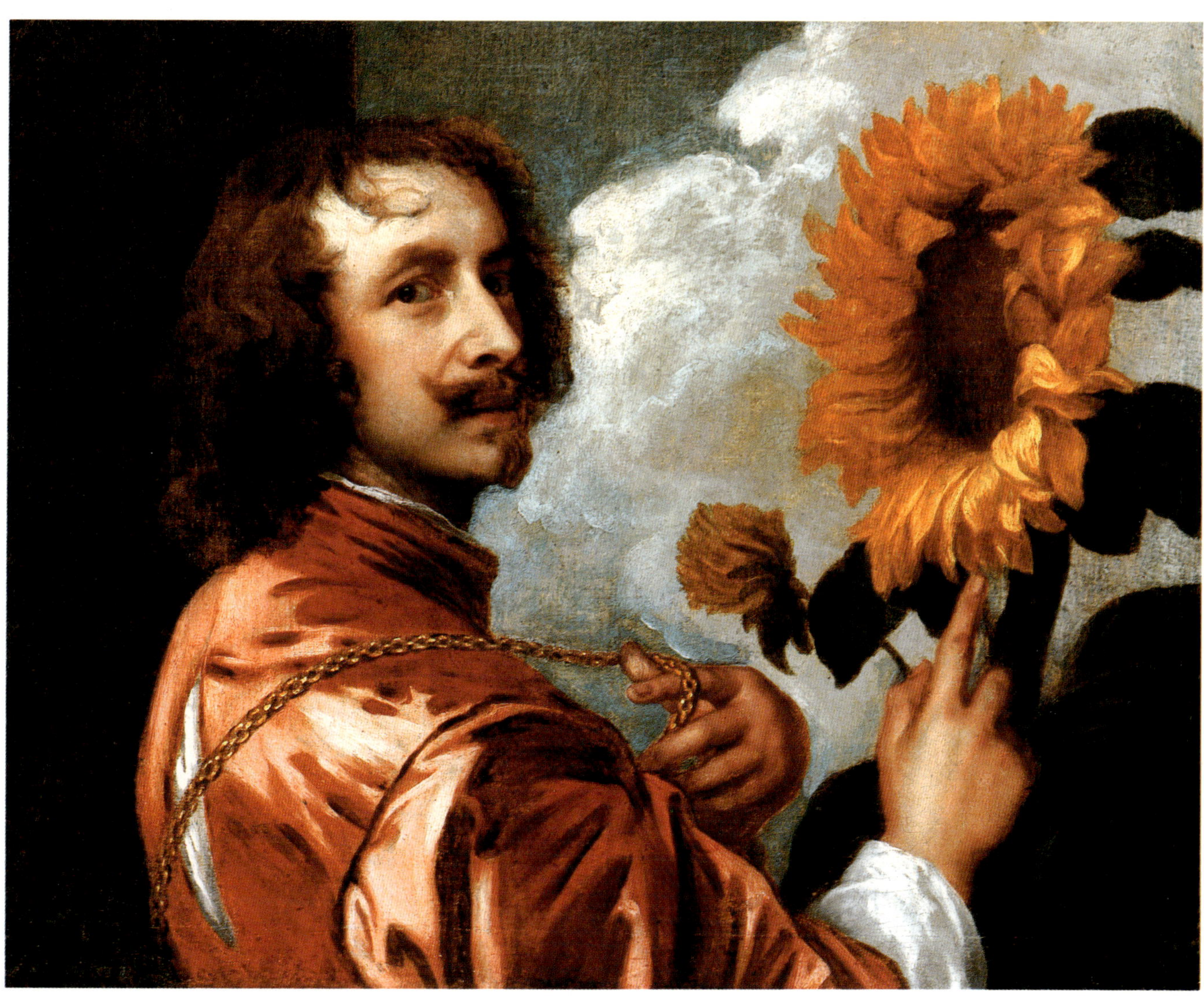

Plate 2
Sir Peter Lely
Self-portrait with Hugh May (Cat.no.7)
(Owned by the Braybrooke Trust on long loan to Engish Heritage at Audley End House)

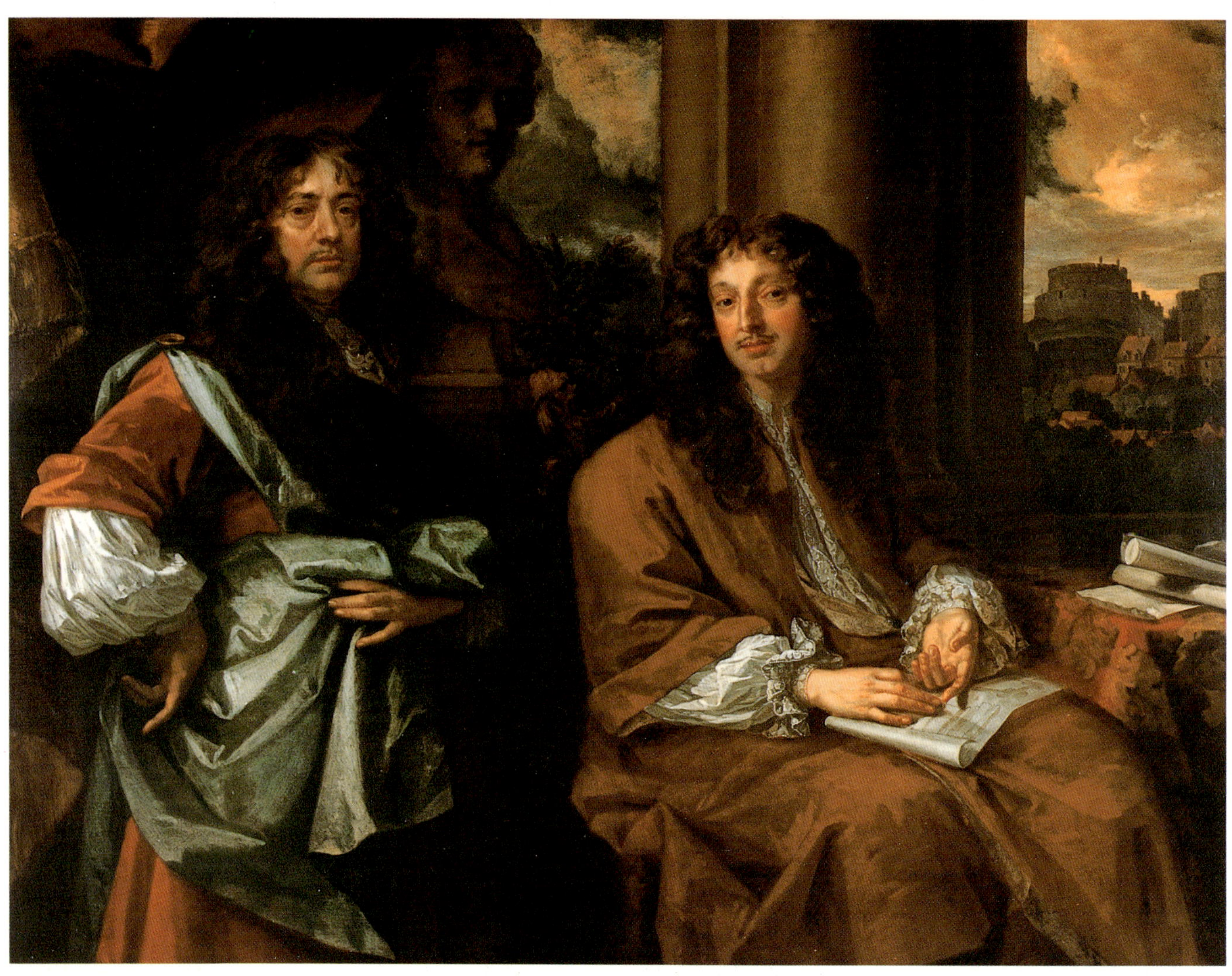

Plate 3
Jan Lievens
Self-portrait (Cat.no.8)
(Trustees of the National Gallery, London)

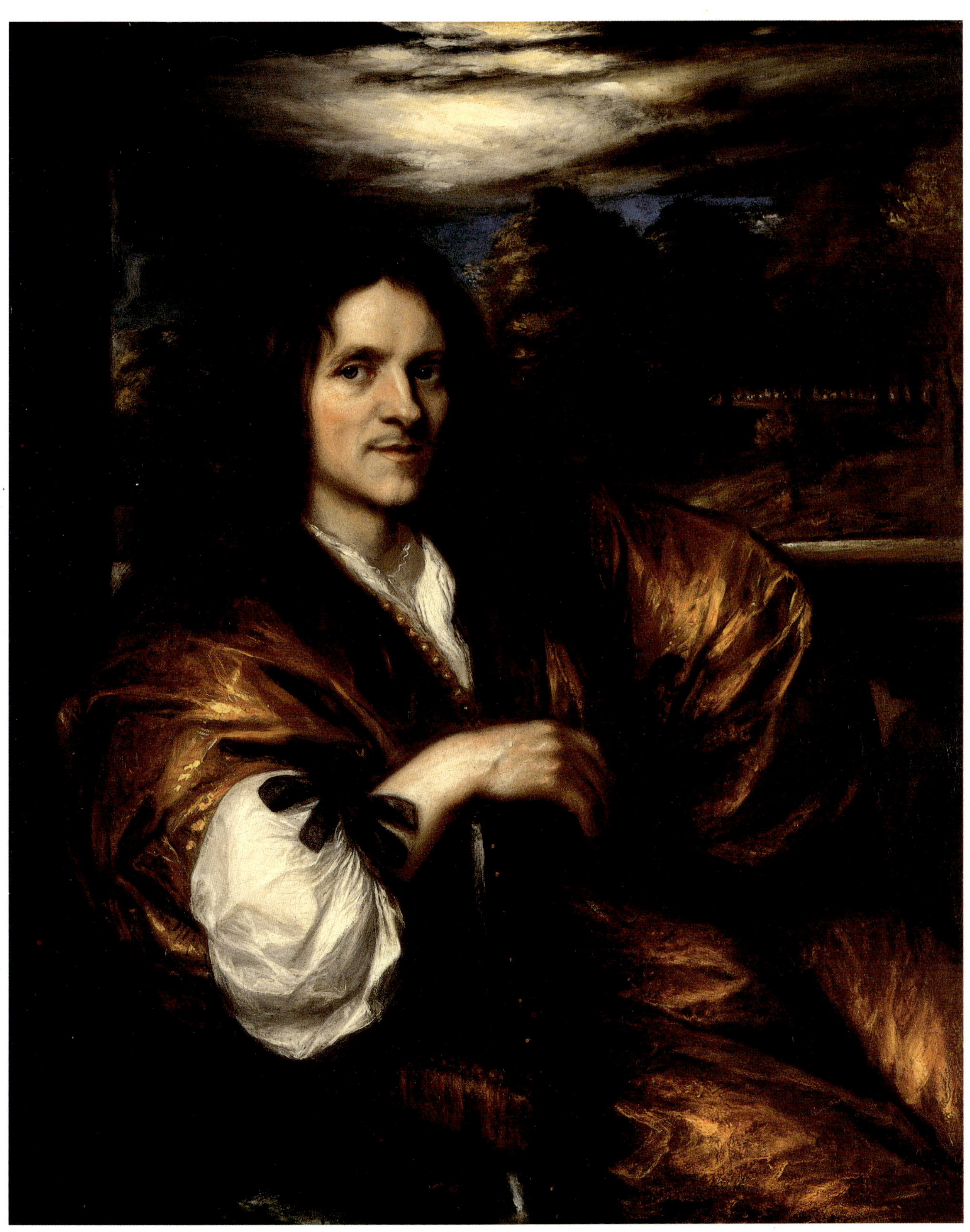

Plate 4
Rembrandt van Rijn
Portrait of the Artist as a Young Man (Cat.no.11)
(Board of Trustees of the National Museums & Galleries on Merseyside, Walker Art Gallery)

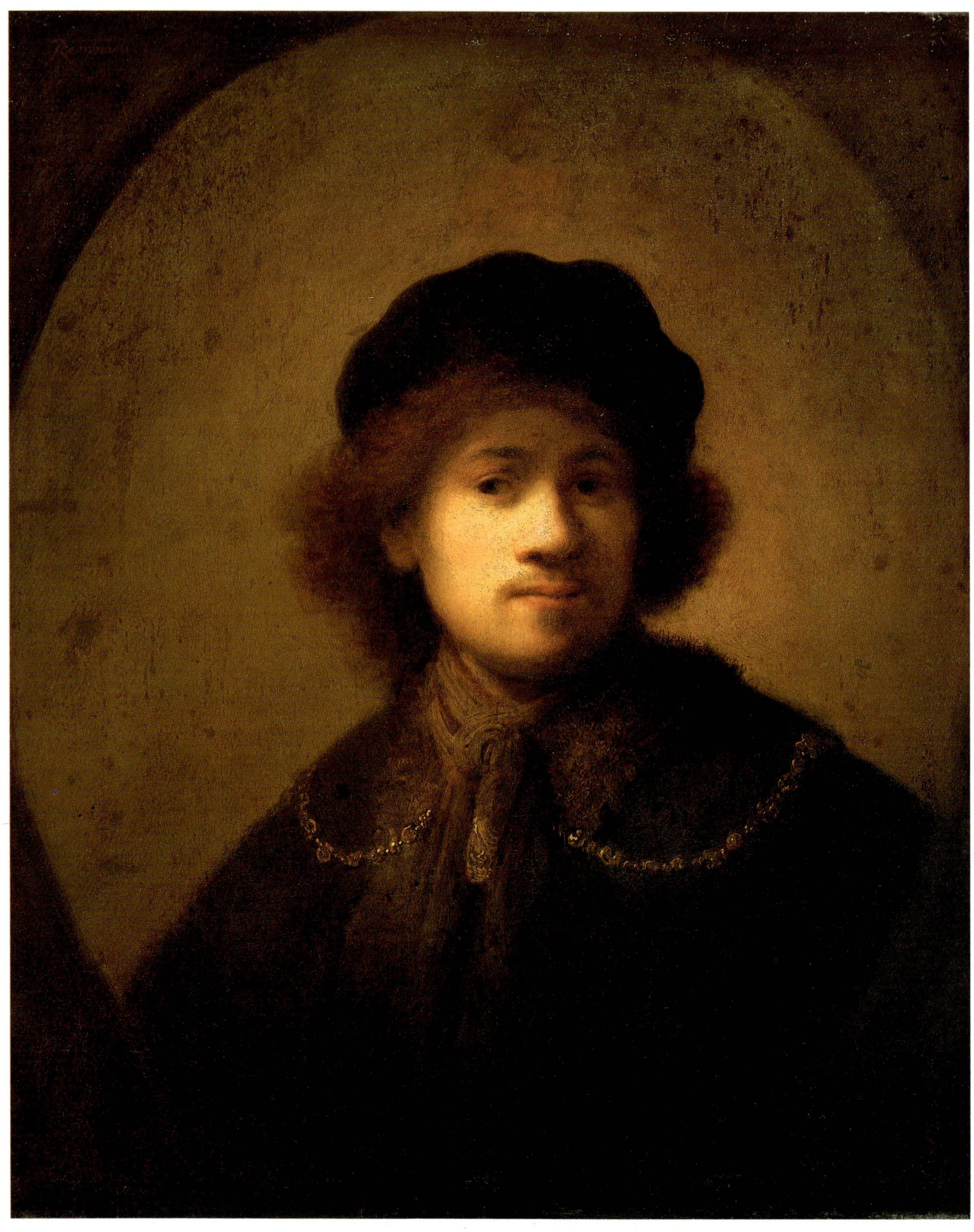

Plate 5
Rembrandt van Rijn
Self-portrait (Cat.no.16)
(English Heritage, (The Iveagh Bequest, Kenwood, London))

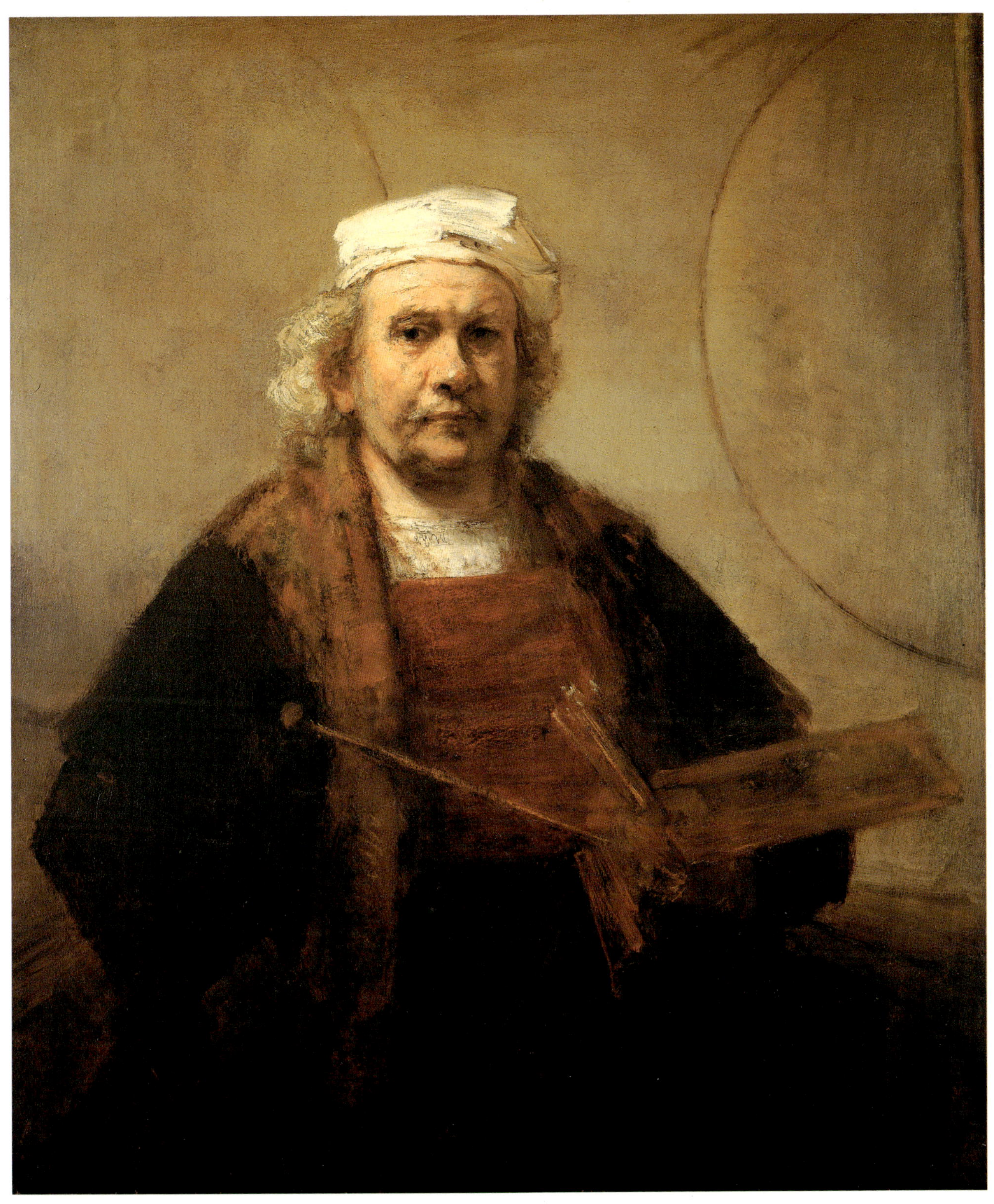

William Hogarth
The Painter and his Pug Dog (Cat.no.23)
(Tate Gallery, London)

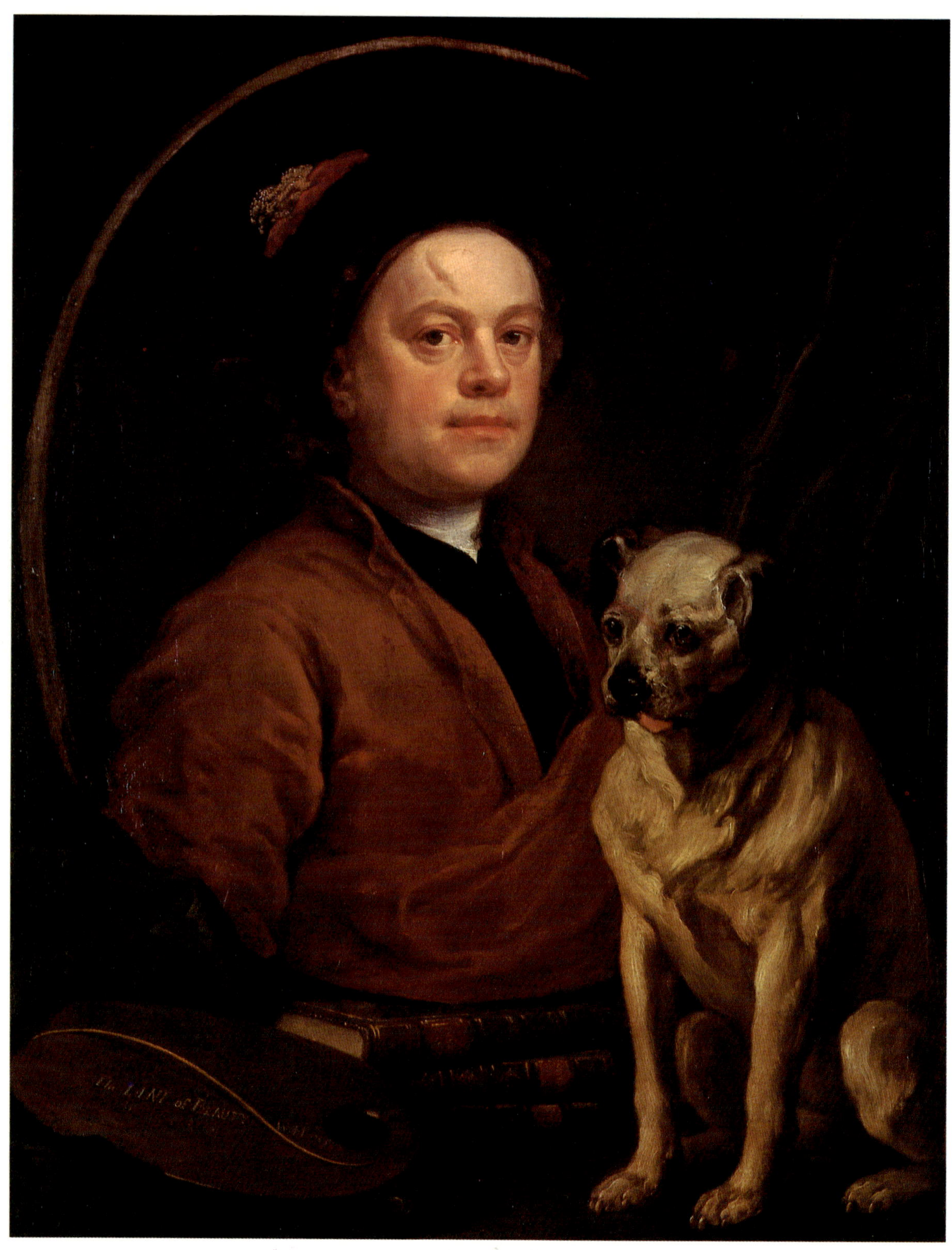

Plate 7
Angelica Kauffmann
The Artist hesitating between the Arts of Music and Painting (Cat.no.25)
(By kind permission of Lord St. Oswald and The National Trust, Nostell Priory)

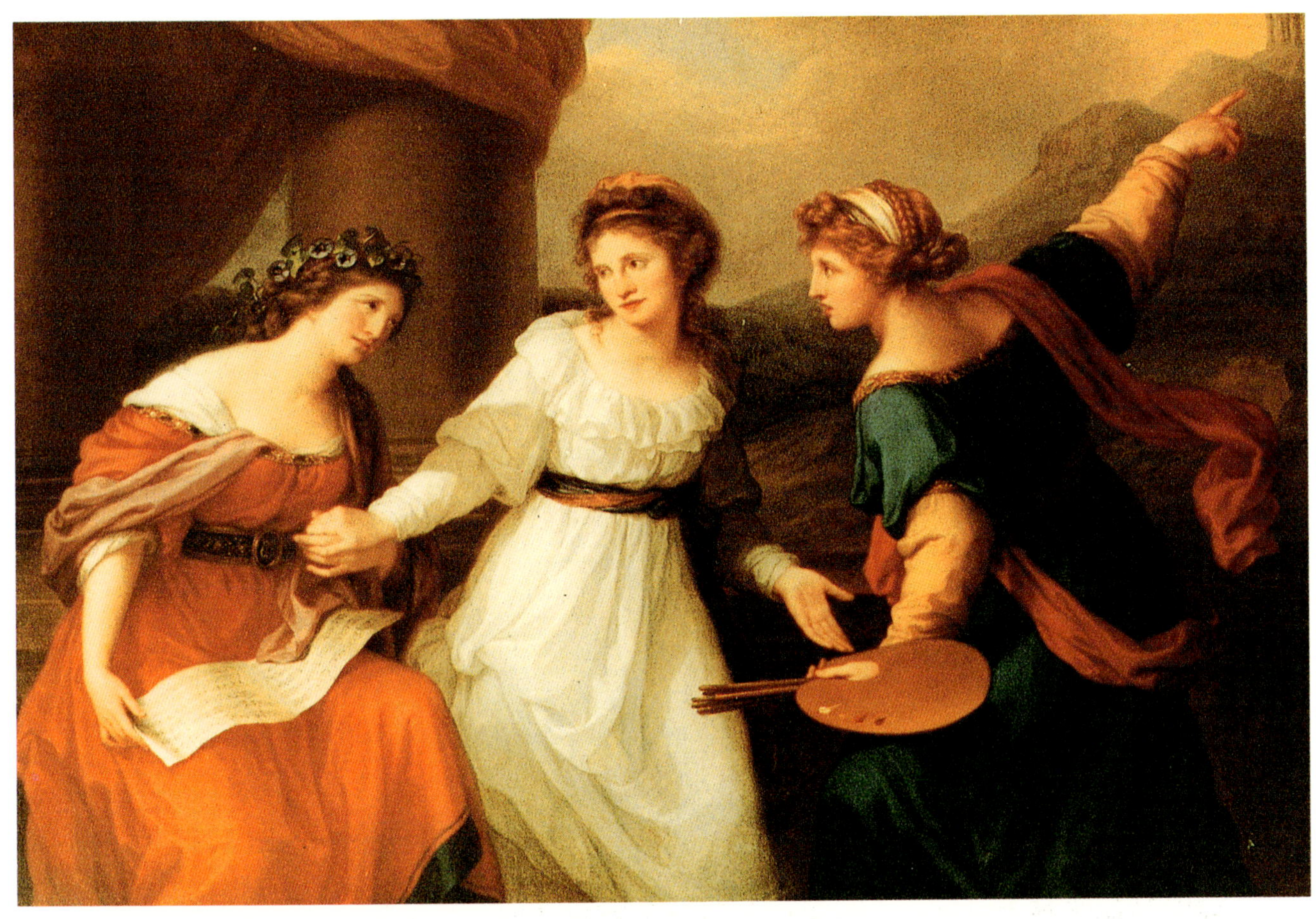

Plate 8
Anton Raphael Mengs
Self-portrait (Cat.no.26)
(Board of Trustees of the National Museums & Galleries on Merseyside, Walker Art Gallery)

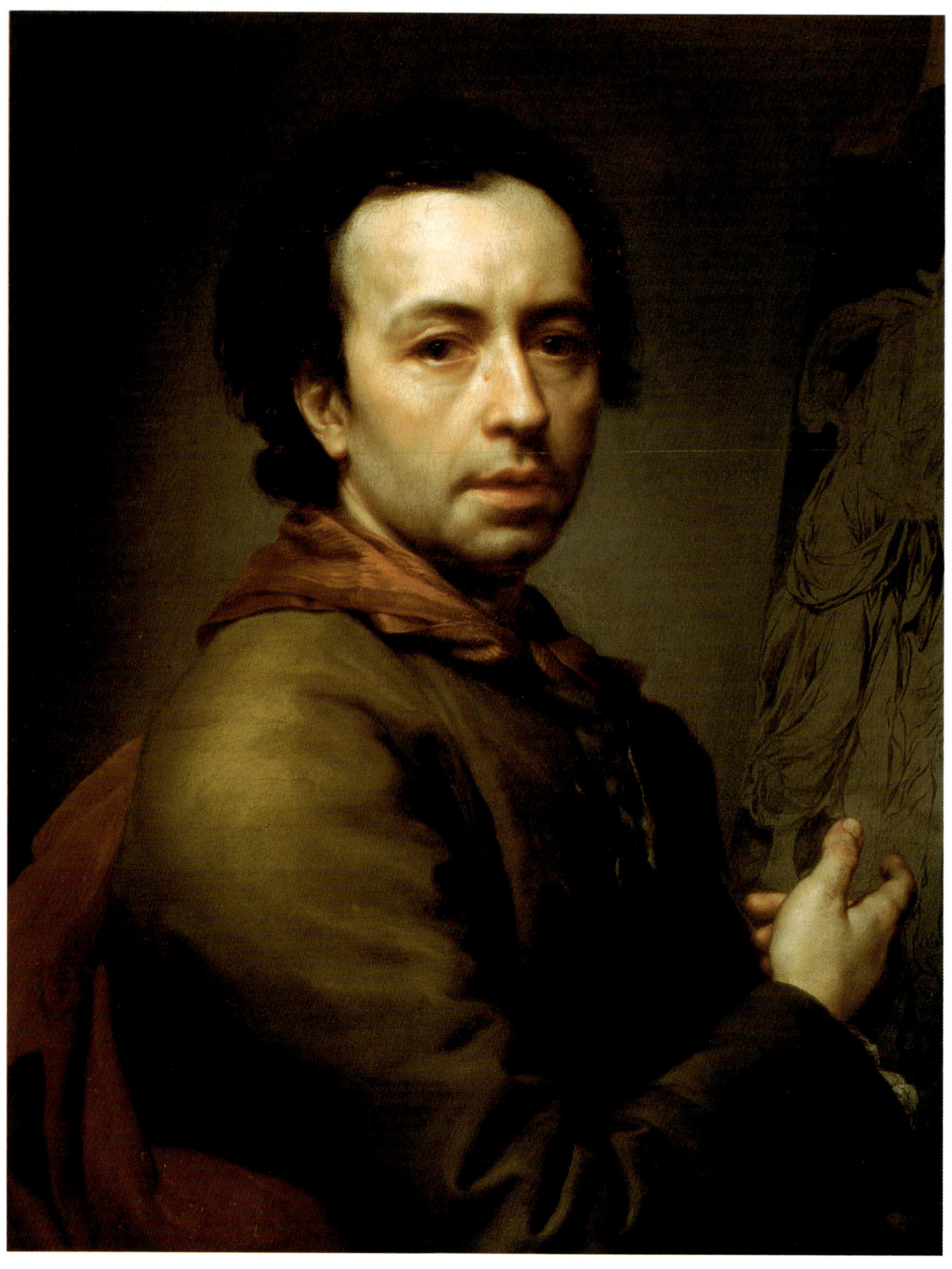

Plate 9
Sir Joshua Reynolds
Self-portrait (Cat.no.29)
(National Portrait Gallery, London)

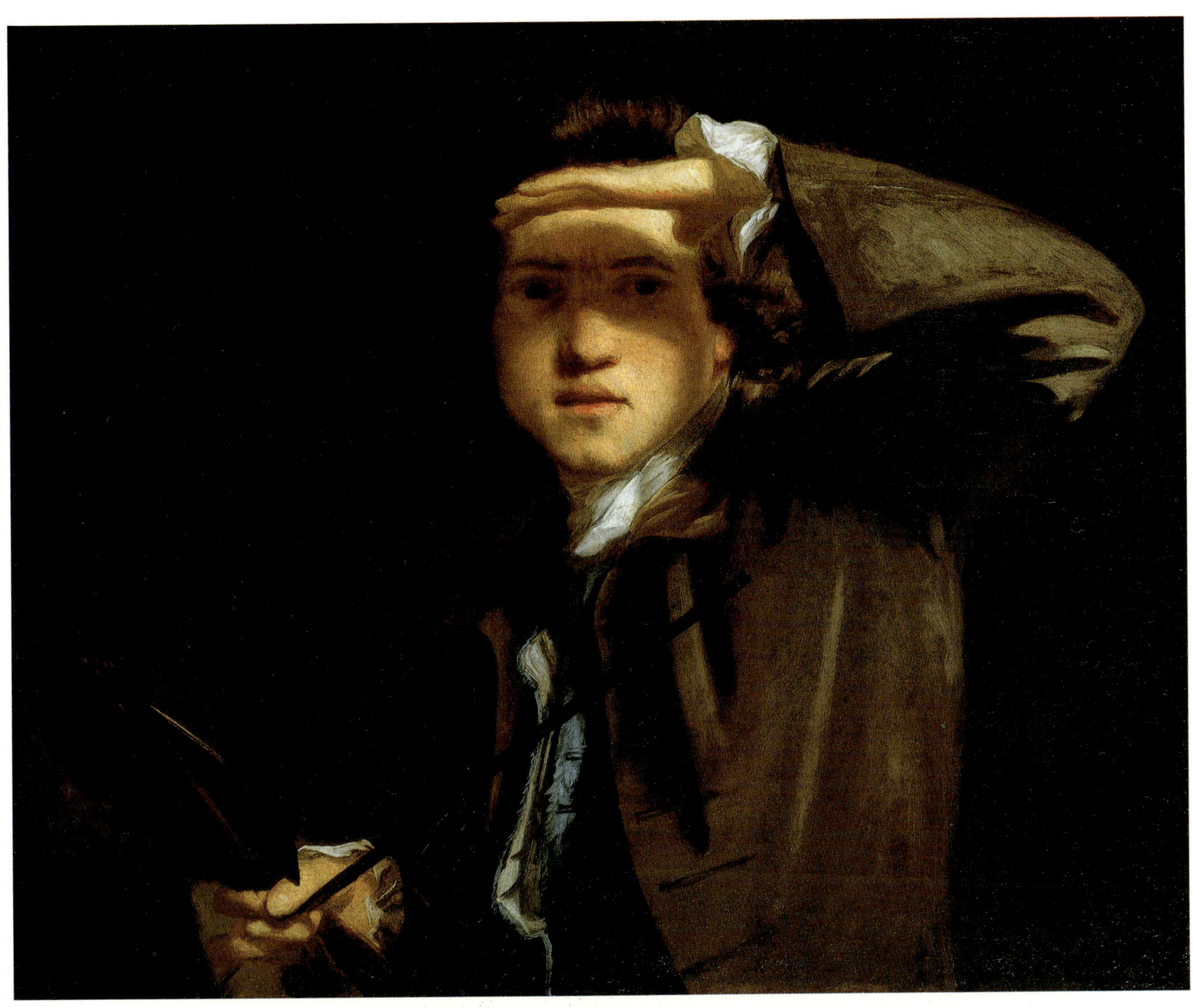

Plate 10
George Stubbs
Self-portrait on a White Hunter (Cat.no.33)
(Trustees of the National Museums & Galleries on Merseyside, Lady Lever Art Gallery)

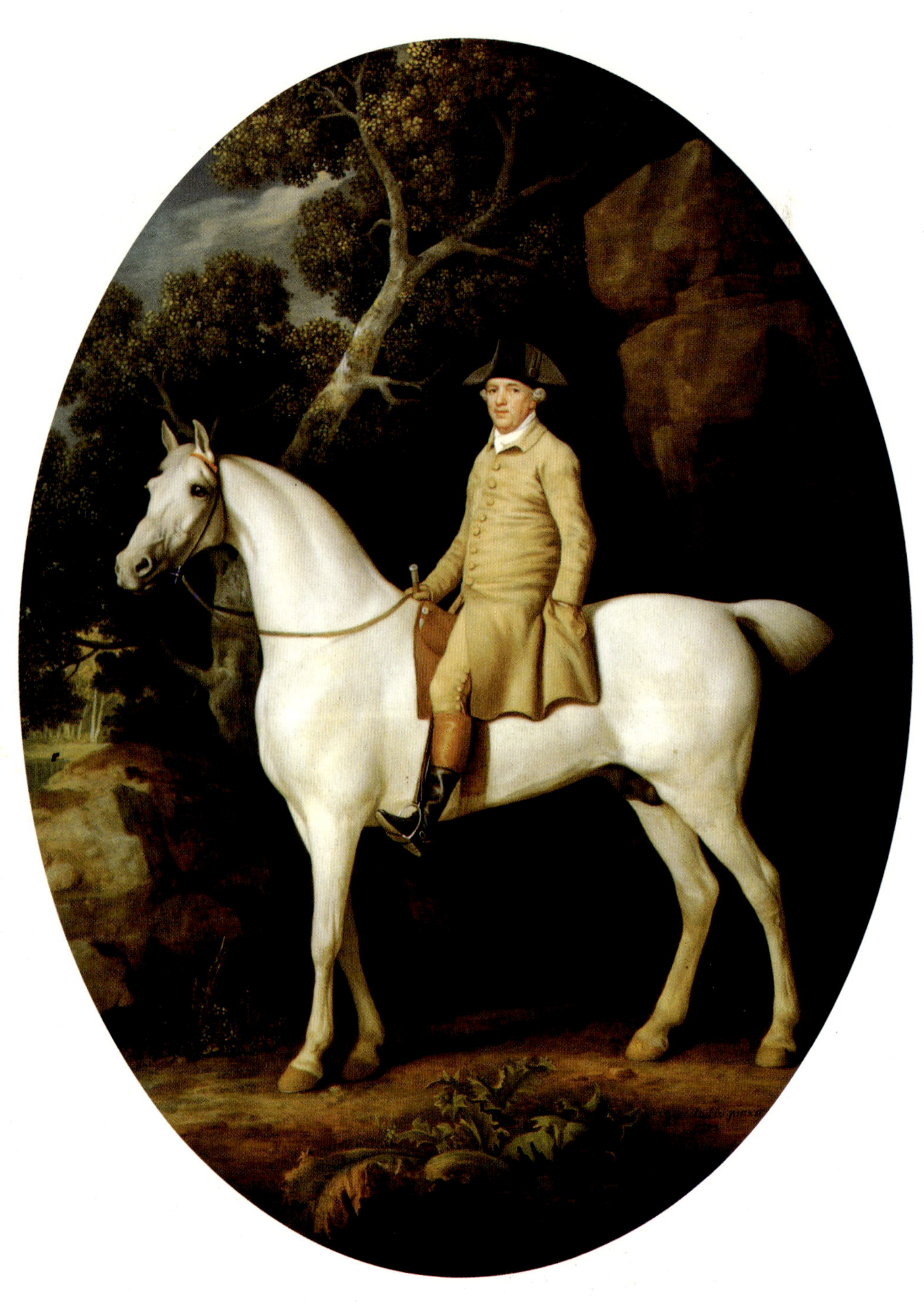

Elizabeth Louise Vigée Le Brun
Self-portrait in a Straw Hat (Cat.no.35)
(The National Gallery, London)

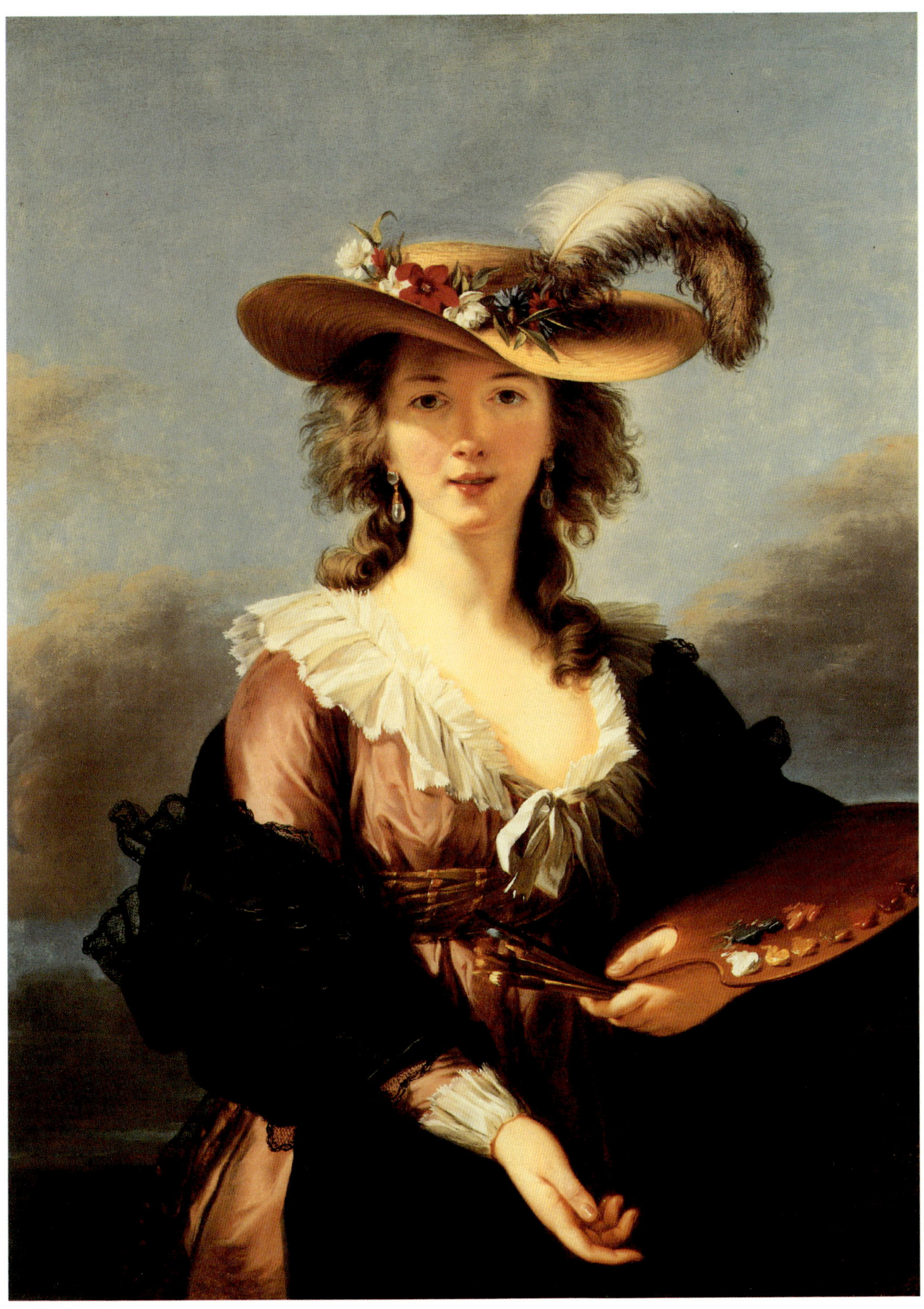

Joseph Wright of Derby
Self-portrait in a Black Feathered Hat (Cat.no.37)
(Derby Museum & Art Gallery)

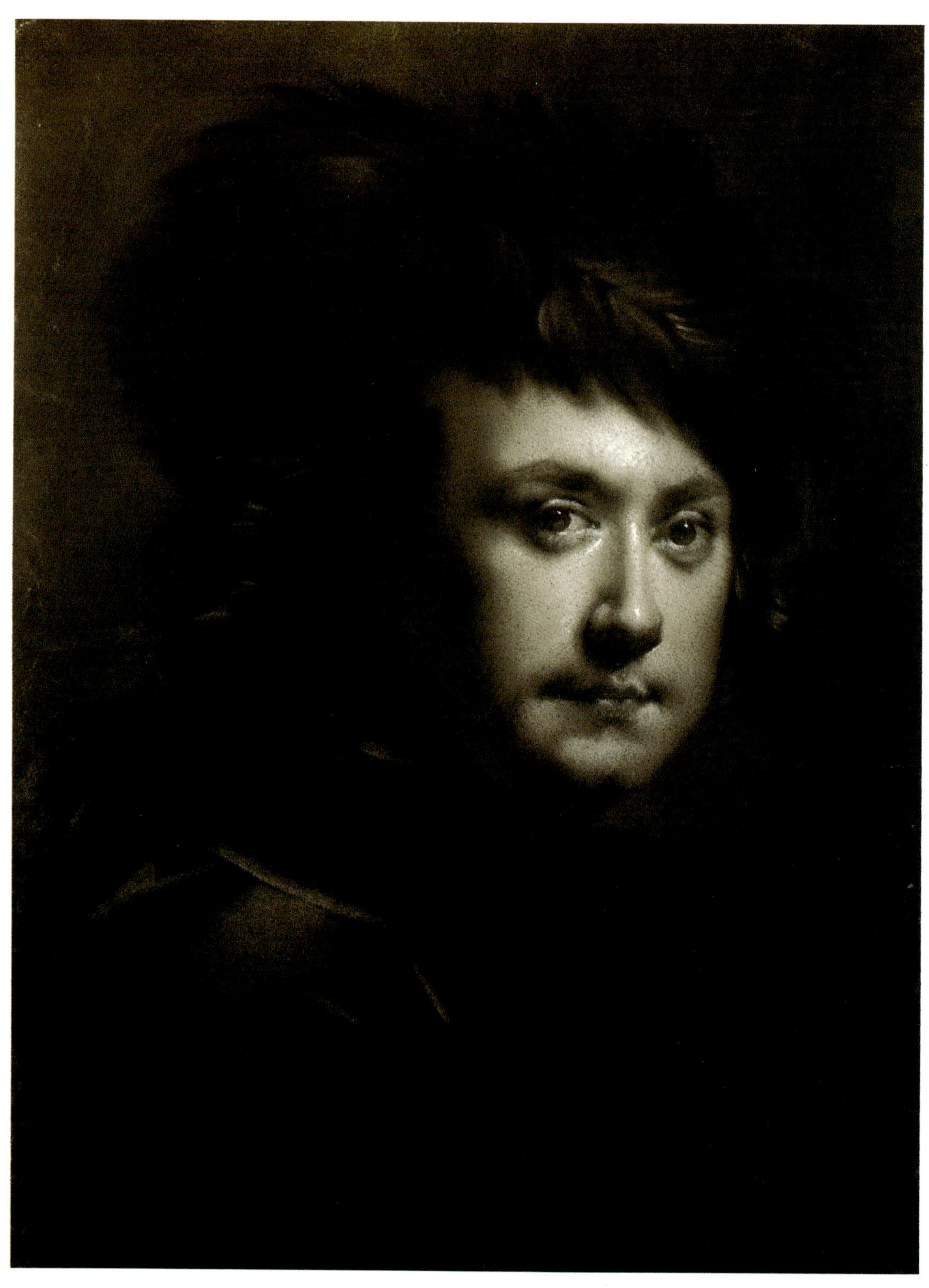

James Barry
Self-portrait as Timanthes (Cat.no.38)
(National Gallery of Ireland, Dublin)

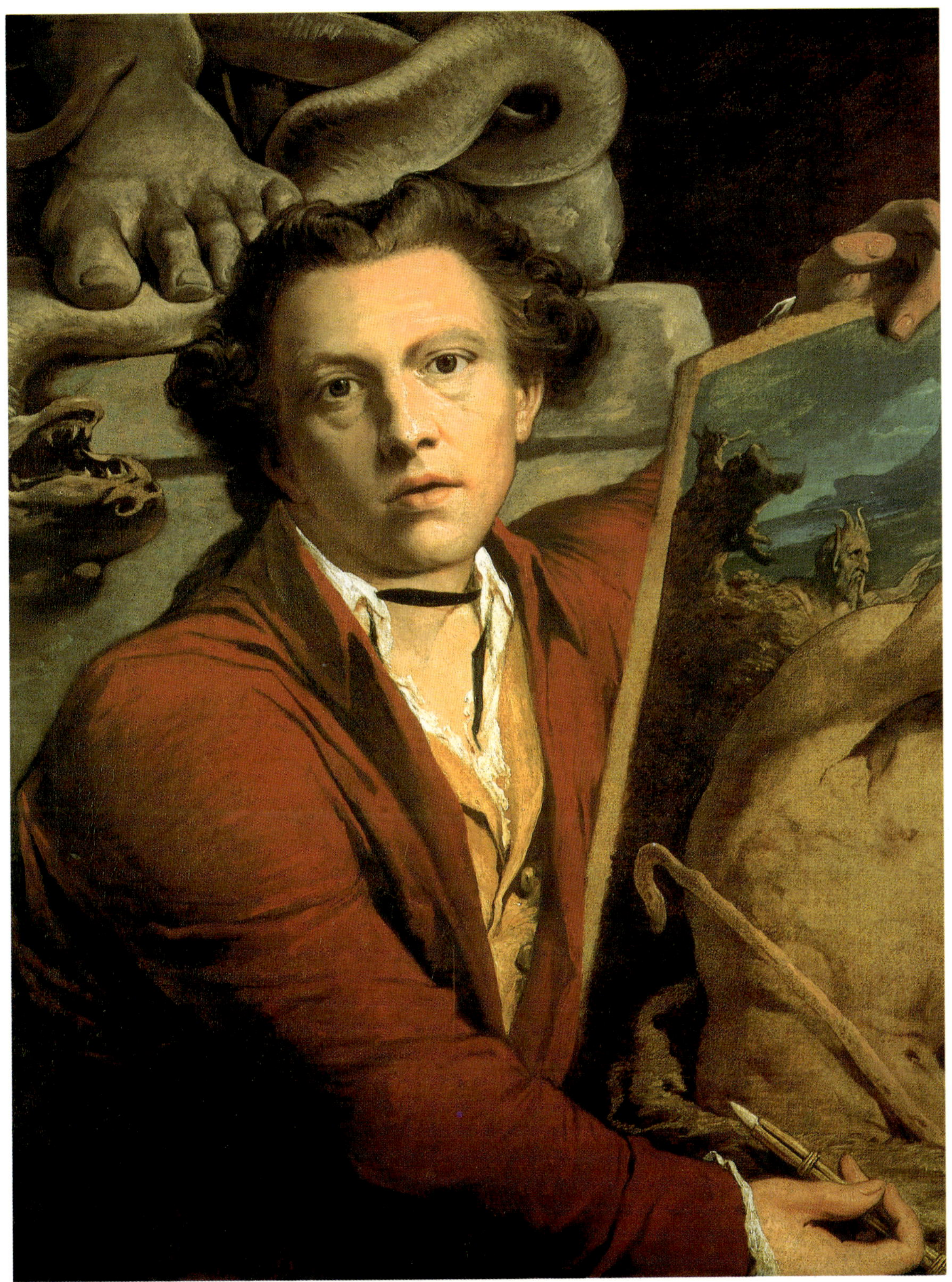

Plate 14
Emily (Milly) Childers
Self-portrait (Cat.no.40)
(Leeds City Art Galleries)

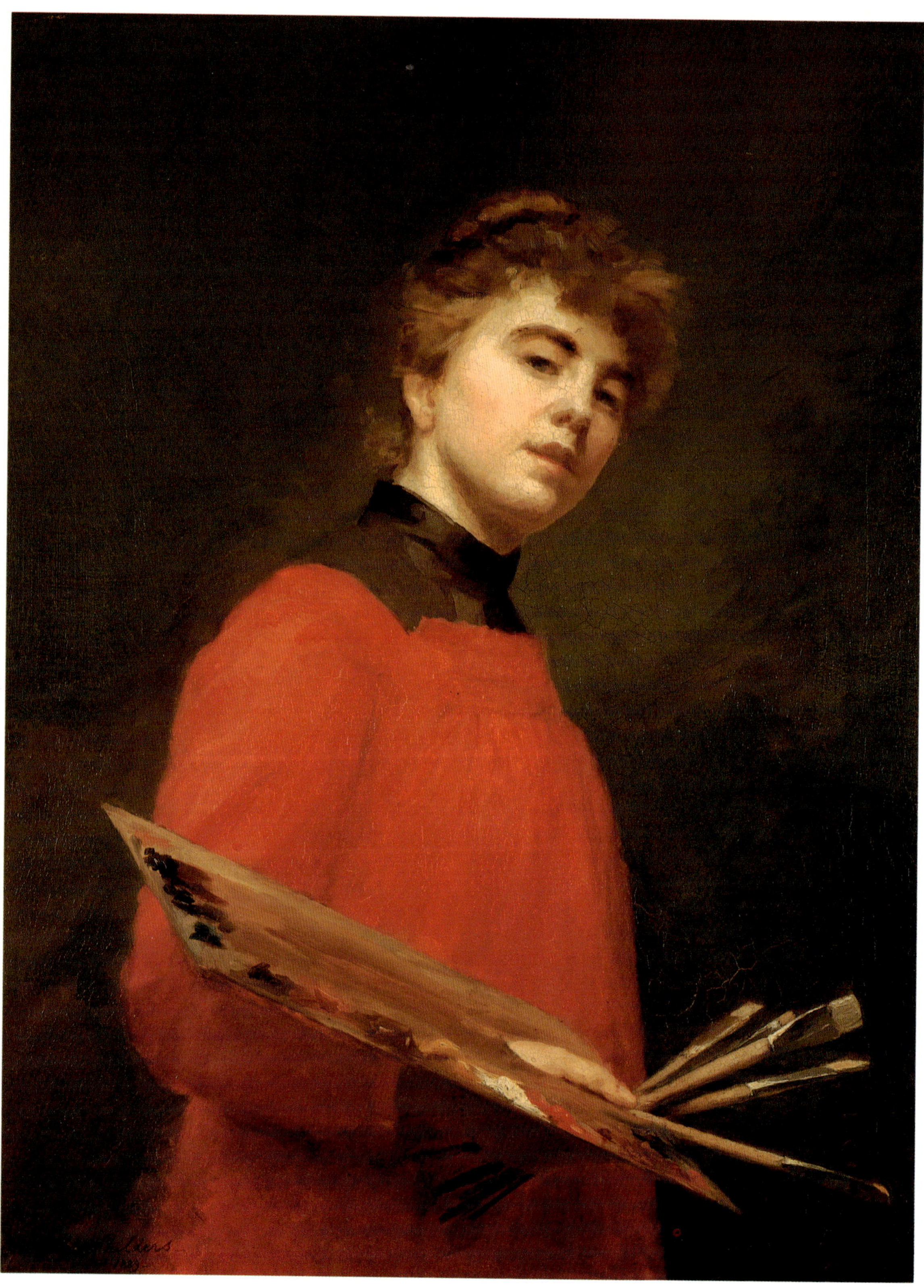

Plate 15
William Davis
Self-portrait (Cat.no.43)
(Trustees of the National Museums & Galleries on Merseyside, Walker Art Gallery)

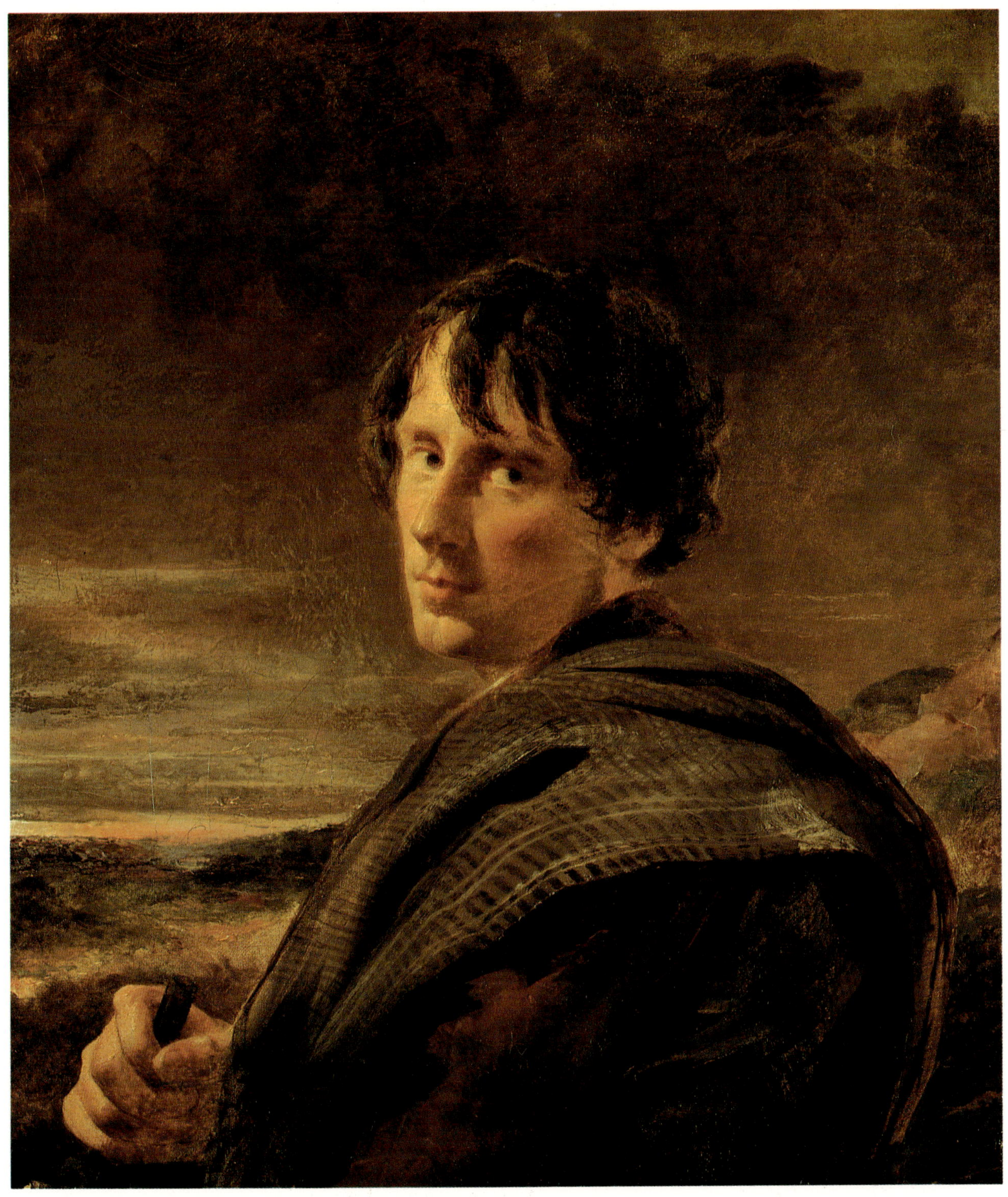

Plate 16
John Phillip
The Evil Eye: Self-portrait of the Artist sketching in Spain (Cat.no.51)
(Trustees of Patrick Allan-Fraser of Hospitalfield, Arbroath)

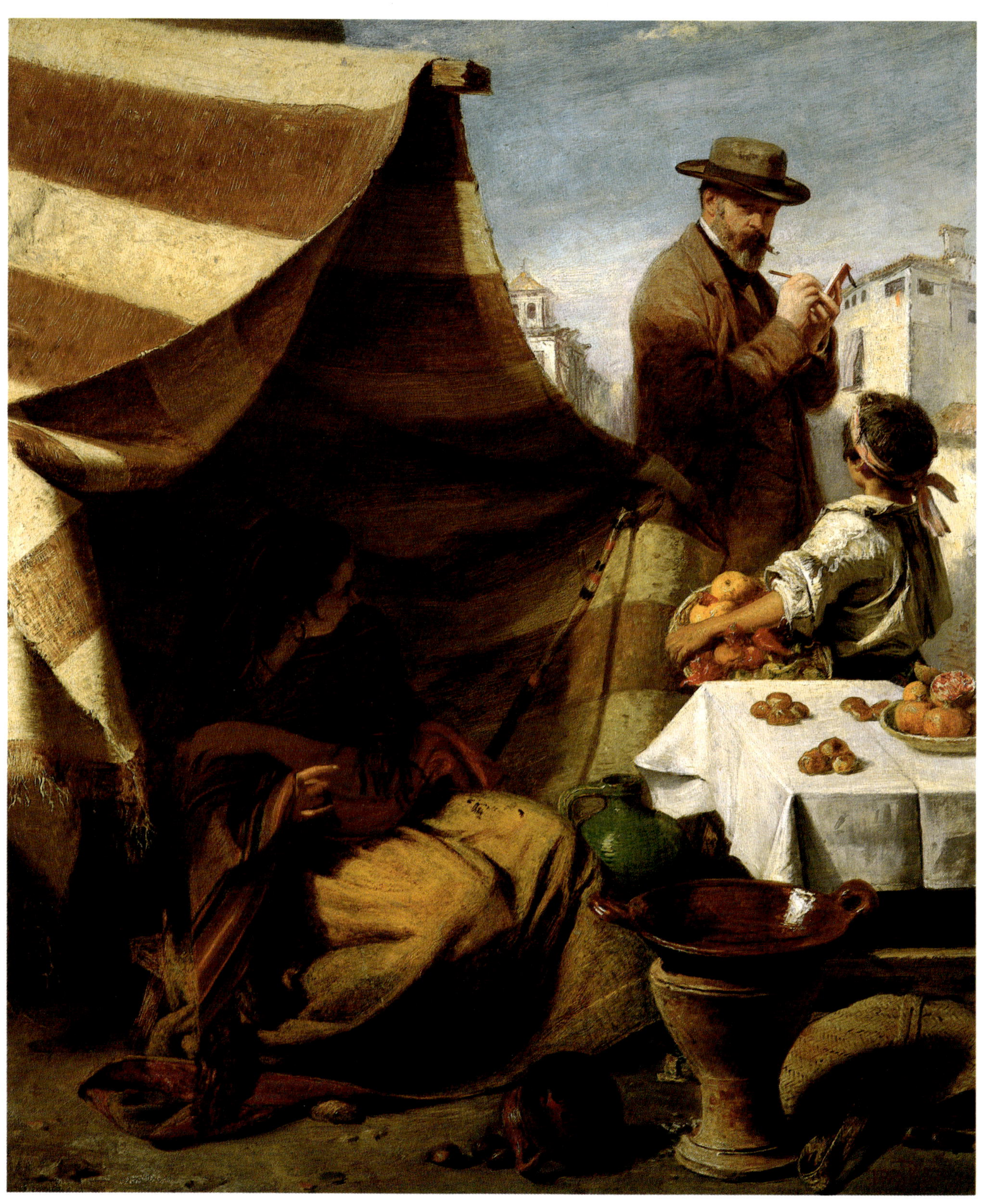

12 **Rembrandt van Rijn** 1606-1669
Self-portrait in a Soft Hat 1631 and 1633-4
Etching and black chalk, 13.2 x 12cm
(Trustees of the British Museum, inv.1842-8-6-134)

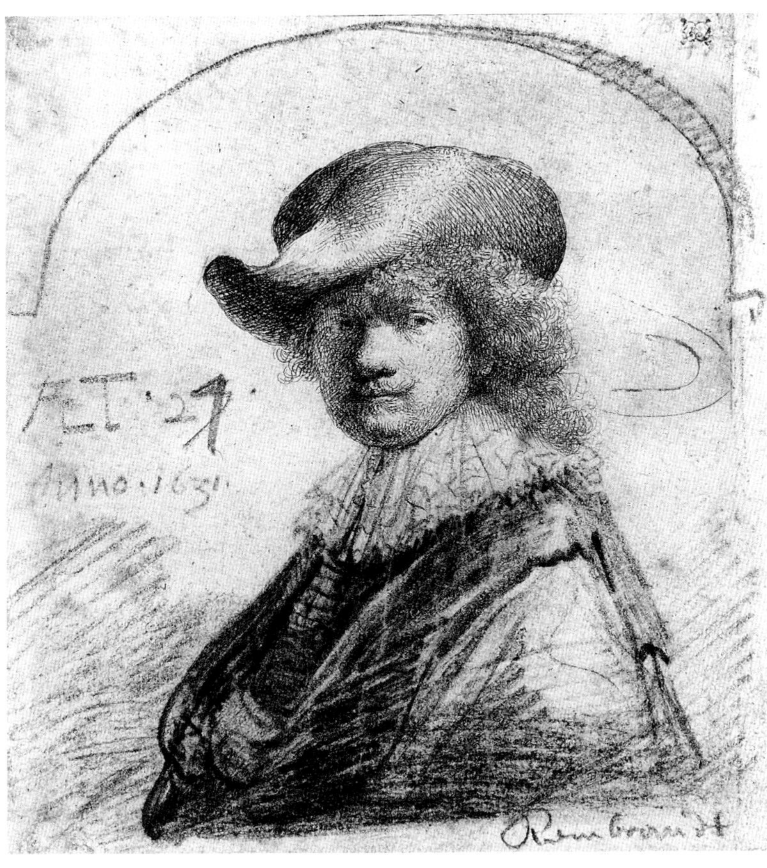

The self-portrait was created from an early state of a major portrait etching touched up later in black chalk. It was dated retrospectively by Rembrandt who corrected his age from twenty-seven to twenty-four, the age he was when he etched the head in 1631. The body and the illusionistic frame above his head were drawn in a couple of years after, when he was twenty-seven. The drawing is distinctively signed with his first name only, the form he used only after 1632-33. The etched head was probably a proof or impression kept in the studio from the second state of his *Self-portrait in a Soft Hat and Embroidered Cloak*, which was Rembrandt's most ambitious portrait etching to date, worked on the largest plate. He expended much effort on working up the plate in eleven states and bringing the art of etching to the highest level of refinement, as is evident in the sheen of the soft hat and the wiriness of his hair. All Rembrandt's early biographers conceded his international renown as an etcher. An etching worked and reworked by Rembrandt to such an extent as this was obviously intended for a connoisseurs' market and the number of examples of the image remaining suggest a fairly large one. It was therefore a more public image than any painted self-portrait of the period. As was common in his practice at this time the etching was an experimental prototype for a painted version, the Burrell *Self-portrait* of 1632 (Cat.no.13), although the pose he eventually adopted for his *Self-portrait in Embroidered Cloak* was more flamboyant, swaggering and courtly than the painted one or this one drawn in chalk. The prototype for the latter pose particularly the turn of the body and the wide-brimmed felt hat derived from Rubens' *Self-*

portrait (fig.9) in Charles I's collection, which Rembrandt knew in its reversed form from Paulus Pontius's engraving published in 1630 (fig.24). The arched frame above his head confirms this source as it is literally drawn from that used in Pontius's print. It is perhaps not surprising that his chalk additions should be modelled on the self-portrait of Rubens, the most famous living artist, for by the time he made them Rembrandt's own self-portrait (Cat.no.11) had joined the Rubens in the royal collection. In this portrait Rembrandt the son of a Leiden mill-owner has given himself the air of a well-bred gentleman, constructing himself in the image of Rubens the embodiment of the gentleman artist-courtier.

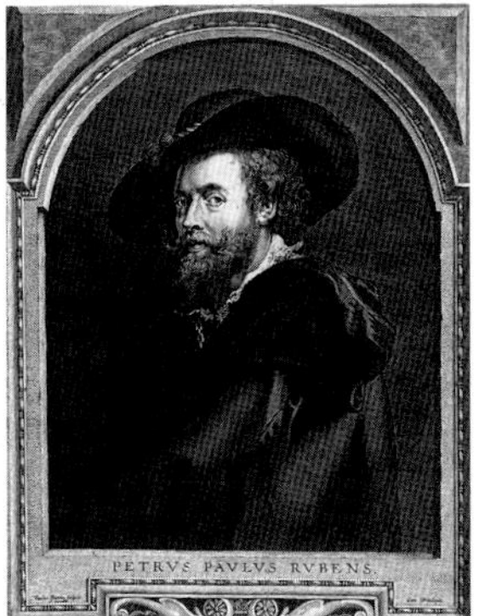

*Fig.24 Engraving by Paulus Pontius after Rubens' **Self-portrait**, 1630, (Manchester, Whitworth Art Gallery)*

Lit: H. Perry Chapman, 'Rembrandt's Fashioning of the Self' in *Rembrandt by Himself*, Glasgow Museums & Galleries, 1990.
Martin Royalton Kisch, *Drawings by Rembrandt and his Circle in the British Museum*, 1992, Cat.8a.

13 **Rembrandt van Rijn** 1606-1669
Self-portrait signed and dated 1632
Oil on panel, 64.4 x 47.6cm
(Glasgow Museums; the Burrell Collection, 35/600)

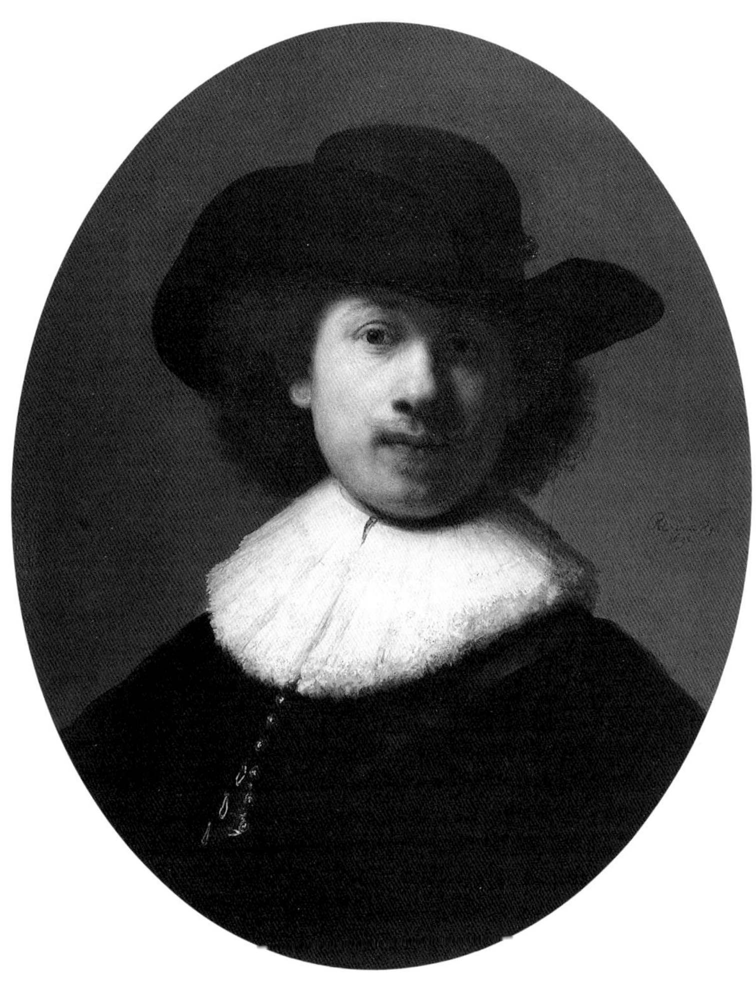

The self-portrait stands out from all Rembrandt's other self-portraits as being the only one in which he painted himself in contemporary formal dress using the conventional oval portrait format popular in the Netherlands in the 1630s. So uncommon was it for Rembrandt to paint himself in this way that by the eighteenth-century it was no longer recognized as a self-portrait.[1] In his early self-portraits of the 1630s he preferred often elaborate theatrical costume with elements drawn from oriental or sixteenth-century Italian dress. Here he is dressed in the black broad-brimmed felt hat, large white collar and black cloak and doublet fashionable amongst Amsterdam's citizens, and worn by the more elegant of Rembrandt's clients. Nowhere is there even a hint that the man might be a painter. The artist's beret of the Liverpool portrait (Cat.no.11) has been dismissed, the unusual and somewhat exotic costume with its glinting gold chain has disappeared and been replaced with discreet small gold buttons, and the somewhat unruly hair has been tidied up. This gives a suggestion of Rembrandt's growing self-identification with the bourgeois sitters he had begun to portray after his move from Leiden to Amsterdam in late 1631, where he hoped for success in the large and rich market for portraits amongst its merchant and professional elite. The self-portrait does not merely reflect his social aspirations. He was also still concerned with learning how to handle paint and light with a confidence that would gain him success as a society portrait painter and finally establish his reputation in 1632 with his group portrait of *The Anatomy Lesson of Dr. Tulp*. The latter inaugurated his busiest and most profitable years as Amsterdam's leading portraitist. He used his own body and face to provide the model formula for such portraits, not only honing his technical and painting skills in the representation of felt hat and linen collar, but his compositional and tonal skills in the artful play of the limited palette of pure black against pure white offset against the gradually changing greys of the background and the creamy pink skin of his face. Rembrandt's pose is the same as in his Liverpool self-portrait (Cat.no.11), but the conventional dress, sophisticated play of cool tones and less shadow makes it seem more composed and self-assured than the tentative moody Liverpool portrait, the light around one eye allowing the viewer to gauge the artist's character. Like the Liverpool portrait it was painted on a reused panel something Rembrandt frequently did with his early self-portraits, but never with a commissioned portrait. The self-portrait enabled him to experiment free of the pressures and obligations imposed by socially superior clients, who would no doubt have demanded the removal of the dark shadow with which one half of his face is still covered.

1. Rembrandt Research Project, *A Corpus of Rembrandt Paintings,* 1986 vol.2, A.58 p.234.

14 **Rembrandt van Rijn** 1606-1669
Self-portrait at the age of 34 signed and dated 1640
Inscribed later: Conterfeycel
Oil on canvas, 102 x 80cm
(The Trustees of the National Gallery, London, NG672)

This is the culmination of a series of painted and etched self-portraits of the 1630s in which Rembrandt celebrated his success as the leading portrait painter in the lucrative Amsterdam market by showing himself dressed up in furs, silks and exuberant plumed hats. It is the most impressive portrait, more dignified and less flamboyant than the ostentatious self-projection of his etched *Self-portrait in Embroidered Cloak* of 1631. However, the self-portrait displays more than a liking for imaginative self-portraiture dressing up in exotic and lavish Renaissance garb fashionable in the first part of the sixteenth-century. The self-portrait also reflected the influence of two paintings by two of Rembrandt's most celebrated predecessors of the Italian Renaissance, Raphael and Titian. Their respective portraits of the Italian courtier *Baldassare Castiglione* (Paris, Louvre Museum) and *A Man* (fig.25), thought at the time to show the poet Ludovico Ariosto, had passed through the Amsterdam auction rooms; the *Castiglione* in 1639 where Rembrandt, who was a frequent auction attender, had sketched it in his catalogue (Vienna, Albertina). Both had ended up, by 1641, in the Amsterdam collection of the merchant Alfonso Lopez, along with at least one work bought from Rembrandt. From the Raphael Rembrandt seems to have derived the beret and its bold silhouetting against a tonally shifting background, whilst the Titian provided the prominent expanse of sleeve draped over the balustrade and the composed posture of a cultured gentleman. Rembrandt was not merely aiming to imitate the 'old masters' who had inspired him, but to rank himself alongside them and make himself the heir to their tradition. By emulating them he could both honour and surmount the challenge their work represented. It was perhaps an even greater source of pride that his knowledge of the work of two such virtuoso Italian painters was gained purely through prints and from viewing the auction houses and collections of Amsterdam, without ever visiting their country, a gap in his training for which he was often to be criticised by his contemporaries and subsequent Dutch commentators on art. Although his costume did not derive directly either from the Raphael or the Titian its choice helped proclaim him as a kindred spirit of the great Italian predecessors.

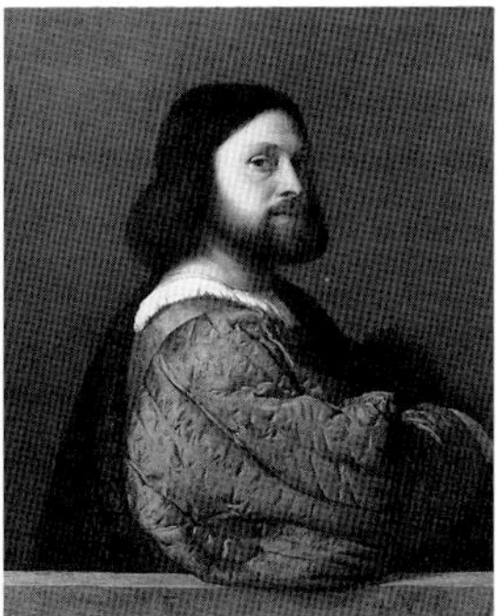

*Fig.25 Titian, **Portrait of a Man**, about 1511, (London, National Gallery)*

Lit: Christopher Brown, *Second Sight: Titian Rembrandt*, National Gallery, 1980.
Rembrandt: the Master & his Workshop, National Gallery, 1992, Cat.no.32.

15 **Rembrandt van Rijn** 1606-1669
Self-portrait drawing or etching at a Window 1648
Etching, 16.5 x 13.4cm
(Trustees of the British Museum, London, inv.1855-4-14-260)

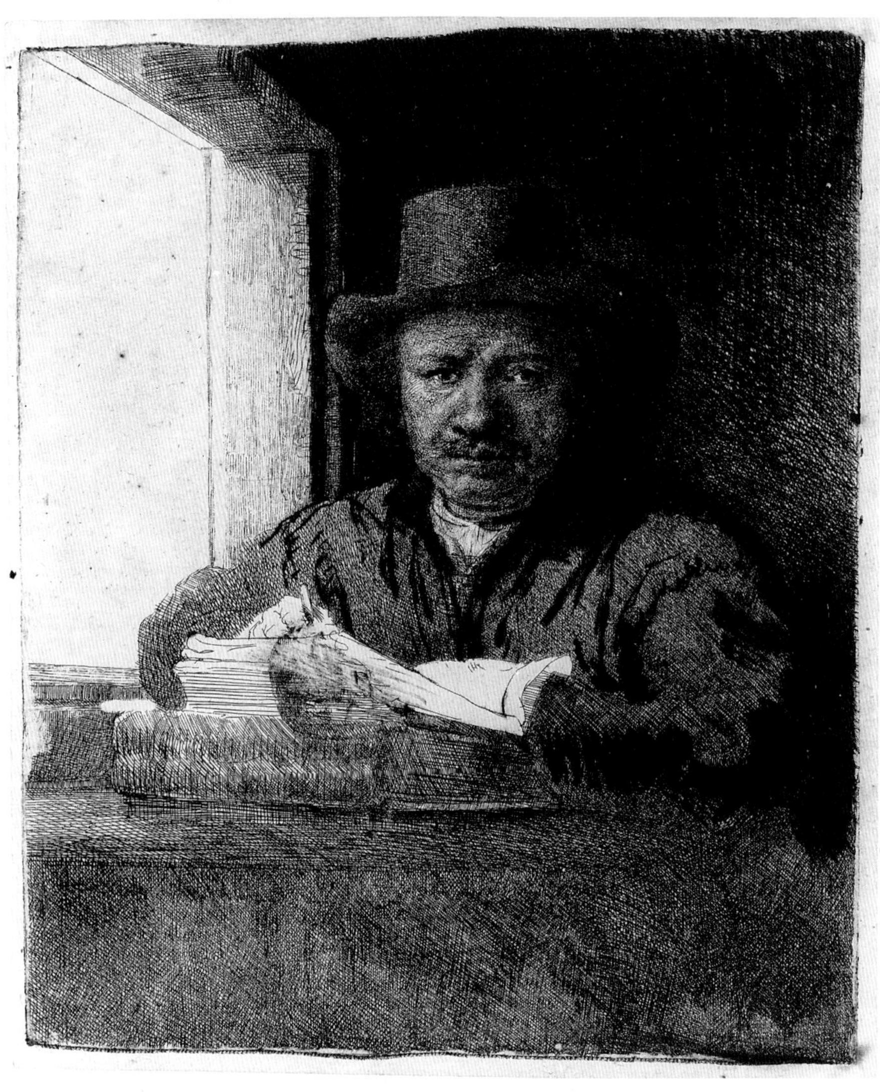

From 1640 to 1648 Rembrandt seems to have lost interest in self-portraiture. When he resumed the practice, with this last etched design, he turned for the first time to showing himself as an artist. The dominant convention in the Netherlands in the previous century had been for a painter to show himself with the tools of his craft, but the artist usually wore fashionable clothes, thus also displaying the wealth and status earned by his profession. Rembrandt, however, sits at the window in his working clothes, the smock and the hat he habitually wore in his studio, a stark contrast from the finery he wore in his etched *Self-portrait leaning on a stone sill* of 1639, which foreshadowed the National Gallery painting (Cat.no.14). Furthermore, this self-portrait is the only time he showed himself actually in the course of producing his work. The tool he holds in his hand and the sloped working surface suggest that he is in the process of etching, indeed that he is in the act of creating the print we now see in front of us. The intense frowning scrutiny he gives himself in the mirror in front of him gives the viewer a startlingly direct impression of eye to eye contact with the artist. The feeling of candour is enhanced by the mechanics of etching which has reversed the inversion imposed by the mirror so that Rembrandt appears to us not as he saw himself but as someone would have seen him on entering the studio. By showing himself as others saw him he produced a subtly different image from that created merely by studying himself closely. The 1648 etched self-portrait fulfilled a similar role to previous etchings, acting as a prototype with which he could experiment with a new motif or format before launching himself into a more formalised painted version of the theme. However, it was not until the 1660s that Rembrandt took up and enlarged upon the theme of the artist at work in painted form, producing in the process some of his most monumental self-portraits in which he was proud to show himself with his palette and brushes.

16 **Rembrandt van Rijn** 1606-1669
Self-portrait about 1665
Oil on canvas, 114.3 x 94cm
(English Heritage, (The Iveagh Bequest, Kenwood, London))
(colour plate 5)

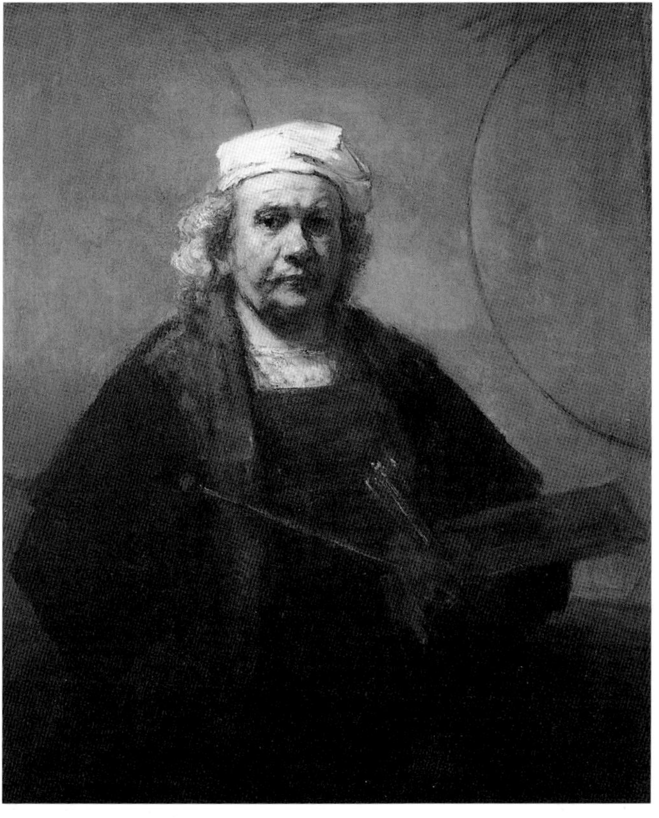

There are only three painted self-portraits, all from the last decade of his life, in which Rembrandt shows himself at work at his easel, dressed in studio garb with the tools of his trade the brushes, palette and mahl-stick, used to steady his painting hand. Of the three paintings this is the most commanding image. But so unused was he to picturing himself with paint-brushes in his hand that, as x-rays of the Kenwood picture have shown, he began work on this canvas by confusedly placing a brush in the 'wrong' non-painting hand, his left, which was originally shown raised holding a brush as if he were about to paint on a canvas positioned at his left. The hand, which as Reynolds commented 'is so slightly touched that it can scarce be made out to be a hand', remained unfinished and as a result appears almost formed out of the brushes he holds.[1] Between the etched *Self-portrait drawing at a window* (Cat.no.15) of 1648 and the Kenwood portrait of the mid-sixties Rembrandt had sufferred professional and personal reverses. Few private patrons now preferred his broad-brushwork to the more fashionable smooth and detailed technique: he was no longer given public commissions; had gone through bankruptcy proceedings in 1656; been dragged before the religious courts by his estranged mistress; and lost the last of his female companions Hendrikje Stoffels to the plague in 1663; his studio equipment was almost all that remained to him. As in the early Liverpool portrait (Cat.no.11) the silhouetting of his head against the background helps focus attention on the flaccid, ravaged features of his face, which he no longer makes any attempt to mask with shadows, as in his youthful more self-conscious days. The vigorous, rougher handling of paint, typical of his late style, serves to emphasise further his craggy features and furrowed brow. Yet the mood is not one of desolation, but of facing the future with equanimity. He confronts us with magisterial gravity, standing with seemingly weary resignation in front of a canvas on which there are drawn two half-circles cut off by the edge of the fictive and real picture. Much has been written about the geometrical forms which dominate the background, some have maintained that they are the outlines of a world map which Rembrandt had left unfinished.[2] They may simply be there to show that he stands before a canvas, about to commence his work, rather than before a bare wall. The circle has always been the symbol of perfection and was used as such in Rembrandt's etched portrait of the Dutch calligrapher Lieven van Coppenol. The circles could also be Rembrandt's allusion to the famous story about the thirteenth-century artist Giotto, which featured in Vasari's *Lives* and was recounted at length by Dutch art biographers, in which Giotto's response to a request from the pope for an example of his work, was to draw a perfect circle without the aid of a compass. When the pope saw the drawing he proclaimed Giotto the best painter of his time.[3] As he addresses us from the canvas, posed in front of two half-formed circles, Rembrandt may have intended a humble and enigmatic comparison with the great Italian artist.

1. Edmund Malone, *The Works of Reynolds*, 1798, vol.II, p.266 reporting Reynolds visit to Flanders and Holland in 1781.
2. C. Brown, J. Kelch & P. van Thiel, *Rembrandt: the Master and his workshop* National Gallery, London, 1992, Cat.no.49, p.286.
3. B. Broos 'The O of Rembrandt', *Simiolus*, 1971, vol.4, pp.168-9.

17 **Godfried Schalken** 1643-1706
Self-portrait by Candlelight about 1695
Oil on canvas, 109.8 x 88.8cm
(Leamington Spa Art Gallery and Museum, Warwick District Council, Inv.A452.1953)

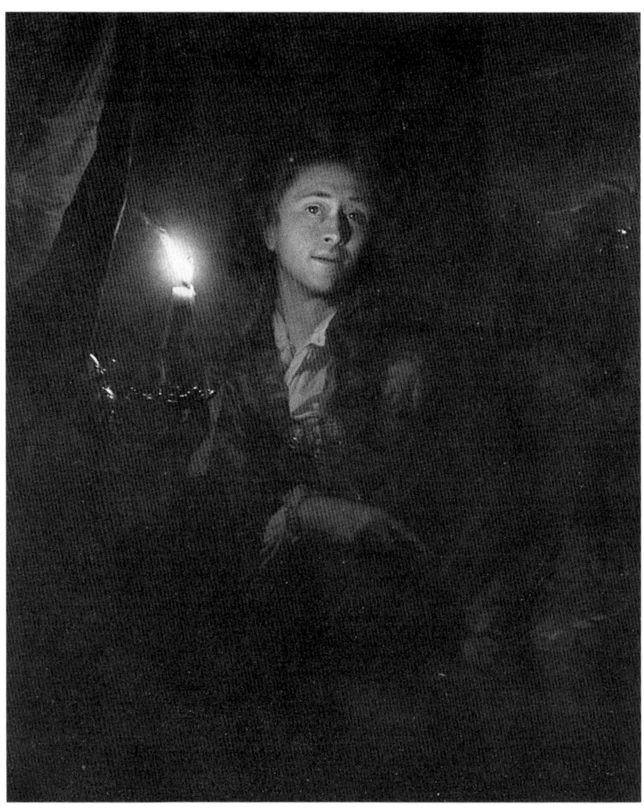

In 1692 when Godfried Schalken moved with his wife from Dordrecht to the court of William III and Queen Mary at Windsor, it was a definite step up the social and artistic ladder. He was determined to make a name for himself at court and to vie for the position as court portrait painter that Godfried Kneller had assumed on Lely's death in 1680. He even enlarged the size of his canvases in order to rival those of Kneller's. Previously he had been known for smoothly-painted small-scale subject pictures, either religious or domestic and sometimes erotic in allusion, but always nocturnal and lit by candle. Whilst in England he continued the use of his distinctive candlelit 'signature' in a series of self-portraits. In 1694 he was commissioned by an English agent of Cosimo III's to paint a self-portrait for the Uffizi self-portrait collection. It was a commission which he was eager to fulfil, even reducing his price for the prospect of new princely commissions and the honour of being hung in the Grand Duke's increasingly celebrated collection, alongside self-portraits by other northern artists including Dürer, Rembrandt, Van Dyck and his own master Gerrit Dou. The Uffizi self-portrait was lit by candle and showed Schalken holding a mezzotint engraving by John Smith of one of Schalken's most popular candle-lit subjects *The Penitent Magdalen*, thus showing that he was an artist eminent enough to have his work engraved (fig.26). The Leamington Spa self-portrait is the only one in which he showed himself with the his brushes, dressed in an informal and artistic way, in open-necked shirt, with long hair curling over his shoulder and gold chain draped over his chest. The picture appears to have been conceived as a companion to the Uffizi self-portrait, sharing the same nocturnal, background landscape and the same room furnishings, but showing him with brushes and palette rather than print and posed as if he were a mirror image, his body turned to his left rather than right. The fact that he painted himself as more youthful than in a self-portrait of 1679 also suggests that the picture was thought of as an allegorized self-portrait, showing Schalken representing Painting. His candle-lit scenes proved an effective marketing technique for Schalken and he used the idea for his portrait of *William III holding a candelabra* (Amsterdam, Rijksmuseum), which caused astonishment at court when it was unveiled.[1] His artificially lit self-portrait remains the only such in the Uffizi collection and his nocturnal scenes were highly valued at the English court.[2] Curiosity over Schalken's painting technique continued into the next century when Vertue described Schalken's method of lighting his subject only by candlelight in a dark room and painting the scene by viewing it through a peephole in another room.[3]

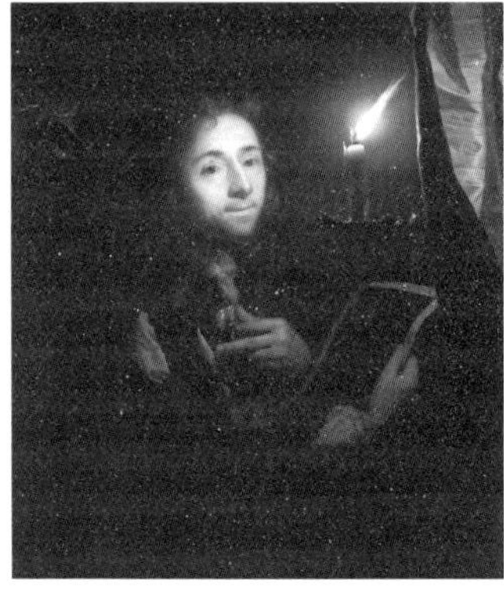

*Fig.26 Godfried Schalken, **Self-portrait**, about 1695, (Florence, Uffizi Gallery)*

1. Peter Hecht, 'Candlelight and dirty fingers or royal virtue in disguise: some thoughts on Weyerman and Godfried Schalken', *Simiolus*, 1980, no.2, p.28-29.
2. G. Vertue, *Notebooks Volume II, Walpole Society*, 1931-2, vol.XX, p.139.
3. Vertue, *Notebooks Volume I*, as above, 1929-30, vol.XVIII, p.29.
Lit: Thiery Beherman, *Godfried Schalken*, 1988.

18 **David Allan** 1744-1796
Self-portrait dated 1770
Oil on canvas, 126.4 x 98.4cm
(Lent by the Scottish National Portrait Gallery, Royal Scottish Academy Loan, Edinburgh, inv.PGL227)

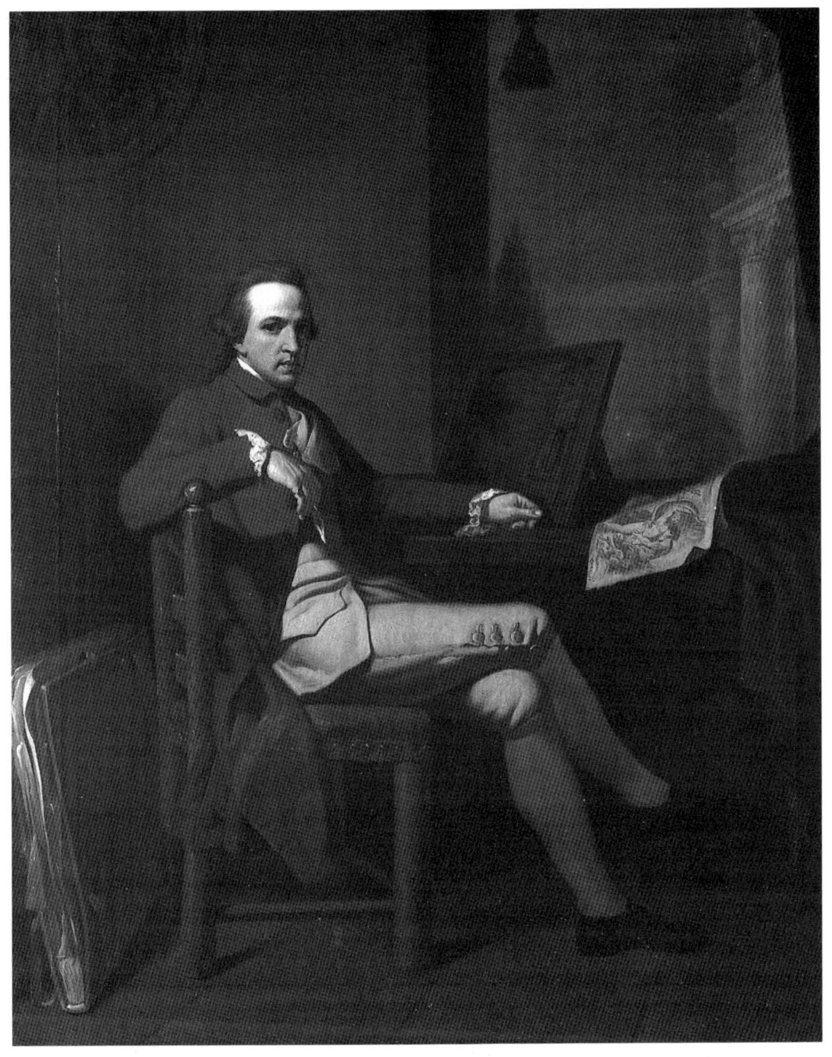

The self-portrait was painted for Allan's patron and supporter Lady Cathcart who had sponsored the artist's long years of study in Italy from 1765 to 1777. In the eighteenth century Italy, and particularly Rome, held a magnetic attraction for artists. It acted as their school, a meeting-place for patrons, their market and above all their inspiration. Whilst in Rome Allan made studies after the antique, painted history paintings and generally followed the example of his Scottish compatriot and teacher Gavin Hamilton, who was playing an important role in the neo-classical revival. The imposing character and classical references in the self-portrait were meant to show his supporter back home how well the young, aspiring artist was using his time. As he sits nonchalantly in his chair, with his porte-crayon in his hand to underline the fact that, despite appearances, he is an artist not a gentleman-connoisseur, he is surrounded by the trappings of artistic study ancient and modern: the portfolio of drawings; the view through the window to a classical Roman facade which he has just paused from sketching; and lying casually on the table a chalk study by the seventeenth-century artist Annibale Carracci, whose classicizing works Allan admired. Allan's features have also been idealised. In 1768 Sir William Hamilton described 'Lady Cathcart's little painter' as having: 'a long, sharp, lean white, coarse face, much pitted by the small-pox and fair hair. His large, prominent eyes of a light colour looked weak, near-sighted and not very animated. ... His whole exterior to strangers , appeared unengaging, trifling and mean. His deportment was timid and obsequious.'[1] Fortunately Hamilton's prejudices were 'soon dispelled on acquaintance'. The portrait's conventional composition makes it feel even more like a souvenir of Allan's academic training, a 'postcard' from Rome to assure those back home that he had arrived geographically and artistically, sent to the patron who had made the arrival possible. In Rome Allan was much thought of and considered an historical painter of promise, winning the Academy of St Luke's gold medal for historical composition. His excursion into the 'grand manner' portrait, however, lasted only as long as his years in Italy, once back in Scotland he found like another of his compatriots Alexander Runciman (Cat.no.31) that there was no call for history painting. He made a successful living instead as a painter of gentry portraits and genre-scenes of Italian and Scottish popular life, becoming known as 'Scotland's Hogarth'.

1. T. Crouther Gordon, *David Allan of Alloa: The Scottish Hogarth*, 1951, p.21.

19 **Giovanni Domenico Campiglia** 1692-after 1775
Self-portrait about 1737-8
Black chalk on paper, 24.8 x 20.3cm
(Trustees of the British Museum, London, inv.1865-1-14-820)

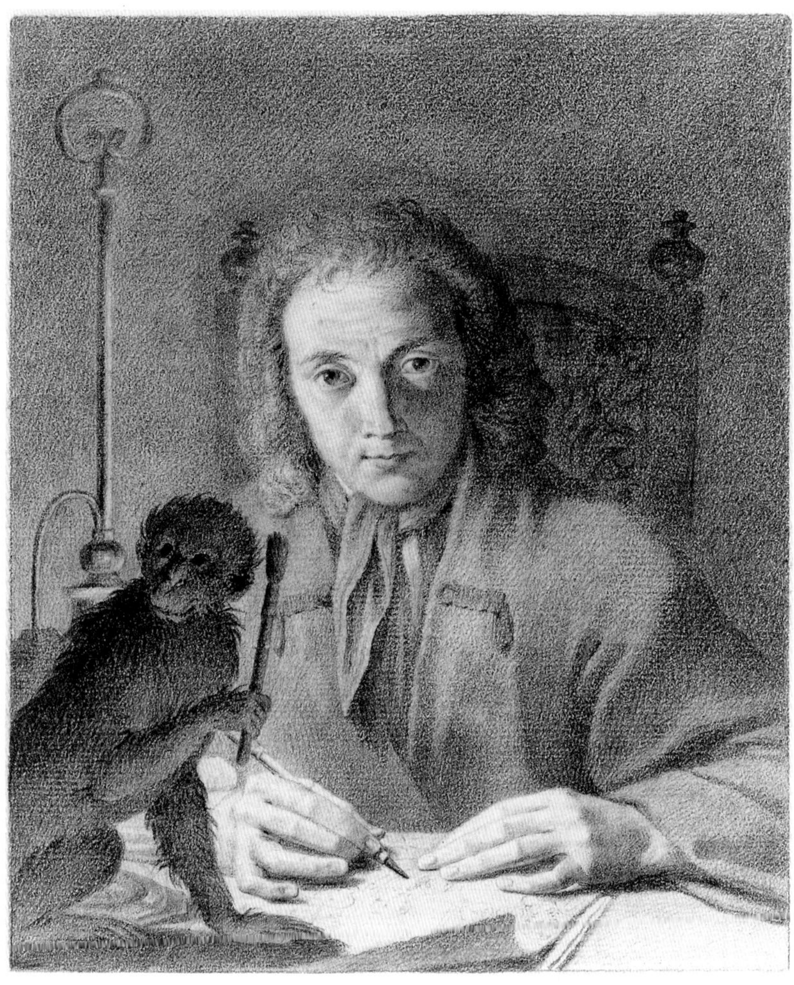

Like the Maratta drawing (Cat. no.9) this self-portrait was acquired by an English nobleman on the Grand Tour. Sir Charles Frederick (1709-85) was in Rome in 1737 and in common with Campiglia was an accomplished draughtsman. He also shared the Italian artist's interest in antiquities. Campiglia had established an early reputation as a portrait painter in Florence before moving to Rome, where by 1720 he had embarked on a profitable career as a professional copyist of classical antiquities. He also produced caricature portrait-groups, like the one he shows himself drawing, and obviously enjoyed a considerable English following. In 1736 Alexander Cunyngham, who met Campiglia in Rome, described him as 'a Florentine gentleman and artist ... employed by the present Pope to make out the grand collection, which he published, of antique statues and bustos, for which he had a large salary. He is a very well-bred communicative man'.[1] Campiglia's combination of gentlemanly good-breeding and fluency made him an ideal guide and tutor for visiting 'tourists' such as Sir Roger Newdigate, who acquired several drawings from Campiglia and took drawing lessons from the artist. When Sir Charles Frederick acquired his drawing in 1738 Campiglia was particularly involved with self-portraiture, as he was preparing drawings of the Uffizi's self-portrait collection for engraving as illustrations to the five volume *Il Museo Fiorentino* (1731-42), whose publication he oversaw. One of the engravers

Antonio Pazzi, a pupil of Campiglia's, was also forming his own self-portrait collection (later sold to enlarge the Uffizi's). Some of Campiglia's frontispiece designs included as illustrations to *Il Museo Fiorentino* show apes animatedly taking part in artistic activities similar to the monkey in Campiglia's self-portrait who, wielding a brush, looks cheekily out at us as if posing for its own self-portrait. An amusing contrast is created between the trim human artist and the scruffy look of the ape-artist. There was a long tradition, stemming from a passage in Aristotle's *Poetics* describing 'art as the ape of nature', which equated apes to artists.[2] In the seventeenth and early eighteenth centuries Flemish and then French artists seized upon the concept to produce humorous sometimes satirical parodies in which monkeys performed artists' tasks. For Campiglia there may have been an additional more personal symbolism related to the fact that his success as an artist derived from copying other's work and imitating everything down to the last detail.

1. *Gentleman's Magazine*, 1853, vol.XL, p.237 as quoted by Hugh Macandrew, 'A Group of Batoni Drawings at Eton College and some Eighteenth-Century Italian Copyists', *Master Drawings*, 1978, vol.16 no.2, p.138.
2. H.W. Janson, *Apes and Ape Lore in the Middle Ages and the Renaissance*, 1952, pp.287-94.

20 **Richard Cosway** 1742-1821
Self-portrait in Fancy Dress about 1770
Oil on canvas, 123.5 x 99.7cm
(The National Trust, Attingham Park (Berwick Collection))

The mask which lies on the table beside Cosway suggests that the artist has portrayed himself as if attending a masquerade party. Van Dyck's portraits provided the inspiration for costume worn at the fancy dress parties and masquerades which were all the rage from the mid-eighteenth century to about 1780. 'Vandyke' dress also provided the stock-in-trade for portrait painters to the aristocracy. Zoffany painted George III and his family in Stuart costume in 1770 and in 1782 Cosway himself painted a miniature of the Prince of Wales in this style. In 1770, when the self-portrait was probably painted, Cosway's gifts as the outstanding miniature painter of his day had led to his election as an Associate of the Royal Academy. Cosway was also a notorious fop, well known for his vanity and sartorial extravagance and a leading member of the *macaroni* set, the fashionable trendsetters of the time, who did much to revive seventeenth-century dress styles. The costume he wears in the portrait allows him to accentuate these aspects of his character whilst also paying tribute to the artist Van Dyck, whom he greatly admired and several of whose works he owned. The allegiance to the Flemish artist is stressed by Cosway's dress - his cloak, collar and sword hilt - and the draped and columned background reminiscent of many Van Dyck portraits. Other artists in this period such as James Jefferys (Cat. no.24) and Joshua Reynolds also portrayed themselves or allowed themselves to be painted in fanciful seventeenth-century dress.[1] The self-portrait's 'Vandykian' dress and Cosway's pose, with his elbow jutting out of the canvas at the viewer are also gestures of an aristocratic style, whilst the portfolio he holds could as easily be that of a noble connoisseur as of an artist. Cosway was always very aware of the importance of exploiting his image, both to enhance his status and, as importantly, to reassure the fashionable clientele of his lucrative portrait miniature business. By being portrayed in 'Vandyke' dress artists immediately linked themselves with the most distinguished painter of British aristocratic society, the role model for the courtier-artist, a fact of particular importance if, like Cosway, one was a portrait painter with artistic and social ambitions. By the 1780s Cosway had become the leading adviser and confidant to the Prince of Wales on all matters of artistic taste and fashion, and in 1785 the Prince made him his principal portrait painter, a post which he held for over twenty years.

1. See Angelica Kauffmann's portrait of *Joshua Reynolds* at Saltram House, Plympton.
Lit.: Stephen Lloyd, 'Richard Cosway, RA: The artist as collector, connoisseur and virtuoso', *Apollo*, June 1991, pp.398-405.
S. Lloyd, 'Forming the taste of a prince: Richard Cosway and George IV's early collecting', *Apollo*, September 1993, pp.192-194.

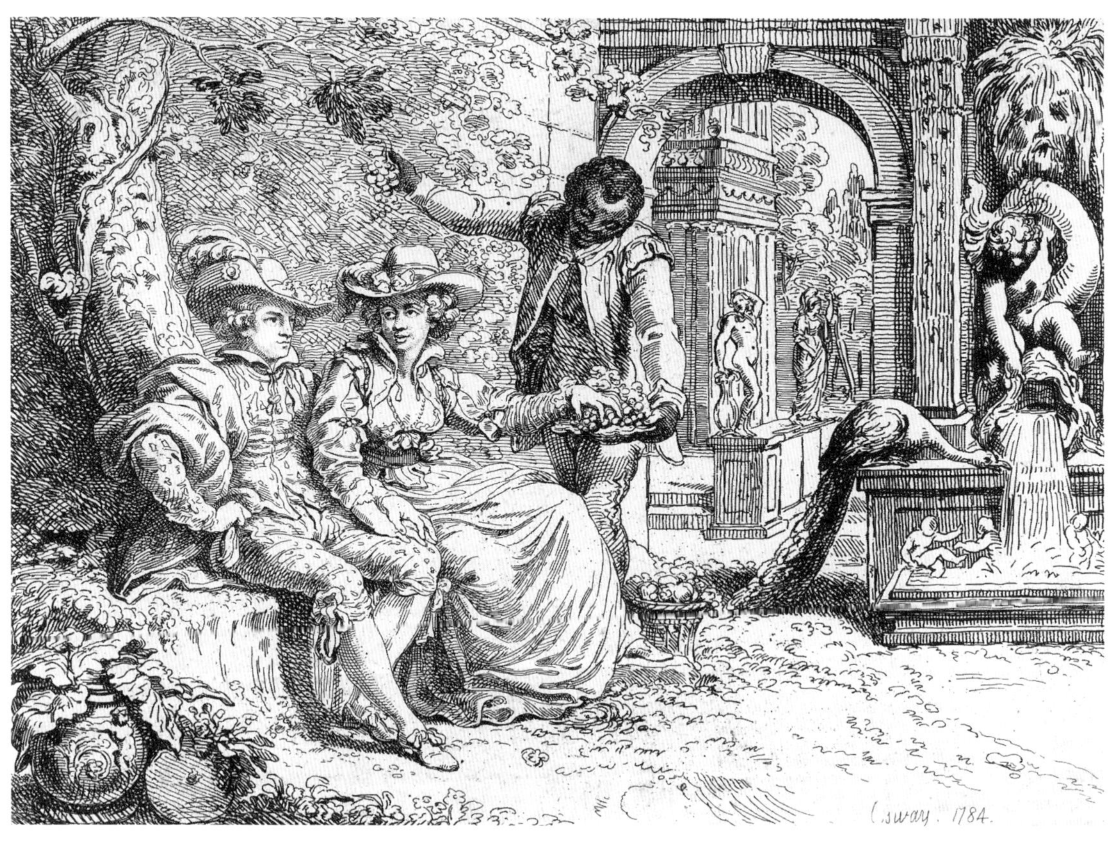

In 1781 Cosway married the Italian born Maria Hadfield, eighteen years his junior, but like himself a youthful prodigy and a talented miniaturist and etcher, who had recently moved to England at the request of her friend Angelica Kauffmann. In 1784 the couple moved into Schomberg House, Pall Mall, where their lavish soirées (at which Maria showed off her musical talents) and sometimes scurrilous entertainments made theirs one of the most fashionable salons in town, attracting numerous artists, collectors and diplomats and the Prince of Wales, who lived nearby. Cosway chose to show his captivation with his young bride by using as an underlying model for the etching the double portrait Rubens painted of himself and his first wife seated under a honeysuckle bower (fig.11). The costume, garden setting, fountains and black servant boy all reflect other Rubensian prototypes. It is somewhat ironic that it should be Cosway who produced one of the rare celebrations by an English artist of a wife as artistic inspiration, for it was an ultimately unhappy marriage which lead (after Maria's celebrated affair with the American Thomas Jefferson) to a separation just a decade later. Maria, however,

presumably approved of the 1784 image of herself, as a Rubens portrait come to life, as the following year she was portrayed in a stipple engraving by Bartolozzi in a costume and pose closely reminiscent of Rubens' *Portrait of Suzanne Lunden* (fig.31). The previous decades had seen a society fashion for seventeenth-century fancy dress (Cat. no.20), but Rubens also held an important almost obssesive place in Cosway's heart. Almost a quarter of Cosway's own connoisseurial collection of old master paintings and drawings was devoted to works attributed to Rubens and his followers. That Cosway greatly admired Rubens as artist and courtier was further reflected in another Cosway self-portrait, a drawing of about 1790, (Lodi, Italy, Fondazione Cosway), in which he presented himself in the guise of a seventeenth-century courtier wearing a Rubensian feathered hat and paying homage to the busts of Rubens and Michelangelo. His self-identification with the artist was such that a couple of years after etching the self-portrait with his wife he purchased what he claimed was Rubens' own colour box, which he later used himself.

22 **Francis Hayman** 1708-1776
The Artist with Grosvenor Bedford about 1748-50
Oil on canvas, 71.8 x 91.4cm
(National Portrait Gallery, London, inv.217)

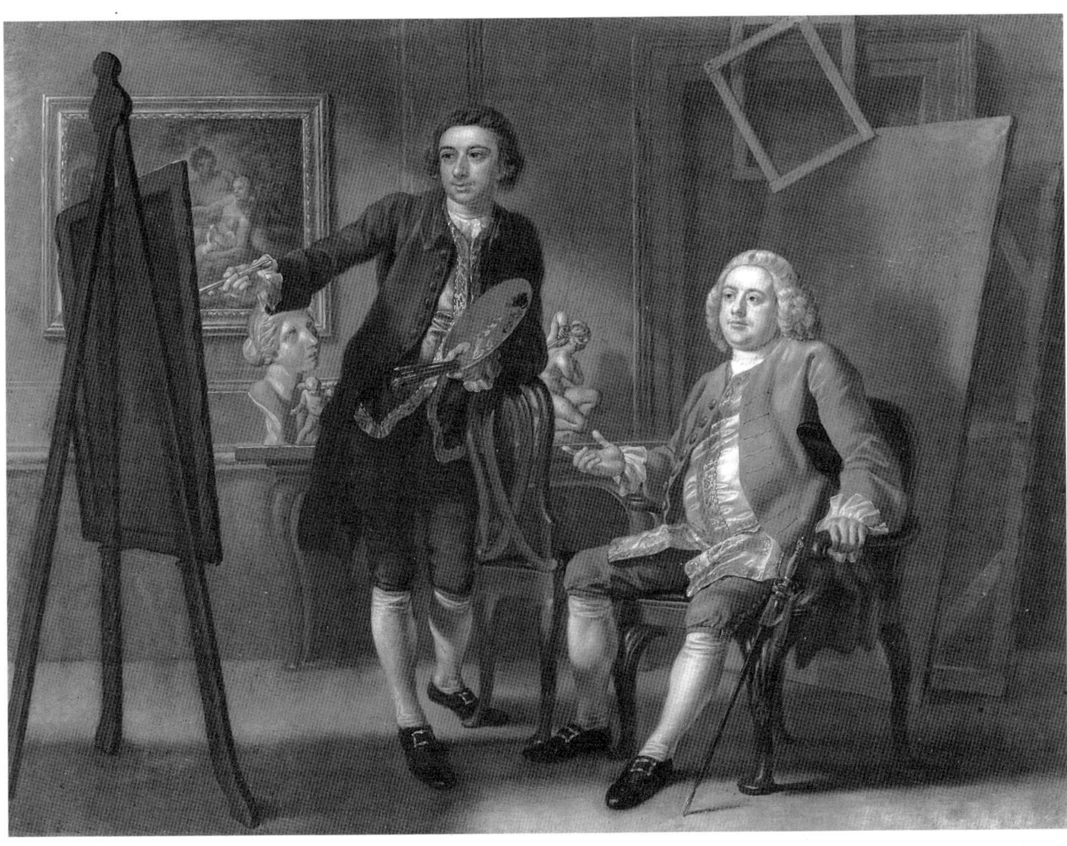

The artist shows himself in a studio discussing the painting he is at work on with Grosvenor Bedford, the long term political ally of Prime Minister Sir Robert Walpole, and one of Hayman's earliest and most constant patrons, who commissioned several family portraits in the 1740s and 1750s. Compared to other Hayman self-portraits which show him alone in the same studio (Exeter, Royal Albert Memorial Museum) or at work sketching his aristocratic friends (New Haven, Yale Center for British Art) the London self-portrait shows him dressed more formally, adopting a slightly deferential pose in honour of the status of his portly, self-confident patron. In the Exeter self-portrait of 1750 he is wigless, wearing an open shirt and slippers and the floppy turban-like cap which in the first half of the eighteenth century symbolised the artist (see Cat.no.36). Hayman was one of the originators of the conversation piece, a type of group portrait in which the figures often appear as if in the middle of some discussion. He introduced a relaxed air into what had become rather stiffly composed group portraits in which those depicted appeared all too conscious of the artist and the viewer. Hayman has created the same convivial informality of a conversation piece in this self-portrait, in which neither painter nor patron appear aware of the spectator. They concentrate instead on the painting in front of them, indeed Grosvenor Bedford appears caught in mid comment on the picture whose subject the viewer can only ever guess at -perhaps they are discussing the progress of the self-portrait itself. The studied informality of pose is extended to the whole composition. Not for Hayman the conspicuous rows of clearly visible paintings displayed by Tillemans in his working studio (Cat.no.34), instead the only work on show, a *Venus and Mars*, is teasingly obscured by the easel's silhouette and the artist's training and collection is merely suggested by the discreetly placed examples of busts and statuettes after the antique. One of the pieces on the sidetable is a variant of the Uffizi's celebrated *Crouching Venus* perhaps based on the marble statue in the Royal Collection at Kensington Palace, where Hayman, whose patrons included Frederick, Prince of Wales, may have seen it.[1] The studio provided an elegant setting, fashionably decorated with small-scale sculpture, in which he could entertain and cultivate his patron. In this way the portrait of Hayman, at ease with his patron, dramatised his rise from provincial obscurity in Exeter to his friendship with national politicians and literati, which culminated in his becoming a founding member of the Royal Academy and its first Librarian.

1. P.P. Bober & R. Rubenstein, *Renaissance Artists and Antique Sculpture*, 1986, pl.18.
Lit.: Brian Allen, *Francis Hayman*, 1987.

23 **William Hogarth** 1697-1764
The Painter and his Pug Dog 1745
Inscribed: The LINE OF BEAUTY And GRACE W.H.
Oil on canvas, 90 x 69.9
(Tate Gallery, London, purchased 1824)
(colour plate 6)

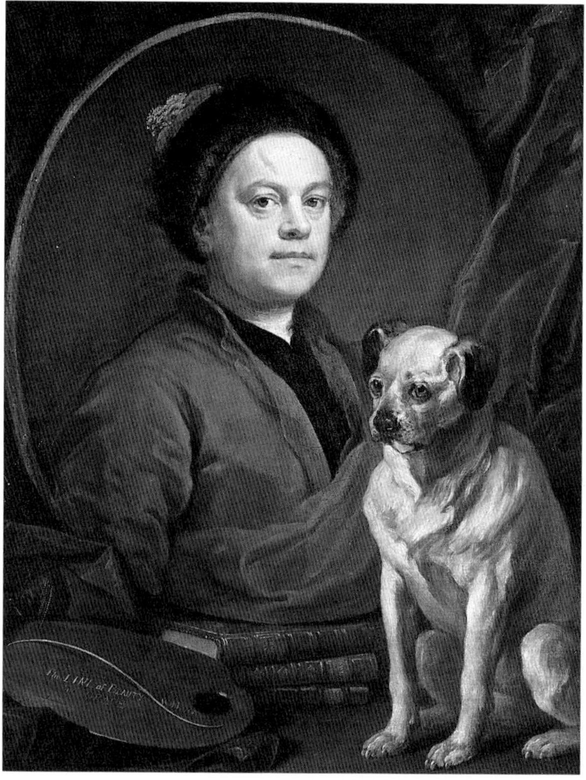

This self-portrait by Hogarth was the most concerted and public statement of his artistic beliefs and as such was engraved as the frontispiece to his collected prints published in 1749. Earlier and later self-portraits either catch him staring inquisitively at us in a simple bust length format holding his palette or show him as a caricatured figure seated at his easel about to paint the muse of Comedy (fig.27). The Tate self-portrait shows the artist as a painting within a painting, one of his own unframed canvases in a contrived piece of still-life in which the portrait of Hogarth is literally supported by volumes of Shakespeare, Swift and Milton, just as in reality Hogarth relied on the writings of these masters of drama, satire and epic poetry for his inspiration. X-ray evidence has shown that the portrait's calculated artifice took time to create. It was finished in 1745 the year in which Hogarth became a public success when he published his satirical *Marriage à la Mode* series in engraved form. Originally Hogarth portrayed himself in a gentlemanly fashion as a more formally dressed bewigged and cravatted figure; the loose artist's robe, the fur-trimmed red cap with its gold tassel and crucially his favourite pug dog, Trump, were an afterthought. The combative looking pug acts as the alter ego of its equally pugnacious master, a fact subtly and amusingly underlined by their facial similarities, a resemblance which Hogarth and contemporaries remarked on.[1] The dog also increased the illusionism of the picture, he is the same size as Hogarth's portrait yet inhabits the same space as the viewer, creating a counterpoint of naturalistic reality as against the artistic reality presented by the oval canvas. The pug exemplified the artist's loyalty to unidealised naturalism and thus acted as a symbolic and compositional counterbalance to the prominently displayed artist's palette, bare apart from the serpentine line and the inscription 'Line of Beauty and Grace', which represented artistic theory. The Line of Beauty, although the most distinctive part of Hogarth's artistic creed, was placed here almost as a teasing joke, for the portrait was painted some eight years before Hogarth published his *Analysis of Beauty* in which he described in detail his belief that the essence of natural and therefore artistic beauty was only to be found in the undulating, sinuous line. The fact that Hogarth's insertion of the 'Line of Beauty' into his self-portrait was meant to intrigue, encourage speculation and so increase the amount of attention the image gained was admitted by the artist in the Preface to his *Analysis*. In describing the reaction to its publication as a frontispiece he wrote: 'The bait soon took; and no Egyptian hieroglyphic ever amused more than it did for a time, painters and sculptors came to me to know the meaning of it, being as much puzzled with it as other people, till it came to have some explanation'.[2] He continued to use the S-line as an advertisement of his artistic beliefs, even having it painted as a crest on his coach.[3]

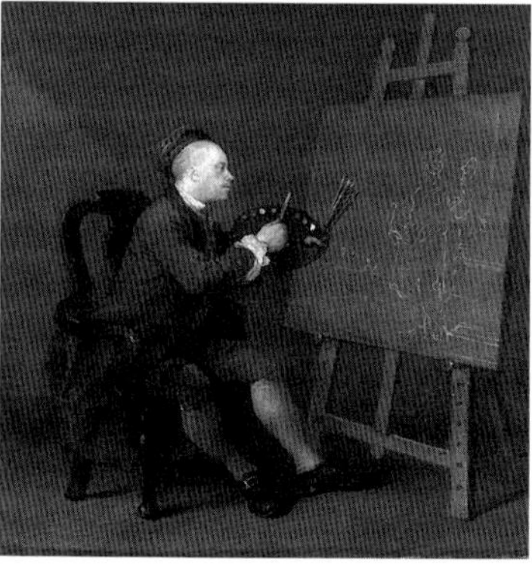

*Fig.27 William Hogarth, **Self-portrait painting the Comic Muse**, about 1757, (London, National Portrait Gallery)*

1. E. Einberg & J. Egerton, *The Age of Hogarth*, Tate Gallery Collections, 1988, vol.2, cat.no.103, p.110.; Ronald Paulson, *Hogarth: his life, art and times*, 1971, vol.II, p.3.
2. *Age of Hogarth*, as above, p.114.; Jack Lindsay, *Hogarth: his art and his world*, 1977, p.119 quoting the Preface to Hogarth's *Analysis*, 1753.
3. Frederick Antal, *Hogarth and his place in European Art*, 1962, p.12.

24 **James Jefferys** 1751-1784
Self-portrait about 1774-75
Pen and ink and pencil on paper, 47 x 41.3cm
(National Portrait Gallery, London inv.4669)

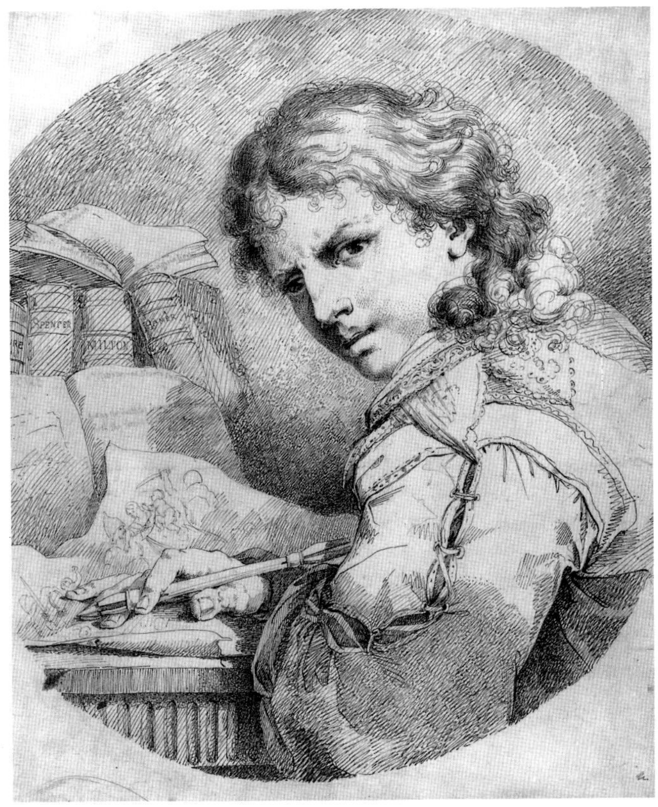

The sharp turn of the head, which gives the impression that Jefferys has been momentarily distracted from his work, was a commonplace in self-portraiture. It enabled artists to forge an intimate link between themselves and the viewer and so make a virtue of the sideways glance that most adopted in order to capture their image in a mirror. But as the intense gaze suggests Jefferys is not being distracted by an external visitor but by his own thoughts. The impression formed by Jefferys' stare, his half-open mouth and unruly hair, of his struggle with his own thoughts and imagination, is reinforced by the title of the open volume lying on top of the row of books ranged in front of him: Addison's *On the Pleasures of the Imagination*. The books represent the metaphorical 'food' for the artist's imagination - Nature, the lyric poet Spenser, the epic moralist Milton and the ancient Greek story-teller Homer, all of whom, like the artist himself, are governed by the lines from *Midsummer's Night Dream* partially and faintly pencilled onto the open book in front of Jefferys: 'And as the youthful Imagination bodies forth the forms [of things unknown]'. The Shakespearean quote poetically summarised an increasing concern, of the late eighteenth-century artistic and literary world throughout Europe, with the workings of the mind and artistic genius as the product of natural and specifically youthful imagination rather than as the result of incessant study of established masters past and present. That such ideas were uppermost in Jefferys mind when he drew his self-portrait is found in the companion portrait (fig.28) showing him with his back to the viewer reading through the disillusioned text of a letter to his godfather and early patron (the Maidstone brewer Mr. Brenchley) decrying the folly and vice of the leaders of Jefferys' profession.[1] The portraits were probably drawn on the eve of a visit to Italy made, at the suggestion of Reynolds, after Jefferys had won the Royal Academy Schools gold medal for historical painting in 1774. The distracted look of the artist as he ponders his thoughts is that of a discontented young student in a crowded art market, who felt his advancement thwarted by the art establishment, and whose appeal to his patron is couched in the only way he knew how - in a virtuoso piece of penwork. The fanciful costume Jefferys wears could relate to the fashion in the 1770s for portraits in 'Vandyke' dress (Cat.no.20), but in the context of this attitudinising self-portrait it is more likely a device to show him as unconventional adding to the romantic image of the artist as young, misunderstood and frustrated. This self-image reflects later accounts of his wild, bohemian behaviour before his early death aged thirty-two from an unromantic cold.

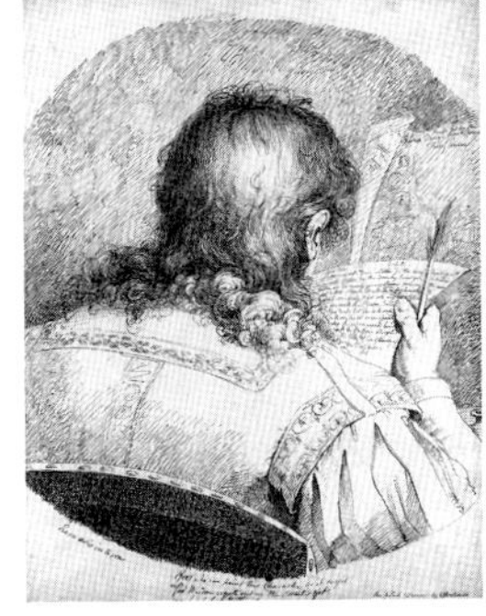

*Fig.28 James Jefferys, **Self-portrait**, about 1774-5, (New Haven, Yale Center for British Art)*

1. The text of the letter reads: 'I flatter myself I have abilities for the Art of Painting wch I hope will appear by the Drawing I send you, but indeed there are so many young Persons pursuing the same Art, that I think it will be a prudent Step to drop it intirely, & get into any other kind of Business you shall think, proper. I make no doubt but you will comply with my desire more especially when you inform yourself how much the Proffession is disgrac'd by the Folly & Vice of many of the Proffessors' quoted by P.J. Noon, *English Portrait Drawings & Miniatures*, Yale Center for British Art, 1979, cat.71.

Lit. T. Clifford & S. Legouix, 'James Jefferys, Historical Draughtsman', *Burlington Magazine*, March 1976, pp.148-157.
Malcolm Rogers, *Master Drawings from the National Portrait Gallery*, 1993, cat.no.29.
J. Sunderland, 'Two self-portraits by James Jefferys?', *Burlington Magazine*, April 1977, pp.279-280.

25 **Angelica Kauffmann** 1741-1807

The Artist hesitating between the Arts of Music and Painting signed and indistinctly dated 1794
Oil on canvas, 147.5 x 218.5cm
(By kind permission of Lord St. Oswald and The National Trust, Nostell Priory)
(colour plate 7)

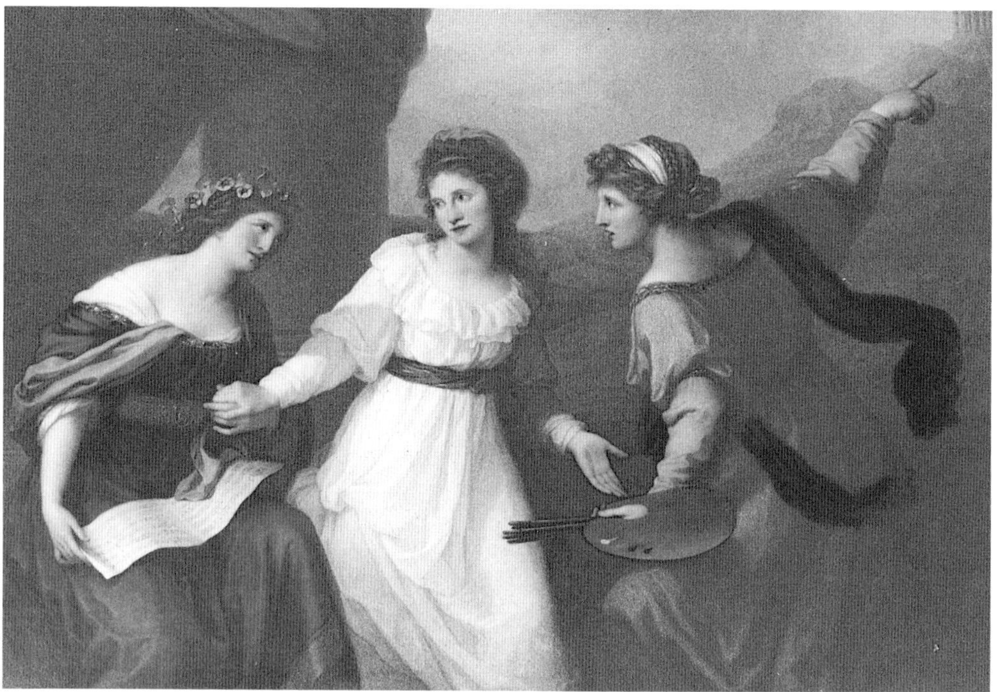

The painting's subject was described in a *Memorandum* written by Kauffmann's husband as showing: 'the moment when the Artist ... says good-bye to Music who is trying to seduce with her charm. Angelica is holding Music's hand as a final adieu, and she gives herself up entirely to Painting, who shows her in the distance the temple to Glory where she will be able to arrive by the road of drawing and painting.'[1] Like many of her self-portraits this picture was given to one of Kauffmann's patrons and close friend, James Forbes of Stanmore Hill, Middlesex, who met her in Rome in 1796 and commissioned several works from her. Although the picture was painted in Rome when Angelica was in her fifties it looks back to her teens when she had faced the dilemma of whether to follow her musical or her painting talents and had made the crucial decision dramatised in the painting. Her earliest self-portrait aged thirteen had referred only to her musical talents showing her holding up a page of sheet music (Innsbruck, Tiroler Landesmuseum). The picture of her *Hesitating between the Arts* is strongly personal in its subject, but in composition as in its monumental size it is a history painting which uses allegorical figures, representing artistic concepts, to make a public statement about the painter's career and personality. The composition is a variant on the theme of the *Choice of Hercules* in which the ancient Greek hero had the, usually erotically charged, choice of the broad often sunlit road offerred by seductive Vice and the narrow difficult path of Virtue. In art theory the subject justified the intellectual status and didactic purpose of painting.[2] Sometimes, as in Kauffmann's picture, the figures also represented different painting styles: Music in its colouring and pose denoting the seductive feminine Venetian style; whilst Painting presents a Raphaelesque profile and masculine, energetic gesture. Kauffmann stands in her favourite white dress symbolic of virtue and her pivotal relationship with the other two figures

also recalls the theme of the Three Graces representing perfect feminine friendship. Kauffmann, however, introduced a note of intimacy into the grand picture style in the wistful glance she throws at Music, the gentle consolatory squeeze of her hand as she parts from her and the apologetic open hand indicating the palette of Painting, who boldly exhorts her to follow the steep road to glory. In this way Kauffmann invested her allegorical figures with human feelings and produced one of the few paintings that worked successfully on several levels, as both autobiographical self-portrait and history painting. That Kauffmann should have chosen history painting as a vehicle for her grandest and possibly last self-portrait is significant, as it emphasised her ambition to be identified with what was considered the art world's highest, most intellectually-demanding and masculine genre. Kauffmann was distinguished from other eighteenth-century women artists in her determination to achieve a standing as a history painter. Despite the lack of patronage in Britain for narrative painting she made a successful living from it during her fifteen years in England and the number of times she painted this composition suggests that she did so as a proud declaration that she had made the right choice.

1. Quoted in Desmond Shawe-Taylor, *Genial Company*, Nottingham University Gallery, 1987, p.21.
2. The theme of the *Choice of Hercules* was an important one in eighteenth-century critical thought on art and had been used by Lord Shaftesbury in his study on the theory and practice of painting in 1713. The theme had also been parodied by Angelica's friend Joshua Reynolds in his portrait of the actor David Garrick in 1762.
Lit.: *Angelica Kauffman: A Continental Artist in Georgian England* Brighton Art Gallery, 1992.

26 **Anton Raphael Mengs** 1728-1779

Self-portrait 1774
Carved on reverse: RITRATTO D'ANTONIO RAFFAELLO MENGS/FATTO
DI LUI MEDESIMO/PER LORD NASSAU CONTE DI COWPER/IN FIRENZE L'ANNO 1774
Oil on panel, 73.5 x 56.2cm
(Board of Trustees of the National Museums & Galleries on Merseyside, Walker Art Gallery, inv.WAG1227)
(colour plate 8)

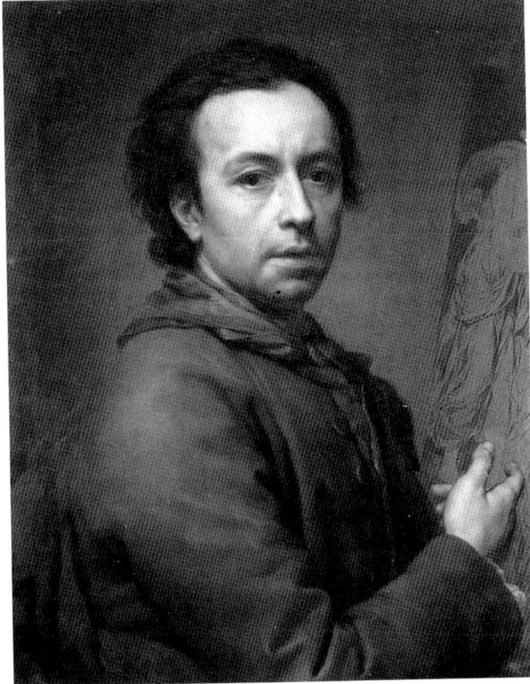

The *Self-portrait* was painted during Mengs' stay in Florence between autumn 1773 and May 1774 and was commissioned by George Nassau, the third Earl Cowper, a great admirer of Mengs' work and one of his major British patrons. As well as the *Self-portrait* he acquired from Mengs two portraits of himself and a *Holy Family*. Contemporaries described Cowper as a vain man who dominated British expatriate society in Florence, holding parties at his Florentine palace and his villa in Fiesole, and enjoying close contacts with visiting artists British and foreign. His ebullience was well shown in another portrait of him by Johan Zoffany (fig.29) By the time of their first meeting in 1770 Mengs was an internationally famed artist, originator of the Neo-Classical style of art and a successful Grand Tourist portrait painter, a former child prodigy, court artist to two of the most cultured courts in Europe, Dresden and Madrid, and recently elected Principal of the Accademia di San Luca in Rome. Mengs' pupils and admirers were often keen to own a likeness of the master and he satisfied this need by producing many half-length self-portraits in oil and pastel.[1] Cowper seems to have had a particular interest in self-portraits. He acquired Raphael's *Self-portrait* (Royal Collection) and then gave it to George III in 1781, as he also attempted to do with this Mengs *Self-portrait* in 1786.[2] Mengs' vividly realised 'speaking likeness' points didactically towards the layed-in figures of what was his final finished major project, his *Perseus and Andromeda* (St. Petersburg, Hermitage Museum), for which Cowper owned one of the many sketches, and which had been commissioned in 1768 by another British collector Sir Watkin Williams-Wynn. However, the painting is more than that familiar device, a self-portrait used to advertise the artist's wares to a patron, although it is the only one of his self-portraits to show him with an example of his work. By showing a work-in-progress with its preparatory underdrawing for obviously classical figures, rather than the more usual finished work, the picture became an exemplar of Mengs' artistic theories. It emphasised his artistic credo that

modern art must follow the art of the ancients to recover its greatness, and furthermore that he was the modern equivalent of that spirit of antiquity. Even the ordinary workday jacket and scarf he wears and the picture's colour scheme recall his colour theories.[3] He recommended green as being the most pleasing of colours not fatiguing to the eyes, whilst red added liveliness and brightness particularly to the flesh and eyes. But the overall mood of Mengs' *Self-portrait* is not that of celebration but of confession. Underlying the picture's seeming propagandising self-advertisement is a pessimistic disillusionment, the result of his searching introspection. His haggard face bears the signs of emotional strain. His lank hair, pallid skin, rheumy eyes, red with weariness, are all painted with intensely observed naturalism, and indicate the incipient illness, probably chronic lead poisoning, that was to kill him in five years time.

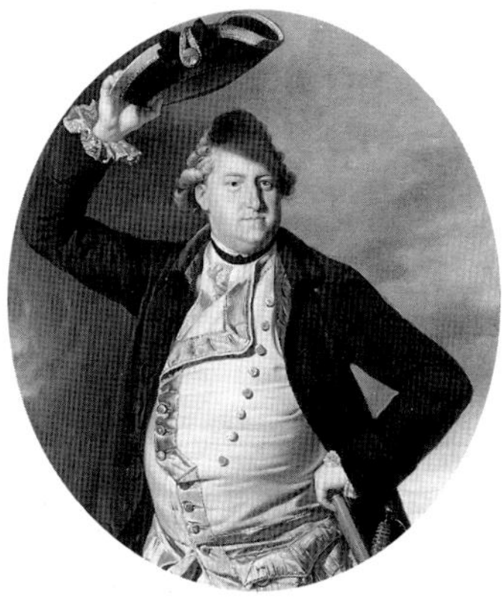

Fig.29 Johann Zoffany,
Portrait of George, 3rd Earl Cowper*, about 1773,*
(Liverpool, Walker Art Gallery)

1. Giuseppe Niccola D'Azara, *Opere di Antonio Raffaello Mengs* 1787, Vol.I, LXXIV.
2. His offer was turned down in favour of a collection of 223 miniature copies also commissioned by Cowper of the Uffizi self-portrait collection. Steffi Roettgen, *Anton Raphael Mengs and his British Patrons*, Kenwood, 1993, cat.no.1. p.46.
3. D'Azara, as above, vol.II, pp.264ff.

27 Sir Henry Raeburn 1756-1823
Self-portrait signed and dated 1792
Inscribed on reverse: Presented to Adam Smith by his much esteem'd friend Henry Raeburn Author of this Medal 1792[1]
Vitreous paste, 9.8 x 7cm
(National Gallery of Scotland, Edinburgh, inv.NG1959)

In 1792 when this medallion portrait was modelled by Raeburn in wax for James Tassie to cast in his unique 'enamel paste' the artist was on the brink of becoming Scotland's leading portrait painter, but he was still relatively ill at ease with large scale portraits in oil. It was only in 1792 that he sent his first double portrait in oils for exhibition in London, where it made a strong impression. As a portrait painter in oils Raeburn was both self-taught and a late starter. He had been apprenticed in the 1770s to an Edinburgh jeweller James Gilliland who had taught him the craft of jewellery including the designing and carving of cameos. By the end of his apprenticeship he had begun painting portraits, but as a watercolourist in miniature, a practice which he continued until at least 1786, perhaps until he was sure that he could establish himself as a full-scale portrait painter. It is not surprising, therefore, that he chose to create what may be his first self-portrait in a sculpted form and on such a small scale only slightly larger than the cameos he would have worked on as a jeweller. The modelling technique was akin to his method of painting, direct and without the intervention of drawings, and allowed Raeburn to display, particularly in the treatment of his hair, the free 'square touch' which he was beginning to use in his most brilliant painted passages. The idea of modelling himself in profile reflected his interest in classical reliefs, which had been spurred by his acquaintance with Reynolds and a friendship he had struck up whilst in Italy between 1784 and 1786 with the antiquarian and art connoisseur James Byres. The 'cameo' format also enabled him to concentrate the viewer's attention on the head a practice which became a trademark of his portraits, for he believed that 'nothing ought to divert the eye from the principal object: the face'.[2] The profile view, although it deprived the viewer of eye-to-eye contact, highlighted those features, the brow, nose and jaw which, under the system proposed by the eighteenth-century French physiognomist Lavater, were thought to produce the most scientific understanding of a person's character. The focus on the head recurred with greater dramatic intensity in 1815 when he painted his self-portrait (fig.30), with the intention of presenting it to the

Royal Academy in London as his diploma piece. In the latter he used striking lighting effects to stengthen the shadows, 'modelling' his face into a compelling presence the glowing light seemingly eminating from Raeburn's forehead.

The late self-portrait, so consistent with the romantic image of the artist, was completely different in character from the classically derived profile portrait whose opaque, white glassy paste was deliberately created to resemble cool porcelain or marble. Yet in both he is dressed in conventional contemporary dress and in neither does he show himself with any artistic paraphernalia, for as one of Raeburn's sitters commented he 'found no professional pedantry about him; indeed, no one could have imagined him a painter till he took up the brush and palette'.[3]

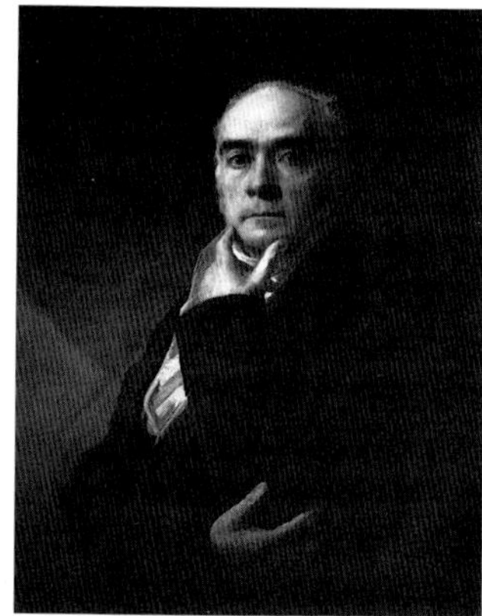

*Fig.30 Henry Raeburn, **Self-portrait**, 1816, (Edinburgh, Scottish National Portrait Gallery)*

1. Adam Smith, the political economist, died in 1790 and there is no evidence to back this claim other than this inscription in a late-eighteenth-century hand which is not that of Raeburn. I should like to thank Helen Smailes for checking this for me.
2. John Morrison, 'Reminiscences of ... Sir Henry Raeburn, etc.', *Tait's Edinburgh Magazine*, new series XL, 1844, p.17.
3. Allan Cunningham, *The Lives of the most Eminent British Painters*, ed. Mrs. Charles Heaton, 1879, vol.II, p.269.
Lit.: John M. Gray, *James and William Tassie*, 1894.
David & Francina Irwin, 'Raeburn', *Scottish Painters at Home and Abroad*, 1975, pp.146-164.

28 **Allan Ramsay** 1713-1784
Self-portrait at the Easel 1756
Oil on canvas, 62.9 x 47.6cm
(Private Collection, Scotland)

In this unfinished portrait which Ramsay began in Rome he points to the canvas on which there is sketched a woman's head, almost certainly that of his second wife Margaret Lindsay with whom in 1752 he had eloped and married against her aristocratic parents' wishes. They travelled to Italy in 1754 as a belated honeymoon Grand Tour arriving in Rome in December with Margaret several months pregnant and in delicate health. In 1755 shortly after the birth of his first daughter Ramsay painted in celebration a gentle and wistful portrait of Margaret holding a parasol.[1] After the birth of his second daughter he painted a similarly commemorative portrait of Margaret (Edinburgh, Scottish National Portrait Gallery), now acknowledged as his masterpiece. Margaret's first children, twins, had died within hours of birth and all three of Ramsay's children by his first wife, Anne, (who died in childbirth) had died in infancy or at birth. Ramsay's compatriot the Scottish architect, Robert Adam, described Margaret as 'a sweet, agreeable, chatty body, tho' silent in Company'.[2] The self-portrait, therefore, shows Ramsay pointing to his portrait of someone extremely dear to him, and it was possibly intended as a present for her or even for her estranged parents. It is more than the conventional self-advertising portrait-type in which the artist displayed a key example of his 'wares' (Cat.no.26, Cat.no.34) or showed himself in the act of painting (Cat.no.36). Ramsay holds neither brush nor porte-crayon in his hand, although a preparatory drawing, dated November 1755, showed him seated holding both palette and brushes and gesturing to an empty space.[3] As was his normal studio practice he has begun the portrait of his wife by drawing her head in vermilion underpaint, which would

later be covered in thin layers of colour.[4] The visit to Rome in 1754-7 was his second, his first as a student in 1736-8 had also resulted in a self-portrait, which had emphasised the young artist's confident mastery of the newly fashionable portrait style developed in Italy by Batoni and Solimena, under whom Ramsay studied. By the mid 1750s Ramsay had no need, as he had done twenty years earlier, to show off in an assertive self-portrait his newly acquired skills and attract portrait commissions from Edinburgh society and the Scottish aristocracy at court in London. He had just published his influential *Dialogue on Taste* and was about to catch the attention of the future George III. In his second major self-portrait in oil he could, therefore, concentrate on more personal matters than he had in his first, and adopt a more reticent and subdued expression and style. His visit to Italy had also been intended to offer him respite from professional pressures and the social whirl of Edinburgh and London. Unlike his first visit to Rome he deliberately lodged away from the city's British community and this desire for seclusion radiates from this intimate and reflective portrait of the artist and his wife.

1. Alastair Smart, 'A Newly Discovered Portrait of Allan Ramsay's Second Wife', *Apollo*, May 1981, p.291
2. Letter to his sister Nelly quoted in Smart *Apollo*, as above, p.292.
3. Edinburgh, National Gallery of Scotland (NGSD.2020) illustrated in A. Smart, *Allan Ramsay*, National Portrait Gallery, 1992, p.120 cat.51.
4. Smart, *Allan Ramsay*, as above, p.129 cat.no.66.

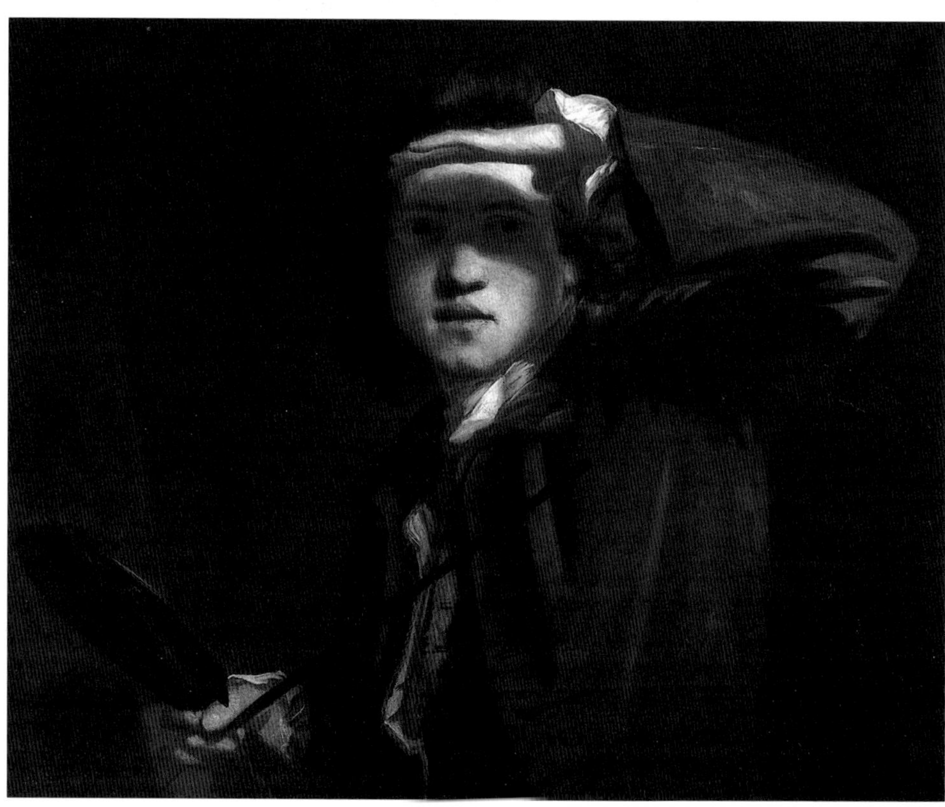

No other British painter left so complete a set of self-portraits covering every key stage of his life and career as Reynolds. The National Portrait Gallery's self-portrait was probably painted just before his trip to Italy in 1749. A visit to Italy and especially Rome was considered as essential to any aspiring artist as to any young aristocrat in the mid-eighteenth century. In 1747 Reynolds was very much the aspiring artist peering enquiringly and rather worriedly into the future as the striking gesture he incorporates into his portrait suggests. He had only recently arrived on the London scene, having trained in his native Devon where he had been supported by patronage from local gentry. He was seeking wider employment and his artistic ambitions are evident in the self-portrait. The shadow cast by his hand across his eyes enabled Reynolds to show off his skill in reproducing a range of tones, his shadowed but penetrating eyes contrasted with the otherwise brightly lit face. The self-portrait was an early example of Reynolds' adeptness at 'borrowing' from the old masters yet concealing the loan with an everyday gesture. The seemingly naturalistic action of shading his eyes from the glaring light to sharpen his study of the object of his attention is also an artful pose allowing Reynolds to try and emulate Rembrandt's mastery of light and shade. Although it did not reproduce a gesture from a Rembrandt self-portrait the pose enabled Reynolds to play around with that typically Rembrandtesque motif, the shadowed eyes (Cat.nos.11,13).[1]

Rembrandt's work was increasingly popular among artists and connoisseurs in the mid-eighteenth century and was the most important influence on the young Reynolds. During his stay in Rome he made a copy of one of the Dutch artist's self-portraits, his *Self-portrait as the Apostle Paul*, (Amsterdam, Rijksmuseum), whose turbanned head was shown half in bright light and half shadowed. As a young artist at the beginning of his professional career Reynolds chose to show himself, for the first and only time, as an artist at work holding his brushes, palette and mahl stick in front of an empty canvas. After his return from Italy his self-portraits became less tentative and more assertive gradually stressing the intellectual side of his ambitions. The casual attitude displayed in this self-portrait was replaced by a more dignified presentation. He produced several portraits of himself in academic robes culminating in his official portrait as first President of the Royal Academy wearing doctoral robes, holding a scroll and contemplating the bust of his artistic hero Michelangelo (fig.16), but still proclaiming his attachment to Rembrandt through its technique.

1. The pose does however appear in an unfinished etching *Old Man shading his eyes with his hand* of 1639 (B.259)
Lit.: David Mannings, *Sir Joshua Reynolds: The Self-portraits*, Plymouth City Museums, 1992.
Reynolds, Royal Academy, 1986.

30 **George Romney** 1734-1802
The Four Friends: William Hayley with his son Thomas, William Meyer and the Artist 1796
Oil on canvas, 123.5 x 99.7cm
(Abbot Hall Art Gallery, Kendal, inv.AH 674/68)

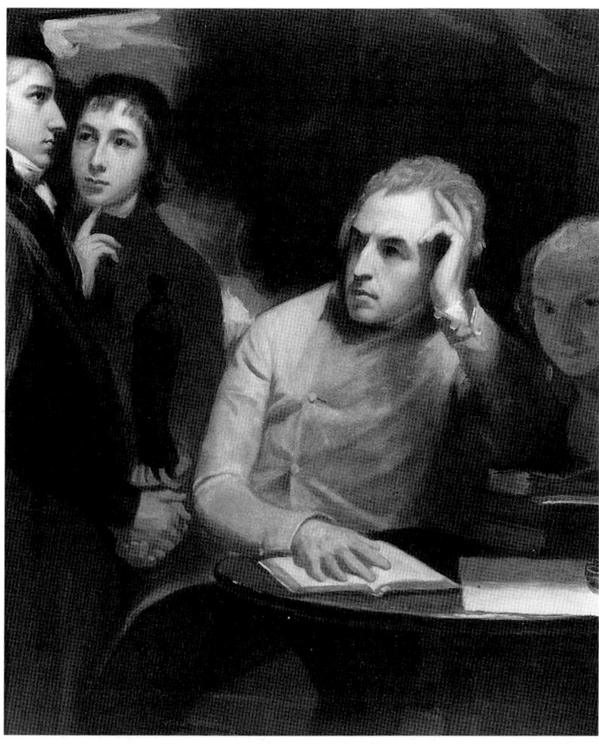

William Hayley, seen seated at the desk, was a poet and long time friend and patron of the artist. He had allotted himself the role as Romney's protector, providing psychological support to the shy and neurotic artist, and in 1809 he published a self-important biography using the letters he had received from the painter over the 25 years of his acquaintance. William Meyer, shown standing in his university gown, was the son of the celebrated miniaturist who had been a great admirer of Romney's work and had introduced Romney to Hayley in 1776. In 1795 Thomas Hayley, William's son, had become a student of the sculptor Flaxman as the result of Romney's promotion of his 'young friend', and to denote his role as a sculptor Thomas holds a statue of Minerva, the Roman goddess of the Arts. Romney had commemorated the occasion by beginning but never completing a portrait for Hayley senior of Flaxman modelling a bust of Hayley attended by his pupil Thomas and Romney. *The Four Friends* was also intended for Hayley senior and started in the summer of 1796 after a visit made by Romney to the two young friends Meyer and Hayley, a visit which he credited with helping him to recover from a bout of depression. The support of his protective friends meant a lot to Romney. He wrote in July 30 1795 'Friendship is then the first of human blessings. Only whilst I can merit friendship do I wish to live, if it fades away IN All I hope to die'.[1] The picture acted, therefore, as both a celebration of the personal benefits of close friendship and, in the form of Meyer junior, a commemoration of a specific friend, Meyer senior, who had brought them all together. In this sense the portrait fulfilled a similar function to *The Four Philosophers* (fig.31) by Rubens, an artist whom Romney admired. In Rubens' picture, which Romney could have studied during his visit to Italy in the 1770s, the artist paid tribute to the posthumous influence of the scholar Lipsius on his students and reenacted their friendship by demonstrating their mutual love for study. The similarity of intent was recognised by Romney's son in his description of the picture and by Romney's aping of its title in that of his own.[2] Romney's shyness, and extreme diffidence is indicated by the way he peers out at us from the corner of the canvas, though his need to wear bifocal spectacles, commented on by his son, might provide a more prosaic reason for his short-sighted gaze. Certainly Hayley senior did not consider the self-portrait to be 'completed', comparing the face to a caricature he commented:'It is rather surprising that the artist whose pencil had delicately flattered so many faces, did not seem to think himself entitled to be commonly civil to his own'.[3] In front of Hayley lies a copy of Cicero's *On Friendship* a treatise which formed the basis of many an eighteenth-century gentleman's moral outlook (see Cat.no.31). The picture has the air of a conversation piece, as if Hayley and Romney were recommending to the young men the usefulness of friendship in 'getting on' in society. The book thus provided a suitable classical and intellectual framework to what was a personal statement of loyalty between friends.

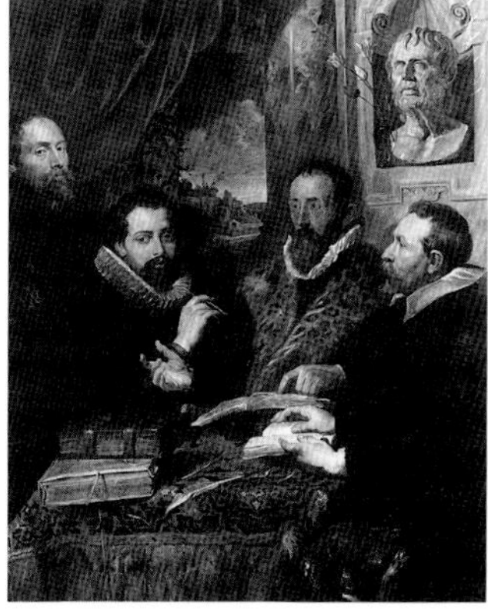

Fig.31 Peter Paul Rubens, ***The Four Philosophers***, about 1612-15, (Florence, Pitti Palace)

1. William Hayley, *Life of George Romney*, 1809, p.232.
2. Rev. John Romney, *Memoirs of the Life and Work of George Romney*, 1830, p.237-8.
3. Hayley, as above, p.253.

Alexander Runciman 1736-85

Self-portrait with John Brown signed and dated 1784

Inscribed on the back: Alexr Runcimanus et Johannes Bruno, Pictores eximii et mihi amicissimi de Poeta Avoniense disputantes. MDCCLXXXIV. Et monere, et moneri, proprium est verae amicitiae et alterum libere facere non aspere; alterum patienter accipere non repugnater. Cicero de Amicitia.

Oil on canvas, 63.6 x 76.5cm

(Lent by the Scottish National Portrait Gallery (National Museums of Scotland Loan) inv.PGL31)

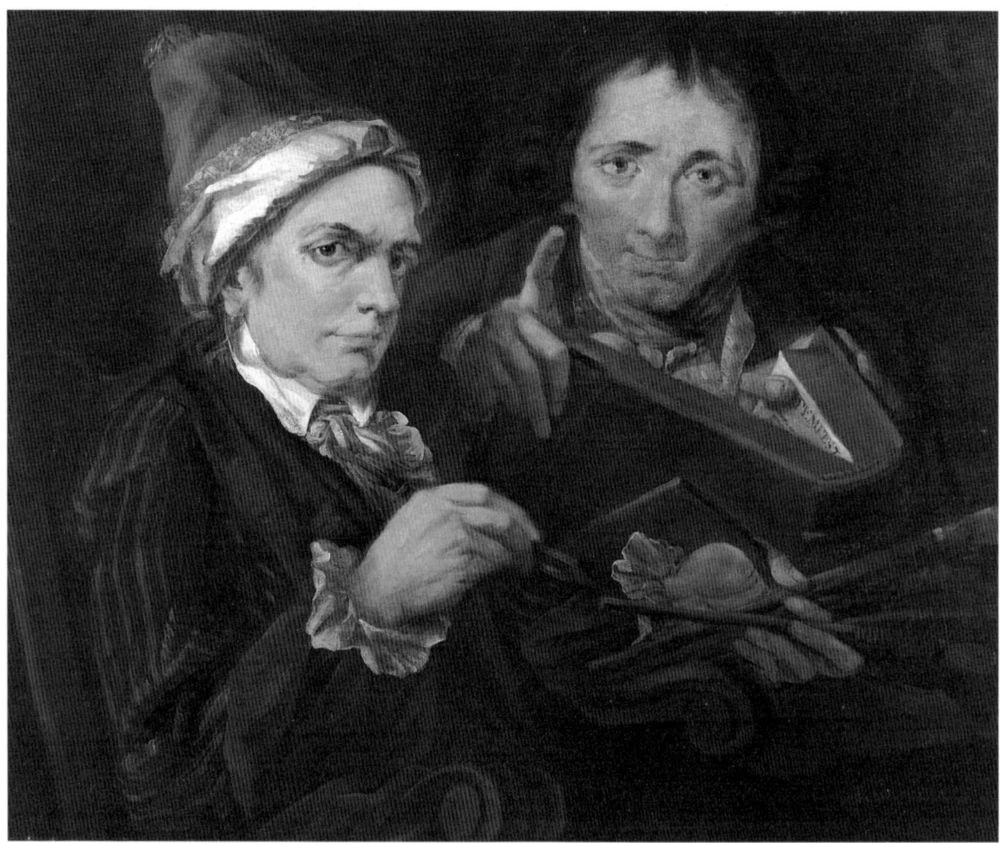

This disconcerting composition was painted for a friend and patron and intended as a joke between friends. The specific circumstances under which it was painted were described by the artist John Brown in a letter of August 1784 to the Earl of Buchan, founder of the Scottish Society of Antiquaries and leading member of Edinburgh's intelligentsia: 'I was yesterday with Runciman and sat for my portrait which he has done a first sitting of on the same canvas on which he has already done his own. The piece is for your Lordship and I think will be an admirable one. He has represented himself sitting at his work, his palette and pencils in one hand and portcrayon in the other. I, behind am seeming to point at and find fault with some part of his work, at which, as being rather irascible and impatient of reproof, he is making a damnable face, as he himself expresses it. I flatter myself your Lordship will be much satisfied with it.'[1] This jesting self-mocking piece of theatre did indeed meet with Lord Buchan's approval. He obviously considered it an appropriate symbol of their friendship and of his with them as he had inscribed on the back in Latin a description of it: Alex^r Runciman and John Brown uncommon painters and my very good friends disputing over the Poet from Avon'; and a maxim taken from Cicero's *On Friendship*: 'To warn and instruct befits a true friendship when on the one hand it is made freely and without harshness and on the other accepted patiently and not rebelliously'. Runciman's own history paintings made similar use of expressively gesturing and confrontational poses, derived from his admiration of the Mannerist works of sixteenth-century Italy with their extravagantly distorted figures. Such admiration, combined with his interest in fantastical themes, makes it even more appropriate that the two artists are portrayed arguing over a passage from Shakespeare's *The Tempest*, a play full of scenes of marvel and horror. Whatever the intended subject of the portrait the unsettling nature of the composition makes the viewer feel as though he or she, rather than a painting, is the object of the painters' criticisms. This paradox was probably meant to add to Lord Buchan's amusement. The fact that by 1784, one year before his death, Runciman was a disillusioned history painter with a dissolute reputation, whose work was frequently left unsold, can probably be gauged from the frank portrayal of himself. Both his demeanour and clothing suggest that he was disdainful of what the mass of people would have thought of his features and his work. Despite despising 'face-painting' as a career he left behind in his self-portrait a lively example of his artistic capabilities in the vigorous brushwork and inventive composition.

1. Letter in the Laing Mss. Edinburgh University transcription in National Gallery of Scotland files.
Lit.: David & Francina Irwin, *Scottish Painters at Home and Abroad*, 1975, pp.105-110.

32 **John Runciman** 1744-68
Self-portrait signed and dated 1767
Oil on canvas, 68.7 x 55.6cm
(Lent by the Scottish National Portrait Gallery (National Museums of Scotland Loan), inv.PGL32)

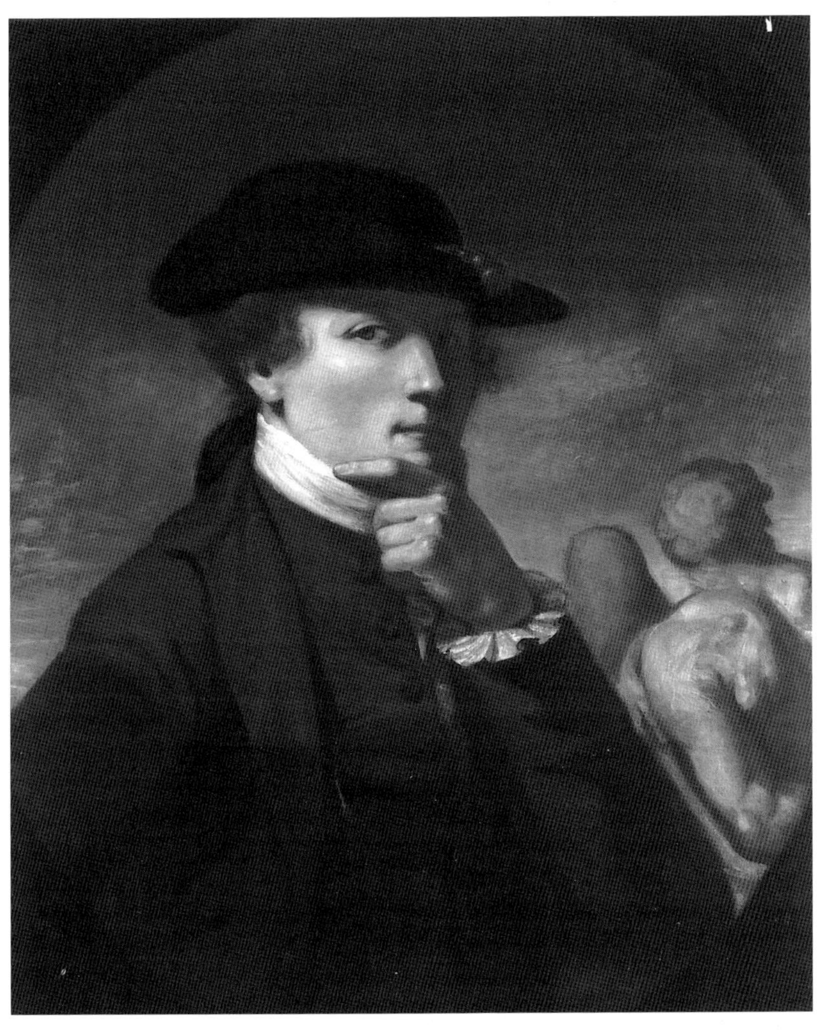

John Runciman accompanied his elder brother Alexander on a study tour of Italy in 1767. Both were determined to make their names as history painters, and rarely painted portraits other than of themselves or their close friends. Soon after their arrival in Rome they had joined the artistic circle surrounding Henry Fuseli, sharing his admiration for the antique and the work of Michelangelo as well as his interest in themes of fantasy and horror. Of the two Fuseli considered John to have 'excited much livelier expectations of his abilities as an artist'.[1] Even before leaving Scotland John Runciman had shown evidence of being an artist of promise. His vigorous drawings on classical themes had shown the influence of Michelangelo and his painting *King Lear in the Storm* (1767) was a dramatic image of wild nature as a symbolic fusion of the disordered mind of the King. The inclusion in Runciman's self-portrait of Michelangelo's sculpture *Day* from the Medici tombs in San Lorenzo, Florence was, therefore, not surprising. Runciman's pose with his hand holding his chin is a less aggressive version of that taken by Michelangelo's figure of *Contemplation* who sits brooding over the tomb of Lorenzo de Medici, his bowed head on hand and his eyes shadowed by the projecting helmet. The striking placement of Runciman's figure silhouetted against the daytime sky also recalls another picture on show in Florence in 1767 the *Self-portait as a Philosopher*, by

the seventeenth-century artist Salvator Rosa (fig.22), whom both Runciman brothers admired greatly. But Runciman's self-portrait was more than a statement of artistic faith, a tribute and response by one artist to the work of others. His choice of models emphasised the intellectual side of an artist's work and this aspect was pictorially symbolised by the bright light that illuminates one side of his face and highlights one eye in particular. Furthermore, Runciman's pensive, questioning expression; the fanciful placing of the sculpture outdoors rather than in an enclosed chapel; and its positioning with its face averted from the viewer, all emphasised the imagination as the source of artistic inspiration, as if the sculpture existed as much in Runciman's mind as in reality. It is a proto-Romantic image of the artist as an inspired creator. Runciman, however, progressed no further. Badly affected by intriguing amongst the closely knit circle of British and foreign artists in Rome, he suffered nervous depression, destroyed most of the work he had done in Italy and appears to have committed suicide in 1768. His brother, who was greatly attached to him, kept the self-portrait until his own death in 1785, perhaps as a form of memento mori.

1. Quoted by David & Francina Irwin, *Scottish Painters at Home and Abroad*, 1975, p.111.

33 **George Stubbs** 1724-1806
Self-portrait on a White Hunter signed and dated 1782
Enamel pigments on Wedgwood biscuit earthenware, 123.5 x 102cm
(Trustees of the National Museums & Galleries on Merseyside, Lady Lever Art Gallery, inv.LL3684
(colour plate 10)

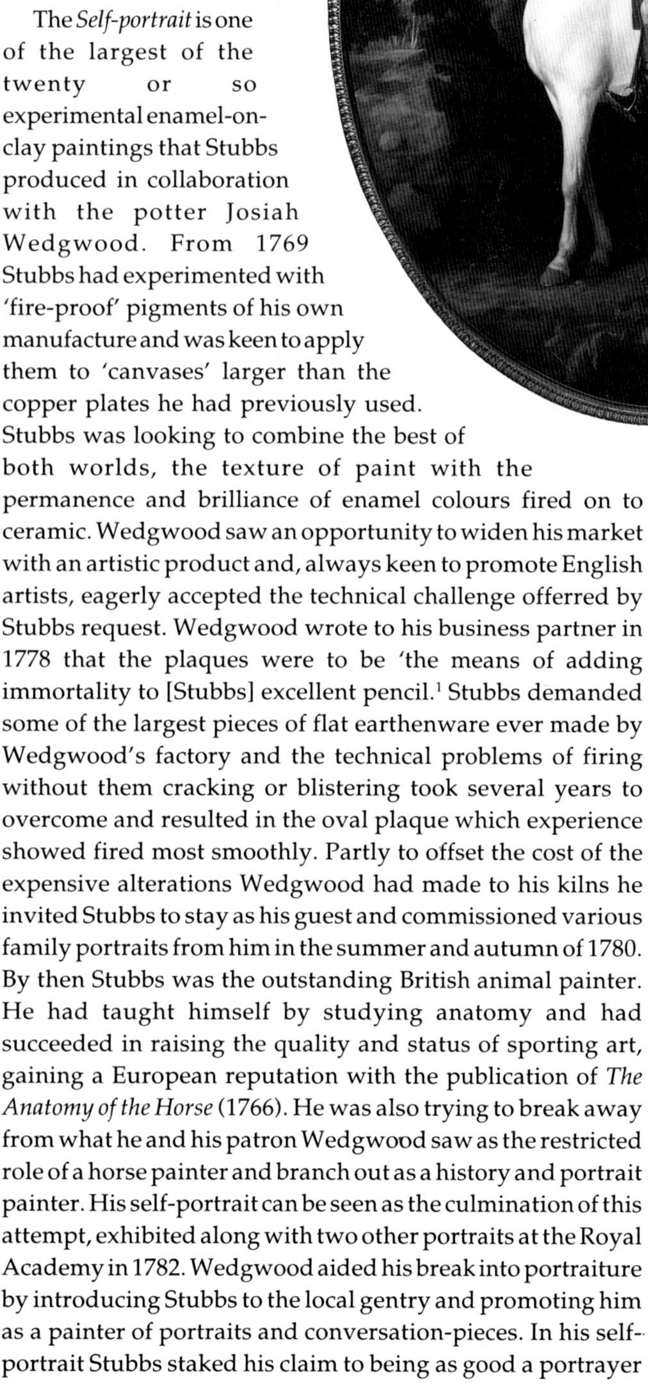

The *Self-portrait* is one of the largest of the twenty or so experimental enamel-on-clay paintings that Stubbs produced in collaboration with the potter Josiah Wedgwood. From 1769 Stubbs had experimented with 'fire-proof' pigments of his own manufacture and was keen to apply them to 'canvases' larger than the copper plates he had previously used. Stubbs was looking to combine the best of both worlds, the texture of paint with the permanence and brilliance of enamel colours fired on to ceramic. Wedgwood saw an opportunity to widen his market with an artistic product and, always keen to promote English artists, eagerly accepted the technical challenge offerred by Stubbs request. Wedgwood wrote to his business partner in 1778 that the plaques were to be 'the means of adding immortality to [Stubbs] excellent pencil.[1] Stubbs demanded some of the largest pieces of flat earthenware ever made by Wedgwood's factory and the technical problems of firing without them cracking or blistering took several years to overcome and resulted in the oval plaque which experience showed fired most smoothly. Partly to offset the cost of the expensive alterations Wedgwood had made to his kilns he invited Stubbs to stay as his guest and commissioned various family portraits from him in the summer and autumn of 1780. By then Stubbs was the outstanding British animal painter. He had taught himself by studying anatomy and had succeeded in raising the quality and status of sporting art, gaining a European reputation with the publication of *The Anatomy of the Horse* (1766). He was also trying to break away from what he and his patron Wedgwood saw as the restricted role of a horse painter and branch out as a history and portrait painter. His self-portrait can be seen as the culmination of this attempt, exhibited along with two other portraits at the Royal Academy in 1782. Wedgwood aided his break into portraiture by introducing Stubbs to the local gentry and promoting him as a painter of portraits and conversation-pieces. In his self-portrait Stubbs staked his claim to being as good a portrayer of humans as of animals, showing himself as a solid horseman on a large hunter, as if he were one of the landed gentry who were the source of his patronage. Contemporaries make no mention of his riding or hunting activities. He successfully hides his origins as the son of a Liverpool tanner and his unorthodox arrangement with his life-long companion Mary Spencer (whom he never wed) under a veneer of a bluff-looking respectable countryman. The self-portrait was radically different from that painted a year earlier for a friend (London, National Portrait Gallery), which conventionally showed him in his brown painting smock holding his brush. The image of Stubbs the 'landowner' was set against a romantic, wild landscape, a craggy woodland glade and river, probably based on the area around Creswell Crags in south Derbyshire. The contrast between the white horse and the darker background provided a good advertisement for the brilliance and durability of his colours. In fact his enamel paintings were received badly by art critics and rarely sold. The self-portrait remained with him until his poverty-stricken death when it was bought in at the studio sale of 1807 by Isabella Saltonstall, his benefactress in his last decades. After a dispute over what Stubbs considered the poor hanging of his enamel pictures at the 1782 Academy he had refused to submit the obligatory diploma picture and become a full Academician and never showed plaques at the Academy again. Such paintings on ceramic were subsequently excluded from the Academy's exhibitions.[2] Ironically what had primarily aroused the hostile criticism was the brilliance of the colours of which Stubbs was so proud and had gone to such lengths to produce.

1. Wedgwood to Thomas Bentley 17 October 1778 transcription published in Bruce Tattersall, *Stubbs & Wedgwood*, Tate Gallery, 1974, p.111.
2. Ruth Vincent-Kemp, *George Stubbs and the Wedgwood Connection*, 1986, p.50.

34 **Peter Tillemans** 1684-1734
The Artist's Studio about 1716
Oil on canvas, 68.3 x 84cm
(Norfolk Museums Service (Norwich Castle Museum) inv.86.989)

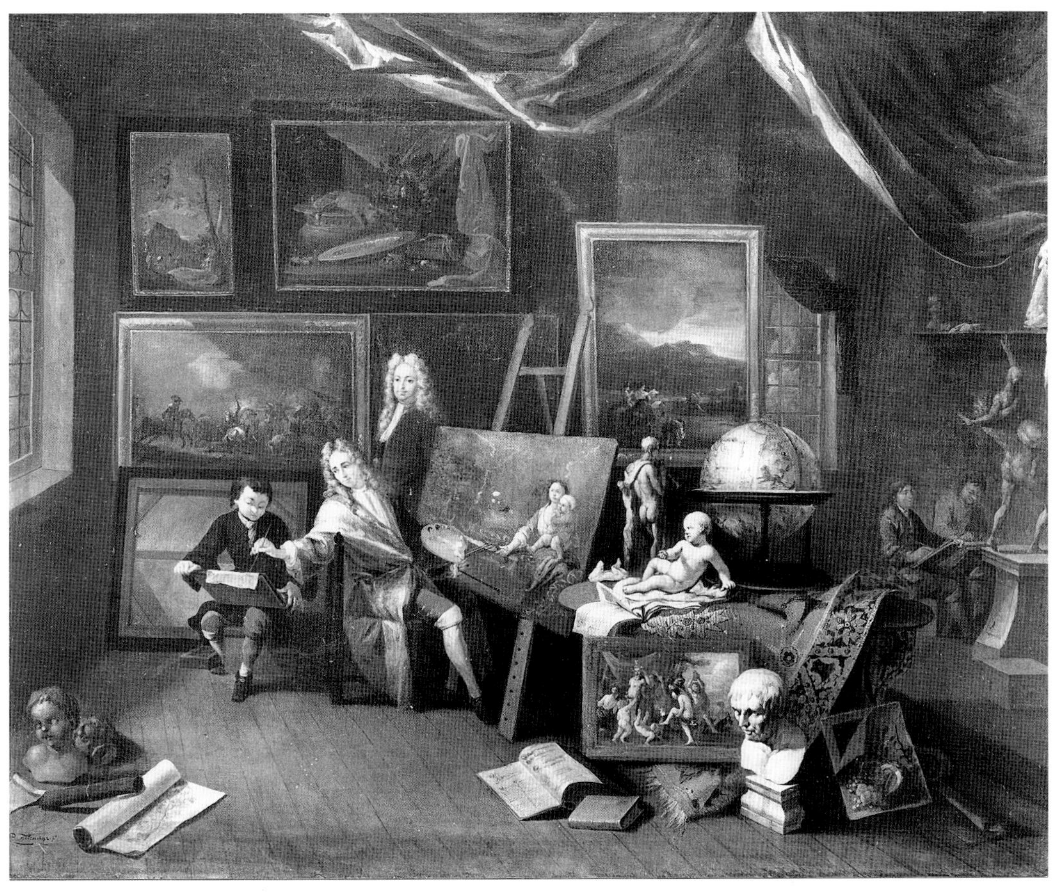

The earliest description of this picture referred to it as 'P. Tillemans in his painting room, instructing a Disciple; Mr Macro standing by him'.[1] Whilst one young apprentice is having his drawing corrected by the artist others are shown studying the figure from a sculpture, that appears to be based on Giambologna's *Rape of the Sabines,* and other busts and statuettes after modern and antique sculpture are dispersed across the studio. Both the sculptor Nollekens and the painter Arthur Devis are said to have passed through Tillemans' studio in London. Although the picture is about the working of an artist's studio, in which activity and instruction revolves around the painter, it is also a portrait of the patron, it is he who looks out at us and engages our attention. By not being involved in any manual activity he is also clearly distinguished as being the patron and of higher status than the painter, despite the latter's formal dress and wig. The Suffolk landowner and antiquary Dr. Cox Macro (1683-1767) was the most faithful patron of the Flemish born Tillemans. From 1715, some seven years after Tillemans' arrival in England, Macro acquired sixteen drawings and twenty paintings by the artist, twelve of which were original compositions and eight were copies after, or painted in the style of, other artists. Macro also commissioned the artist to decorate his house, Little Haugh Hall near Bury St. Edmunds, where Tillemans was to die suddenly in 1734. He also employed him to restore paintings and even to add figures to pictures in his collection. For these commissions Tillemans had to be able to work in a wide variety of styles and a number of genres. It is probable, therefore, that the pictures shown in the studio have been chosen to display his skill in the painting of landscape, still life, battlepieces and figures in styles as various as those of Rosa and Poussin, rather than purely to advertise his own pictures. Macro's own collection included works by Italian and Dutch masters including paintings attributed to Rembrandt. Through his self-portrait Tillemans not only publicised his wide-ranging experience but also his capabilities as a teacher, showing the studio as the training ground for the future artist. The introductions he was able to make through his early association with Macro probably helped Tillemans progress from his position as jobbing restorer and country house decorator to make a successful living from painting country house views, showing their owners enjoying sporting pursuits. In 1725 he became prominent in the London art world when he was made steward of the select Society of Virtuosi of St. Luke. On Tillemans' death his admiring patron commisioned a bust of the artist from Michael Rysbrack (along with a self-portrait of the sculptor) perhaps intending to place it in the temple of honour he contemplated raising to Tillemans.

1. Andrew Moore, *Dutch and Flemish Painting in Norfolk,* 1988, p.125, cat.no.78.

Lit.: Robert Raines, 'An Art Collector of Many Parts', *Country Life,* June 1976, pp.1692-4.

R. Raines 'Peter Tillemans, Life and Work, with a list of representative Paintings', *Walpole Society,* vol.47, 1980, pp.21-59.

35 **Elizabeth Louise Vigée Le Brun** 1755-1842
Self-portrait in a Straw Hat about 1782-3
Oil on canvas 97.8 x 70.5cm
(The National Gallery, London, NG1653)
(colour plate 11)

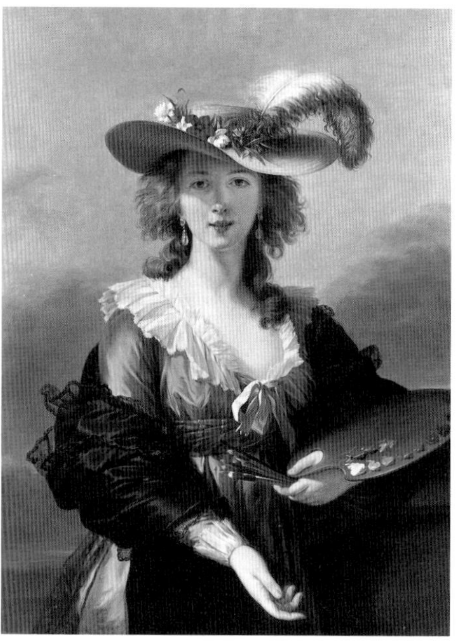

The self-portrait was inspired by Vigée Le Brun's first sight of Rubens' portrait of his future sister-in-law, Susanna Lunden, wearing a black feathered felt hat (fig.32). The portrait made such an impression that, as she described in her memoirs, she determined to paint her own in an attempt to capture the same effects. The straw hat worn by Vigée Le Brun is obviously a playful reference to the mistaken nickname the Rubens portrait had already acquired by the late eighteenth century, 'le chapeau de paille'. She was particularly fascinated by Rubens' brilliant use of luminous shadows and her appreciation is made clear in her own subtle pastiche of the original. 'Its great power lies in the subtle representation of two different light sources, simple daylight and the bright light of the sun. The highlighted parts are those lit by the sun and what I must refer to as shadow, is, in fact, daylight.'[1] The clear daylight filtering through the straw hat serves to accentuate her own eyes (as in Rubens' coquettish portrait) instead of hiding them. Although she borrowed elements of lighting and setting she played down the original's more provocative sensuality and transformed it into a chaster more decorous pose which would appeal to late eighteenth-century taste. She also played with Rubens' dramatic red and black colour scheme to produce the sweeter colour tones of black against pink, more palatable to her public. As a female artist who had had to teach herself outside the academic and studio system she was used to continuosly copying and improvising from other artists' work. Vigée Le Brun's *Self-portrait* was more than just a personal tribute from one artist to another it also advertised, almost flaunted, her artistic talents and her fashion-plate attractiveness, of which she was very much aware. This was certainly how it was viewed by critics when it was displayed at the 1783 Paris Salon, which it took by storm. As one observer wrote: 'When someone announces that he has just come from the Salon, the first thing he is asked is: Have you seen Madame le Brun? What do you think of Madame le Brun? And immediately the answer suggested is: Madame le Brun, is she not astonishing?'[2]. Although an acknowledged beauty (her nephew described her as a lively blue-eyed blonde with a long neck, delicate mouth and slightly retroussé nose[3]) Vigée Le Brun may well have decided to accentuate her charms in the self-portrait, as the first version was acquired by her patron, friend and supposed lover, the Comte de Vaudreuil.[4] It was the self-portrait's success at the Salon that led to her being proposed for membership of the Académie Royale and to her acceptance, with the crucial backing of Queen Marie Antoinette, of one of its four seats reserved for women, despite the fact that her husband's position as a commercial art dealer had officially disqualified her. The impression left by the self-portrait may be that of an elegant society beauty but the palette and brushes, with their colours matching those used in painting, makes viewers aware that they are in the presence of a working artist as well as a woman.

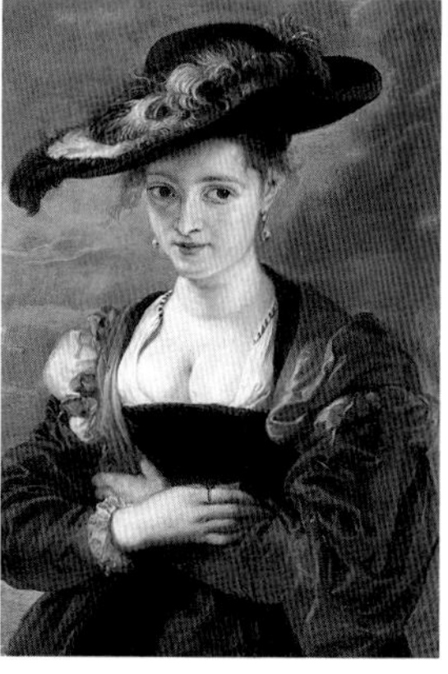

Fig.32 Peter Paul Rubens, **Portrait of Suzanne Lunden (Chapeau de Paille),** *about 1625, (London, National Gallery)*

1. *The Memoirs of Elisabeth Vigée Le Brun*, trans. Siân Evans, 1989, p.32 describing her visit to Flanders in 1782.
2. Quoted in Joseph Baillio, *Elisabeth Louise Vigée Le Brun*, 1982, p.8.
3. Baillio, as above, p.44 cat.no.11.
4. Bailio, as above, p.51 cat.no.14.

Self-portrait before 1731
Oil on canvas, 125.6 x 100.5cm
(Trustees of the National Museums & Galleries on Merseyside, Walker Art Gallery, inv.10396)

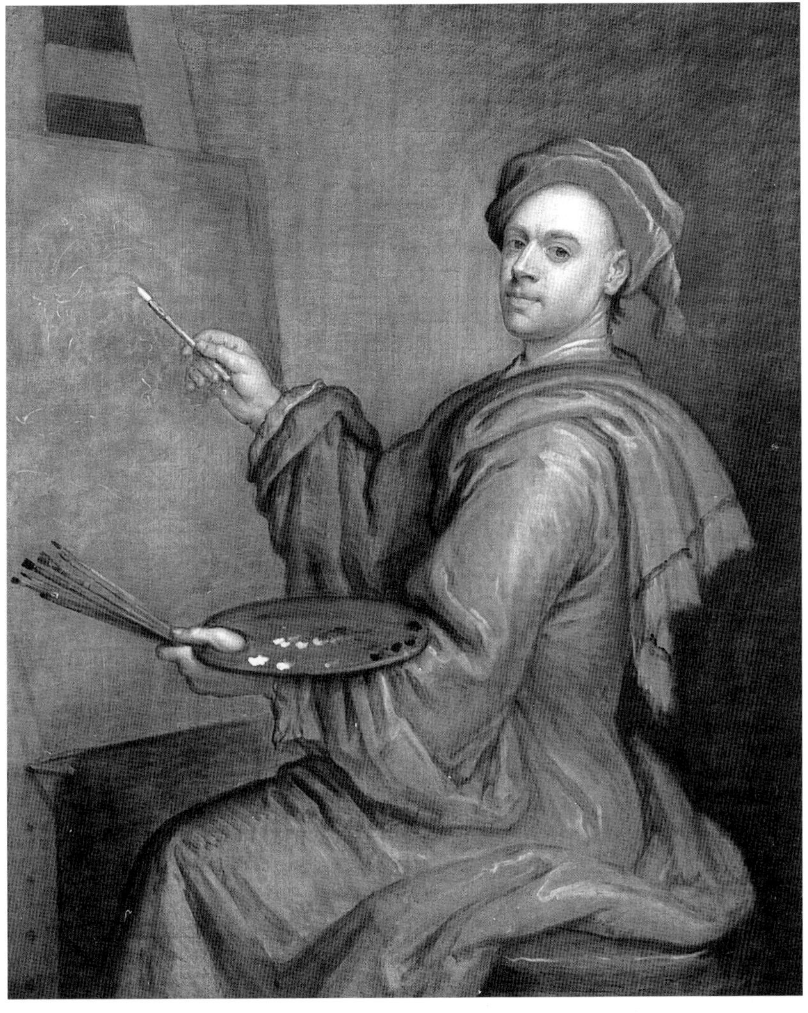

Throughout his career Winstanley, who was born and died in Warrington, depended on the patronage of the Lancashire gentry and aristocracy, and in particular the Earls of Derby. He relied on copying drawings and oils from local collections to teach himself painting before seeking improvement by moving to London in 1718, where he entered Sir Godfrey Kneller's Academy and received personal instruction from the court portrait painter. On his return to Lancashire in 1721 he was taken up by the Stanley family and in 1723 the 10th Earl of Derby, James Stanley, supported his two year tour of Italy to complete his artistic education by copying and purchasing paintings for the Earl's collection. After his return the Earl commissioned from Winstanley further copies of works in his collection, and original portraits and landscapes of his family and estate at Knowsley. In 1728 Winstanley published the Knowsley collection in etched form after which he was better known as an engraver than a painter.[1] By about 1740 when another local self-taught artist, George Stubbs, was seeking a local mentor Winstanley was the obvious choice, although his insistance on a pupillage that stressed the traditional values of copying works at Knowsley, rather than studying from nature, ensured that Stubbs' apprenticeship was short-lived. Despite or perhaps because Winstanley was predominantly self-taught his self-portrait shows him as the epitome of the professional artist, appropriately dressed and correctly posed. He is seated at his easel in the act of outlining on his canvas in white chalk the features of a woman, his palette, held firmly with the thumb flat against the crook of his elbow, is laid out ready for use with neatly ordered paints. The portrait he is sketching could be that of his wife Catherine, whose hair is dressed in a similar manner in her portrait by Winstanley, engraved as a companion portrait to his own in 1731, although her pose is different.[2] His wigless head covered by a red turban-like cap and impressive dressing-gown, which protects his everyday clothes, provide a note of relaxed informality, already considered an essential element in any image of artistic or literary genius. The casual dress was intended as a deliberate contrast to the heavily-wigged status-conscious self-image of the late seventeenth century. Winstanley's *Self-portrait* is a grand statement of pride in professional status, painted by a provincial artist who had returned from his study tour to Italy with a veneer of sophistication.

1. Horace Walpole, *Anecdotes of Painting in England*, edn.1876, vol.III, p.235.
2. Mezzotint engraving by John Faber II.

Lit.: Mary Bennett, *Merseyside Painters, People & Places*, Walker Art Gallery, 1978.

37 **Joseph Wright of Derby** 1734-1797
Self-portrait in a Black Feathered Hat about 1767-70
Charcoal heightened with white chalk on blue-grey paper, 53.3 x 36.8cm
(Derby Museum & Art Gallery, inv.DBYMU 1953-186)
(colour plate 12)

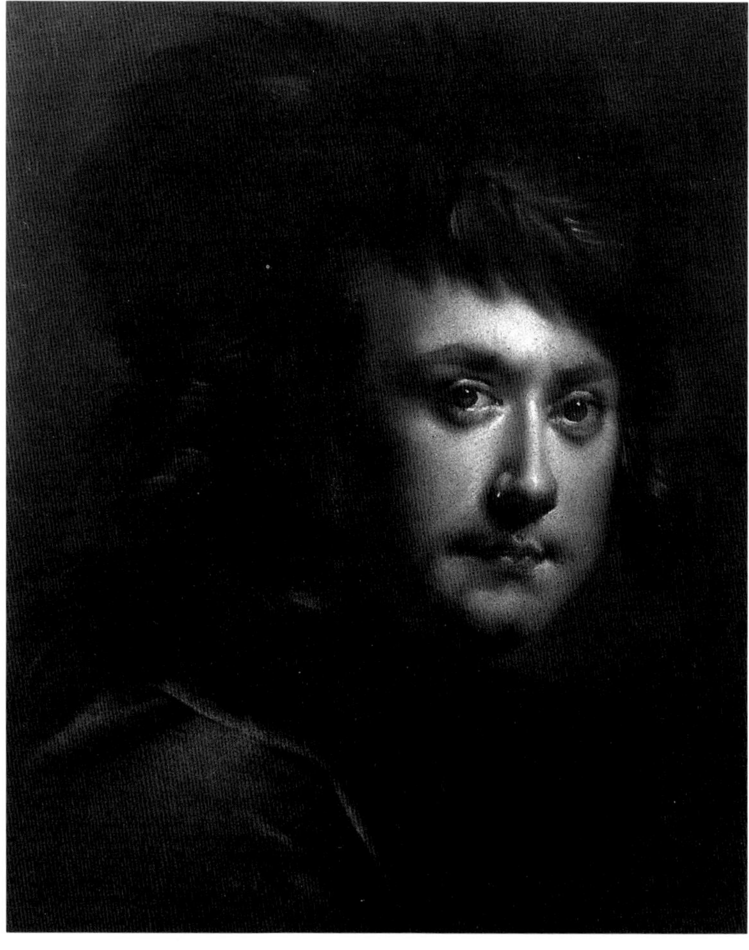

In the late 1760s and early 1770s when Wright was working in Liverpool he painted and drew several self-portraits in exotic or romantic headgear, referred to in an 1814 sale catalogue as 'fancy dress'. John Leigh Philips to whom this drawing probably belonged was a friend and patron of Wright's who left a fulsome description of him in his 'Memoir' of the artist in 1797. He recalled a modest unassuming but very handsome young man with eyes that were 'prominent and expressive'.[1] Wright's beautiful handling of charcoal and chalk and his use of chiaroscuro to suggest the effect of moonlight highlighting the centre of his face and merging the rest into the shadows, skillfully made the most of this expressive feature, turning his eyes into the enigmatic yet penetrating centrepiece of the composition. The dramatic light effects emphasise the introspective mood of the image as if, as Judy Egerton has suggested, 'Wright felt himself that day to be the embodiment of melancholia'.[2] Like other artists who created melancholic images of themselves (Cat.no.3) Wright also sufferred from periodic, sometimes prolonged bouts of depression and lethargy, which he dated back to about 1767 when he began to achieve fame. His subject pictures like *The Orrery* and the *Air Pump* were known for their nocturnal light effects, popularly referred to as 'Mr Wright's candlelights', and were perhaps inspired by the work of Dutch artists such as Schalken (Cat.no.17), whose own work could be found in English collections and had been engraved in mezzotint. The

mezzotint technique, in which the artist worked from dark to light, was closely studied by Wright and provided him with the method to master the use of chalk as superbly as in this self-portrait, where the various textures of luxuriant feathers, sensuous fur and smooth skin have been translated onto paper. Wright would also have encountered Rembrandt's work through engraved copies by his friend William Pether. Rembrandt had frequently posed himself in cap and fur-trimmed cloak (Cat.no.11) exploiting the dramatic contrast of light and shade to emphasise textures. One finds a similar Rembrandtesque style in Wright's self-portraits of the late 1760s as if he wished to pay tribute to the Continental master. That the artist saw himself in the context of an historic artistic tradition is evident from his earliest painted self-portrait of about 1753-4 in which he dressed in 'Vandyke' style. Unlike Rembrandt whose hats, berets and chiaroscuro were used to shadow his eyes, so frustrating the viewer's curiosity, Wright makes his 'expressive' eyes the mesmerizing focal point of his self-portrait.

1. Judy Egerton, 'Joseph Wright of Derby: *Self-portrait in a Fur Cap*', *The Art Institute of Chicago Museum Studies*, 1992, vol.18 no.2, p.113; *Realism through Informality*, Leger Galleries, Oct.-Nov.1983, Cat.no.24.
2. J. Egerton, *Wright of Derby*, 1990, Cat.no.54, p.111

38 **James Barry** 1741-1806

Self-portrait as Timanthes about 1780 and 1803
Oil on canvas 76 x 63cm
(National Gallery of Ireland, Dublin)
(colour plate 13)

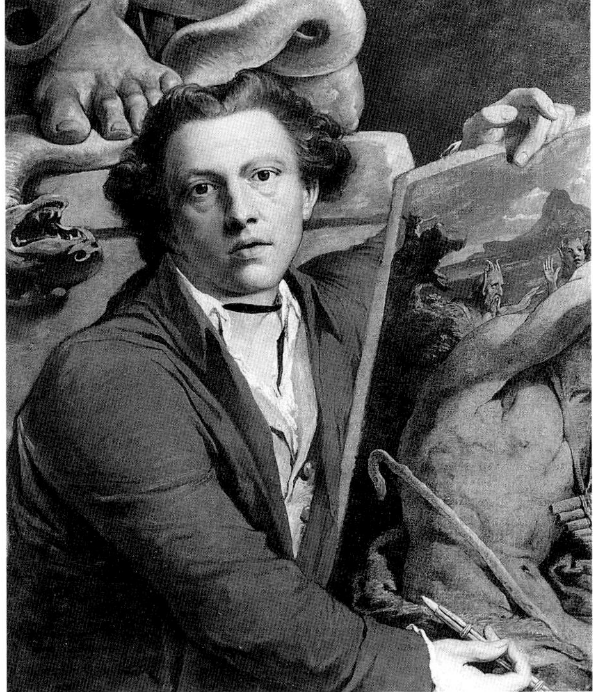

In 1780 Barry painted the head of the self-portrait as a model for his portrait as the classical Greek painter Timanthes in the huge mural of the *Crowning of the Victors at Olympia* for the Great Room of the Society of Arts. Timanthes was described by Pliny as 'the only artist in whose works more is always implied than is depicted and whose execution, though consummate, is always surpassed by his genius'.[1] Barry holds a recreation of one of Timanthes' lost paintings, 'a small panel of a Sleeping Cyclops, whose gigantic stature he aimed at representing even on that scale by painting at his side some Satyrs measuring the size of his thumb'.[2] Barry thus associated himself with the celebrated work of an ancient master who used radical changes in scale to evoke the sublime, effects which fascinated Barry as much as his ancient predecessor and which he put to use in his self-portrait. *The Crowning of Victors* was part of *The Progress of Human Culture*, a decorative scheme full of portraits of heroes past and present, commissioned from Barry in 1777, and to which he dedicated his life for the next six years. He was approaching the height of his career as one of Britain's leading history painters. In 1779 he was appointed Professor of Painting at the Royal Academy. Eventually the combination of his revolutionary political beliefs with his notoriously cantankerous and increasingly eccentric behaviour led to his expulsion from the Academy in 1799 after accusations made against its members in his publications and professorial lectures. By 1803 when Barry completed the self-portrait he was in a very different position. He had fallen gravely ill in January and was living alone in a ramshackle house in the 'greatest of misery'.[3] In the spring of 1804 the Society of Arts decided to help him out of financial difficulties and honour him by approaching him for a self-portrait to be engraved as the frontispiece to their *Transactions*. He offerred them the early self-portrait which he had finished off in the summer of 1803 by 'painting in the hands, drapery, cyclops &c'.[4] Barry claimed that the face was still thought a good likeness by his friends, but perhaps he was also reluctant to publicize later images of himself. It was the 1803 additions which turned a mesmerizing but relatively straightforward portrait head in contemporary dress into a dramatic and complex official image of himself as the heroic artist. The picture was a summary of his self-image in the *Olympic Victors* except that by moving the statue of *Hercules treading down Envy* (placed to the side of the artist in the mural) directly behind himself, he created a startling juxtaposition, as the snake of envy, in its death throes, appears ready to strike at the artist's head. The confrontation was deliberate as the statue had a personal significance for Barry. The Roman author Horace had described how the hero Hercules was only able to conquer the envy his virtue attracted by dying and so depriving the living of the provocation of his greatness. Barry interpreted the passage to show that envy encouraged one to excel, the evil conduct of others reinforcing a hero's virtues.[5] His belief in the symbiotic relationship between envy and greatness must have provided some solace to the seriously ill Barry. He had always identified with the image of the artist as isolated and execrated, subscribing fully to one of the maxim's of his contemporary and mentor Fuseli: 'It is the lot of genius to be opposed and to be invigorated by opposition'.[6] That attitude informed Barry's last public statement in oil of his official persona, the defiant yet wearied *Self-portrait as Timanthes*.

1. Quoted in William Pressly, *The Life and Art of James Barry*, 1981, p.98 from Pliny, *Natural History*, trans. H. Rackham, 1968, Book xxxv, p.74.

2. Quoted in W. Pressly, *James Barry: The Artist as Hero*, Tate Gallery, 1983, p.34, Pliny as above.

3. *The New Monthly Magazine*, vol.V, March 1816, p.134.

4. Barry to the Society of Arts, 2 May 1804, copied in 'Minutes of the Society of Arts', 6 June 1804, quoted Pressly, *Artist as Hero*, p.35.

5. Pressly, *Life and Art*, p.192 quoting from Barry's *An Account of a Series of Pictures in the Great Room of the Society of Arts*, 1783 and Horace, Book II Epistle I.

6. Quoted in Desmond Shawe-Taylor, *Genial Company*, Nottingham University Art Gallery, 1987, p.62.

39 **Ford Madox Brown** 1821-1893
Self-portrait signed and dated 1850 and 1853
Inscribed: Ford Madox Brown aetat 29 - Sept.1850 retouched oct./53
Black chalk on light brown paper, 25 x 23cm
(Trustees of the National Museums & Galleries on Merseyside, Walker Art Gallery, inv.WAG10505)

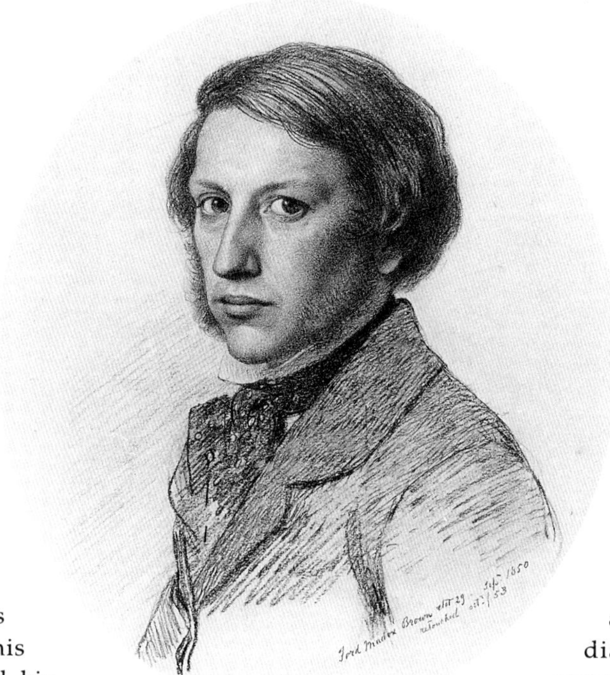

The drawing's dates coincide with two key years in the artist's life which saw the birth of his daughter Catherine in 1850 and his marriage to her mother Emma Hill in 1853.[1] The unadorned, clear-cut image shows the strong influence on Brown's work of German portraiture historic and contemporary, especially the work of Holbein and the nineteenth-century Nazarene group. Brown had arrived in England in 1844, lured by the chance to enter the competition to decorate the new Houses of Parliament and had finally settled after his first wife's death in 1846. The wary but piercing glance thrown out at the spectator from Brown's self-portrait by all accounts gives a good impression of Brown's often despondent, and at one point melancholic, mood in the early 1850s. Unlike his friend Millais (Cat.no.49) the late 1840s and early 1850s were not successful years for Brown. In 1850 while he was working on the large canvas of his *Chaucer* he was described by fellow artist Arthur Hughes as emerging from his gloomy studio 'with the impressive and rather severe face he seemed habitually to wear in those days ... His picture of the *Last of England* represents exactly his earlier face, where it looks at us from the ship's stern disappointed and half-resentful'.[2] For *Chaucer* Brown made many studies in oil and chalk of his friends, one such was William Michael Rossetti who at one time owned the self-portrait drawing, and whose conversation did much to alleviate Brown's gloomy thoughts.[3] By 1852 when he began work on *The Last of England* (Birmingham Art Gallery) in memory of his friend Woolner's departure for Australia, using himself and Emma as the models for the foreground figures, his depression was such that he contemplated emigrating to India. Later he was to describe himself in this period as 'most of the time intensely miserable, very hard up and a little mad'.[4] His worries were increased by the enforced secretiveness of his relationship with the teenage Emma whom he lived with but did not marry until April 1853. Later in 1853 his concern for his wife and growing family and his lack of artistic success led to him being diagnosed melancholic and prescribed a change of scene. Towards the end of the year he spent much time, isolated and morose, away from Emma and their baby, in contact with her only by letter. He spent most of the year retouching old studies, a habit of his that was reinforced by a lack of patrons which made him keep many of his works in his studio. That some of this withdrawn, prickly, personality struggling to create his best pictures is reflected in his self-portrait is evident when comparing the intensity of his moody gaze with that seen in Dante Gabriel Rossetti's portrait of Brown drawn in November 1852 (fig.33).

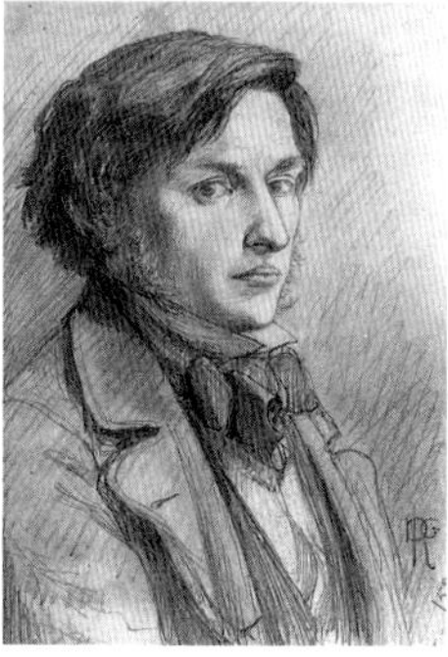

Fig.33 Dante Gabriel Rossetti, **Ford Madox Brown**, 1852, (London, National Portrait Gallery)

1. *Diary of Ford Madox Brown*, ed. Virginia Surtees, 1981, p.72 n.1. Catherine was born on 11 November 1850 and the marriage occurred on 5 April 1853.
2. Quoted in Ford M. Hueffer, *Ford Madox Brown A Record of his Life and Work*, 1896, p.69.
3. Ownership when illustrated in Hueffer, as above, opposite p.67, p.70.
4. Diary entry for 16 August 1854, Surtees, as above, p.78.
Lit.: Mary Bennett, 'Family Drawings of Ford Madox Brown', *National Art Collections Fund Review*, 1985, pp.128-132.
The Pre-Raphaelites, Tate Gallery, 1984.

40 **Emily (Milly) Childers** worked 1888-1920
Self-portrait signed and dated 1889
Oil on canvas, 92 x 68cm
(Leeds City Art Galleries, inv.26.6/37)
(colour plate 14)

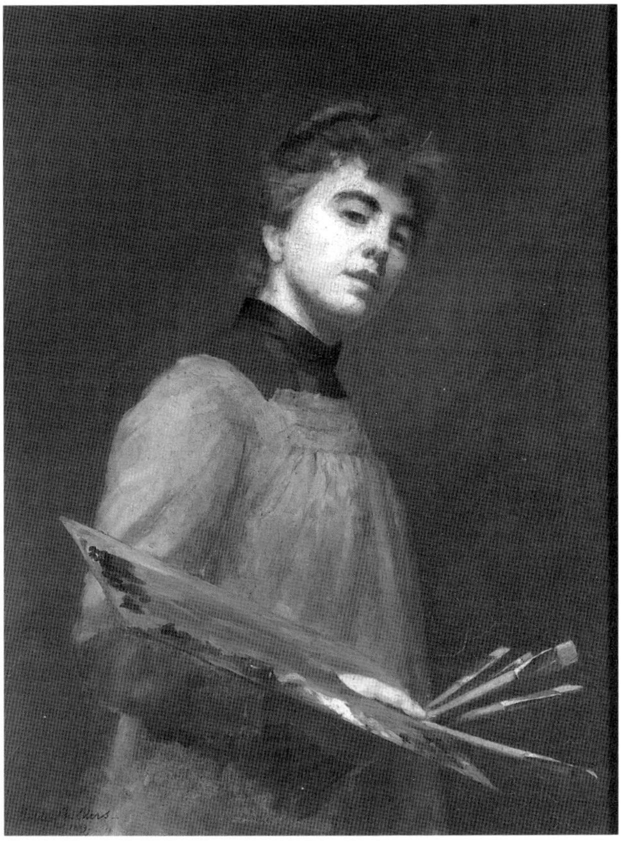

Emily Childers, or Milly as she was called, was the daughter of Hugh Culling Eardley Childers (1827-96) M.P. for Pontefract, in his native Yorkshire, between 1860 and 1885, Chancellor of the Exchequer (1882-5) and Home Secretary (1886) in Gladstone's cabinet. Her background would suggest that she was not a 'career' artist. But like many women painters of the Victorian period, whose position in the artistic hierarchy lay in a limbo between amateur and professional, very little is known about her artistic career or training and what is has to be pieced together from her known works. Her startling self-portrait may have been painted shortly after she had completed her training, for her first exhibited painting was a portrait sent to the Royal Society of British Artists in 1890. A year later she painted her father, shortly before his retirement, seated reading, formally dressed, in a sunny garden in Menton (National Portrait Gallery). Thereafter she seems to have concentrated on producing impressionistic landscapes and church interiors as she accompanied her father on his travels in England and France. It was presumably her father's political contacts that led to her 'employment' by Lord Halifax at Temple Newsam near Leeds, where she acted as a copyist and restorer (rather like Peter Tillemans almost two centuries earlier, Cat.no.34), making copies of royal portraits from the royal collection and of Temple Newsam paintings for other Halifax houses. It was probably also her political connections that provided her with the commission for the group portrait *A Scene on the Terrace of the House of Commons* which she was photographed with on November 4th 1909 (fig.34). The photograph shows a somewhat matronly, formally dressed woman literally overshadowed by her large, plumed Edwardian hat. The painted self-portrait of twenty years earlier creates a sharply different characterisation of Milly Childers. She is shown silhouetted against a dark background looking down at us as if sizing up her audience, a rather imposing figure, whose conventional artist's pose with brushes and very large palette is vividly brought to life by the eye-catching combination of vibrant red painting smock set off against a black blouse. Like Angelica Kauffmann (Cat.no.25) and Elisabeth Vigée Le Brun (Cat.no.35) before her Milly Childers had realised that how one dressed could radically affect the image one presented. Childers with her large palette placed prominently and strategically between the viewer and the artist presents herself proudly, and even more emphatically than Vigée Le Brun, as both woman and artist.

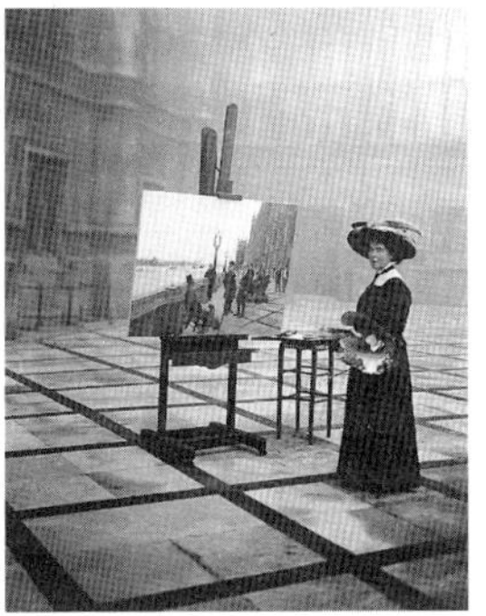

*Fig.34 Photograph by Benjamin Stone of Milly Childers with her painting **A Scene on the Terrace of the House of Commons**, 1909, (London, National Portrait Gallery)*

Lit.: Lieut.-Colonel Spencer Childers, *Life & Correspondence of H.C.E. Childers*, 2 vols., 1901.

41 **Charles Conder** 1868-1909
Self-portrait about 1895-1900?
Inscribed: C.C. TO WILL. R. SOUVENIR DE NOTRE LONGUE AMITIE
Oil on millboard, 47.5 x 35cm
(Manchester City Art Galleries, inv.1925.291)

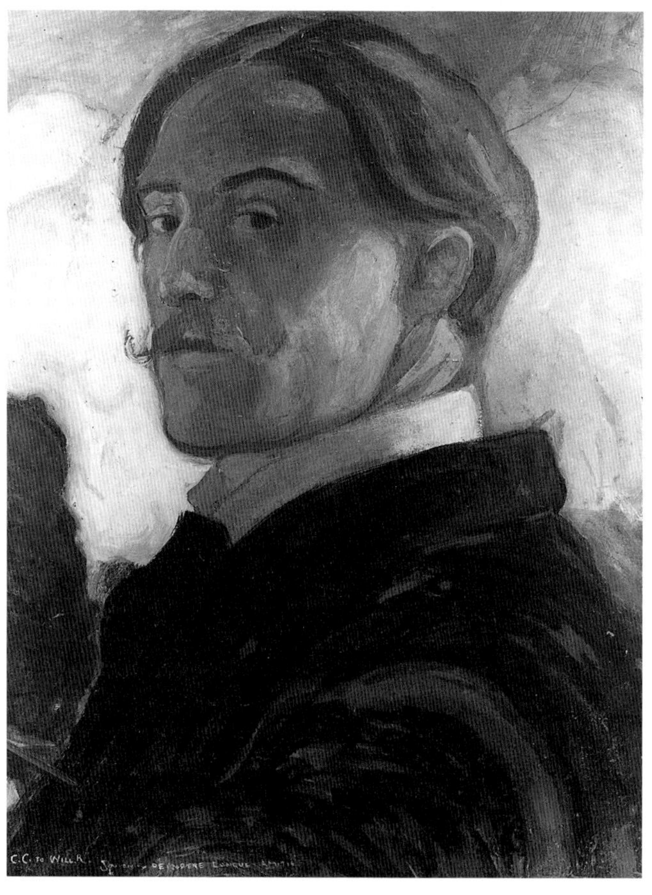

Conder was the archetypal anti-hero who, until his marriage in 1901, led a wholehearted bohemian life of drinking bouts and debauchery. Part of Conder's naturally suspicious character, even deviousness according to some of his detractors, comes over in this self-portrait as he turns enquiringly towards us silhouetted against a white cloud. The painting's inscription in French refers to the 'long friendship' between Charles Conder and William Rothenstein, who first met as students at Julien's studio in Paris in late 1890. From the mid 1890s Rothenstein acted as Conder's informal representative in London overseeing the framing of the pictures sent over from France and dispatching them to exhibitions. When ties of friendship proved strong he acted as his banker. From 1897 Rothenstein organised the exhibitions in London at the Carfax Gallery which did much to shape Conder's career, assuring him of a regular income and, after his one man show in 1898, an established reputation as a landscape painter and a personality among avant-garde London society. Conder made a tempestuous friend at the best of times. Drunken slander from Conder, who accused Rothenstein of getting him to agree to a disadvantageous financial agreement with the Carfax Gallery, provoked physical and verbal retaliation from Rothenstein leading to an abrupt ending to their friendship at the end of 1899. It prompted Rothenstein to sell or give away almost all the works by Conder that he owned. Presumably it was the dramatic caesura along with the fin de siècle air of the self-portrait which has led to its dating between 1895 and 1900. The breach between the two was healed in the spring of 1902 when Conder wrote offering 'mes bonnes Amities' and Rothenstein accepted glad to end the quarrel 'with one of my oldest friends'.[1] It is therefore possible that this testimony to a 'long friendship' dates from near the end of his career, when he was recuperating from one of his increasingly severer bouts of syphilitic-derived illness. On September 8th 1906 Rothenstein wrote to Conder: 'My few friends take a large place in my life ... & who can have more claim on my affection more than yourself, in spite of quarrels and occasional bitterness ... I can never love a man whose work I do not admire ... And to you dear Conder, may I say to you once in a letter, I love you, love you very dearly, and although Newquay is a long way off, I have a constant vision of you by a turquoise sea, vague to the eye, but sharp and living in the mind', adding that he would 'look after any pictures or drawings you may think of sending about this autumn'.[2] In his reply Conder enquired where he might get hold of the special oil-less white with 'wonderfully stiff impasto' that Rothenstein was using. The paintings he worked on at this time, like this self-portrait, are full of a tension suggestive of an awareness that they would be his last.

1. John Rothenstein, *The Life and Death of Conder*, 1938, p.194.
2. Rothenstein, as above, p.232.
Lit.: Frank Gibson, *Charles Conder his Life and Work*, 1914.

42 **William Daniels** 1813-1880
The Brigand dated 1837
Oil on panel, 28.8 x 22.8cm
(Trustees of the National Museums & Galleries on Merseyside, Walker Art Gallery, inv.WAG650)

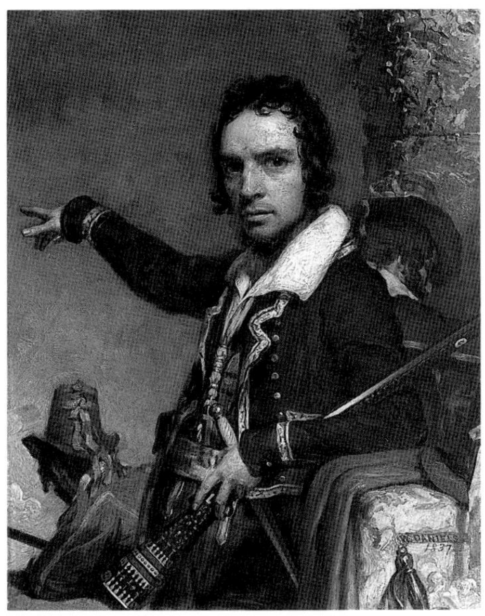

In life and art Daniels played out the 'romantic' image of the artist as a social misfit on the small-scale stage of Liverpool. Discovered as a young boy drawing and making clay models on the brickfields where he worked for his father, he was taken up by a local artist Alexander Mosses as his pupil at the Liverpool Academy Schools (1827-31), and employed by him as an apprentice wood-engraver between 1826 and 1833. Despite receiving no instruction in painting, and teaching himself after work by candle-light, he met with early success as a portrait painter and producer of nocturnal genre scenes. He found his subjects and his friends among Liverpool low-life centered around pubs, theatres and the boxing-ring. Whilst still a student in his late teens in 1829 he exhibited his first self-portrait and was described as a well-built, handsome six-footer 'bronzed and ruddy with eagle eyes and long curling black hair'.[1] Thereafter he frequently used his own image in various guises: once painting himself in action in the boxing ring; at other times as a sailor at the wheel during a moonlit storm; or about to strike a billiard ball out of the picture; or viewed from behind as in *The Card Players* (Liverpool, Walker Art Gallery). He also featured as the Moor in his *Othello and Iago* and as the Jew in *Shylock*.[2] Both in real life and in his self-portraits Daniels played on an image of himself as an outsider, a rough diamond who sympathised with the poor and other outcasts from society. His attitude was probably partly engendered by his working-class background and his self-taught status as an artist, which led him to shun Liverpool's institutional artistic society. Daniels' swarthy appearance and dark lustrous eyes with their piercing glance were often put down to his supposed gipsy blood and contemporaries gossiped about his fondness for depicting vagabonds. *The Brigand* in which Daniels portrayed himself holding a gun amongst a group of brigands in elaborate Italianate costume plays on this bohemian gipsy image. A memorial article on Daniels, headlined 'The Story of a Failure', described disapprovingly how early local adulation went to his head, 'Pats on the back being more confounding to some natures than thumps on the head' and how he then 'took to self-decoration and expressed his professional advance by much gaiety of costume and life'.[3] His eccentric character and ultra-bohemian manner of living, in which spells of hard work alternated with drunkenness, meant that he derived no great financial benefit nor career advancement from his early success and prolific output. He is thought to have made an unsuccessful attempt to establish himself in London, which may have coincided with the first of the few times he exhibited at the Royal Academy in 1840 and '41, shortly after his marriage in 1839. Significantly the early 1840s was also the period of his only conventional self-portrait (fig.35) in which Daniels celebrated his artistic 'coming of age' by showing himself as the professional artist. However, Daniels' penetrating stare and his typical heavy shadows and dark palette, exacerbated by the all black attire of coat, trousers and cravat, create an unsettling intense mood for such a traditional format.

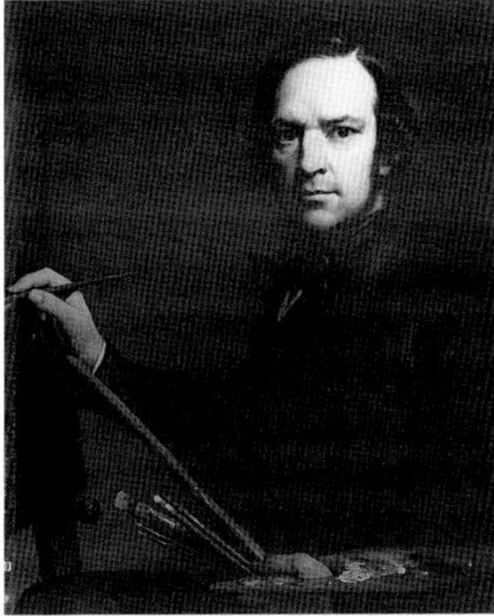

*Fig.35 William Daniels, **Self-portrait**, about 1840, (Liverpool, Walker Art Gallery, WAG1724)*

1. Description in his obituary *Liverpool Lantern*, October 16th 1880.
2. William Tirebuck, *William Daniels* 1879, pp.43, 26, 33, 41; Obituary in *Liverpool Argus* Oct.16th 1880.
3. *The Magazine of Art*, 1882, vol.V, p.342.
Lit.: Ralph Fastnedge, 'William Daniels of Liverpool', *Apollo*, September 1951, p.79-80.

43 **William Davis** 1812-1873
Self-portrait about 1852
Oil on canvas 35.8 x 30.7
(Trustees of the National Museums & Galleries on Merseyside, Walker Art Gallery, inv.WAG10825)
(colour plate 15)

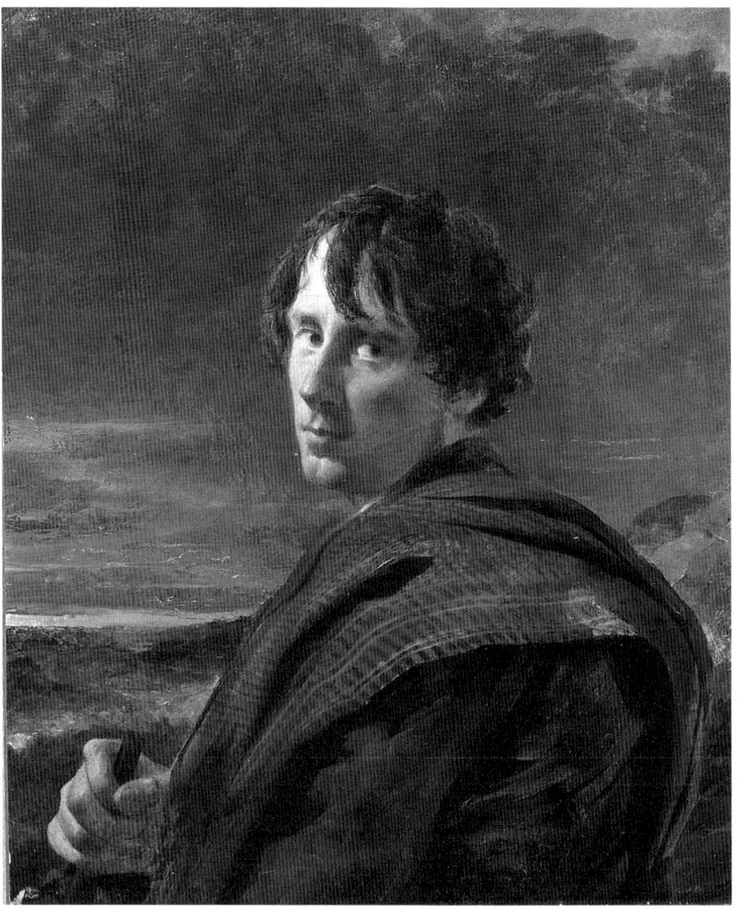

In 1851 Davis was elected an Associate of the Liverpool Academy and was made a full Member in 1853. In 1853 he also began to concentrate on landscape painting. Previously during his art training in Dublin and his move to England in 1837 (first to Sheffield and then to Liverpool) he had painted portraits, figure subjects and still life. Thus the self-portrait was painted at a turning-point in his career, after which he became the leading Liverpool-based Pre-Raphaelite landscape artist. His move to landscape art, which brought him to the attention of the Pre-Raphaelites in London, was possibly due to the encouragement of his first and for many years only patron, the Scottish-born tobacco merchant John Miller (?1795-1878) of Liverpool. Miller belonged to the Hogarth Club whose other members included Millais, Ford Madox Brown and Holman Hunt and his art collection was heavily weighted to landscape artists such as Constable, Turner, Linnell and Cox. His patronage also took the form of supporting Liverpool-based artists by buying their works and entertaining them in Liverpool and Scotland. He organised meetings at which individual pictures could be discussed and arranged painting trips into the countryside. Miller had a house on the isle of Bute at which Davis may have stayed in the early 1850s, as he submitted paintings entitled *Highlander*, *Grouse* and *Dead Game - Capercailzie* to the Liverpool Academy exhibitions of 1850 and '51. He certainly stayed with Miller on Bute in the autumn of 1857 as the inscription on his *Bute from the High Ground* (Liverpool, Walker Art Gallery) states. As is suggested by the tousled, wind-swept figure of Davis prominently sporting his plaid he was known as an ' open air type', a thick-set boxer and athlete as well as a noted singer, though otherwise rather reserved and humourless in character 'for an Irishman' according to Marillier the biographer of the Liverpool School.[1] His dependency on his patron was perhaps not to his advantage, especially as he had a ten children to support. Certainly in 1856 Ford Madox Brown believed Davis to be 'one of the most unlucky artists in England ... a man with a fine-shaped head & well cut features & his manners not without a certain modest dignity, but as it were all crushed by disappointment & conscious dependency of Millar [sic] who has entirely kept him for years'.[2] Brown's gloomy view may have been exaggerated by his own patronage problems. Davis's patronage may have been restricted, but nevertheless it was crucial to a rather retiring man, whose painting technique was painstakingly slow, and whose refusal to use dealers meant that patrons and private sales took on an even greater importance.

1. H.C. Marillier, *Liverpool School of Painters*, 1904, p.110-111.
2. *Diary of Ford Madox Brown*, ed. V. Surtees, 1981, p.190.
Lit.: Mary Bennett, *Merseyside Painters, People & Places*, 1978.
Anne MacPhee, 'Two Patrons of Victorian Art' in *Riches into Art: Liverpool Collectors 1770-1880*, ed. Pat Starkey, 1993.
The Pre-Raphaelites, Tate Gallery, 1984.

44 Augustus Egg 1816-1863
Self-portrait as David Fallen in Not So Bad As We Seem signed and dated 1858
Inscribed: In every scene some moral let it teach And if it can at once both please and preach
Oil on canvas, 76.5 x 64.5cm
(The Trustees of Patrick Allan-Fraser of Hospitalfield, Arbroath, inv.16)

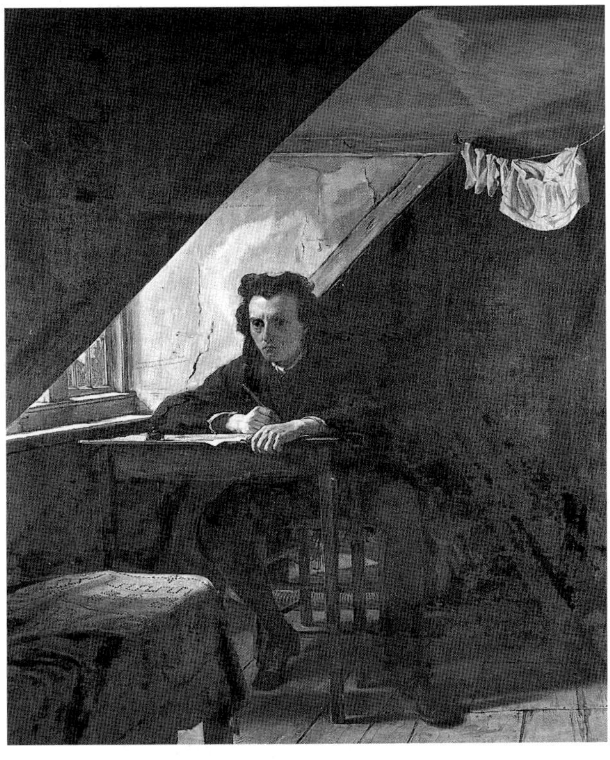

The picture is one of a group of self-portraits 'in character' (see also Cat.no.51, fig.37) that Patrick Allan-Fraser commissioned, to decorate his home, from artist-friends whom he had known in London and Rome. Allan-Fraser had been a professional artist until his marriage in 1843 when he became master of his wife's estate at Hospitalfield. He then embarked on a long-term plan to found an institution for the advancement of art by supporting young but poor artists of talent, using Hospitalfield and other family estates to provide a financial and residential base. Egg shared many of Patrick Allan-Fraser's philanthropic concerns and was particularly worried by the financial problems of painters and writers. Throughout the 1850s the altruistic Egg had been a consistent supporter of the Pre-Raphaelites and so knew well the struggles of poor artists. In 1851 he joined his friends Charles Dickens and Sir Edward Bulwer-Lytton in staging an amateur theatrical tour of Bulwer-Lytton's *Not So Bad as We Seem*, written especially to raise money for the Guild of Literature and Art, established by the two authors as a self-help organisation providing pensions and funds for needy artists and writers. The Self-portrait provided his friend and patron with a very specific message of support for and a symbol of their mutually held philanthropic and artistic beliefs. As the minute inscriptions on the painting reveal Egg painted himself in the guise of David Fallen the hero of Bulwer-Lytton's play and the part that Egg had acted in its nationwide tour. The play was set in the first half of the eighteenth century and its hero was an author and pamphleteer whose decline in fortune and eventual death were the result of the lack of patronage that the Guild, Egg and Allan-Fraser hoped to alleviate with their own projects. In the self-portrait as in the play the 'backdrop' of the scene in which David Fallen broods on his misfortune was based on Hogarth's *The distressed poet* (fig.36) which also depicted the troubles of a destitute, patronless hack shown seated at a table in a roof-lit garret. Like Egg Hogarth had also sought to join the arts of painting and drama. The close relationship between Egg's self-image symbolic of the theme of genius neglected through society's philistinism and Hogarth's attitude to his moral pictures was further stressed by the couplet written on the attic wall in Egg's picture. The concept that art could both entertain and improve was not only Hogarthian in sentiment but was an attitude shared by Egg and his patron, whose activities at Hospitalfield aimed both to delight and improve society.

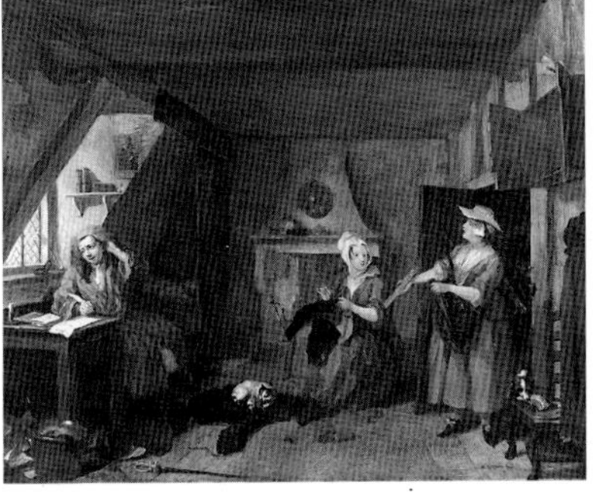

Fig.36 Wiliam Hogarth, **The Distressed Poet**, about 1735, (Birmingham Museums and Art Gallery).

Lit.: Hilarie Faberman, *Augustus Leopold Egg* Phd. Dissertation, Yale University, 1983.
H. Faberman, 'Augustus Egg's *Self-portrait as a poor author*', *Burlington Magazine*, April 1983, pp.224-226.
William Payne, *Hospitalfield: Patrick Allan-Fraser and his art collection*, 1990.

45 **William Etty** 1787-1849
Self-portrait 1825
Oil on paper on canvas, 43 x 33.2cm
(Manchester City Art Galleries, inv.1882.147)

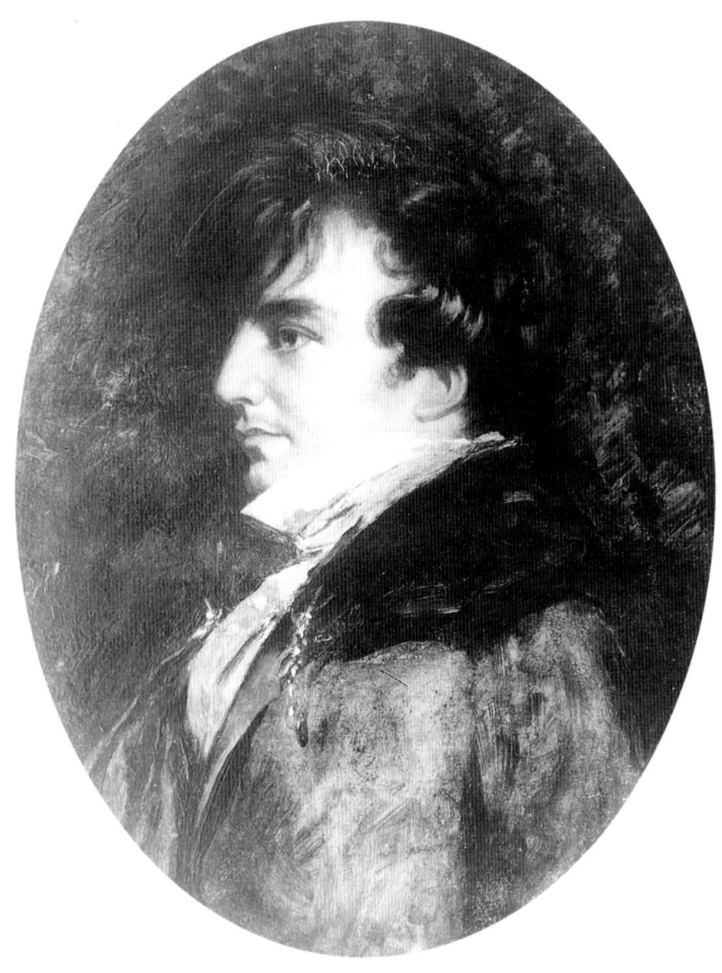

Etty was an Academy artist par excellence. He had been an assiduous student at the Royal Academy since 1807 and continued to attend its life drawing school, overlapping with the young Pre-Raphaelite students, until his retirement to York in 1848. He had also been the favoured pupil of the Academy's President Sir Thomas Lawrence. The year 1825 was one of reassessment for Etty, a time when he was hoping to advance his fame, launch himself as a painter of history subjects and make good use of the one and a half years in Italy from which he had recently returned. In October of 1824 he had, after several attempts, been elected an associate of the Royal Academy and had moved into a larger studio in anticipation of commissions. He spent the spring and summer of 1825 at work on one of his large canvases which was well received at the Academy exhibition, and the autumn visiting, with great pleasure, his native city of York, where after a long absence he took to painting portraits again. Other versions of this self-portrait were painted for members of his family including his youngest brother Charles a captain in the merchant service. The self-portrait shows the artist in an idealized classical profile, his smallpox scars obliterated and the dark background shadows flattening his prominent hooked nose, seen in a portrait of Etty drawn twenty years later.[1] The oval painting itself recalls a classical cameo in its shape, but the dark tones, disordered hair and introspective, slightly melancholic mood, are also suggestive of the work of the French Romantics, whose leading representative, Eugène Delacroix, Etty had met on his visit to London in 1825. Though the self-portrait merged a classical format with a romantic mood and brushwork Etty essentially treated it as a formal academic study in alternating lights and darks - the fur-trimmed brown cloak with its glistening brass fastening, contrasted against the bright white dash of his thickly-painted collar and the rich creamy flesh tones set against his loose mop of hair, which he seems to have darkened from its original sandy colour in order to complete the portrait's alternating tonal harmonies. The overall mood is mysterious but restrained and reveals little of his frenzied working practice as superbly described by Holman Hunt: 'He was intoxicated with the delight of painting ... after a careful reloading of his brush he drove the tool upwards in frequent bouts before his half-closed eyes, I don't think that, had he been asked suddenly, he could have told his name'.[2]

1. Drawing by C.H. Lear illustrated in Dennis Farr, *William Etty*, 1958, fig.1.

2. William Holman Hunt, *Pre-Raphaelitism and the Pre-Raphaelite Brotherhood*, 1905, vol.1, pp.95.

Lit.: Alexander Gilchrist, *Life of William Etty*, (1855) republished 1978.

Arts Council, *William Etty*, 1955.

46 **William Powell Frith** 1819-1909
The Sleeping Model dated 1853
Oil on canvas, 63.5 x 71.8cm
(Royal Academy of Arts, London)

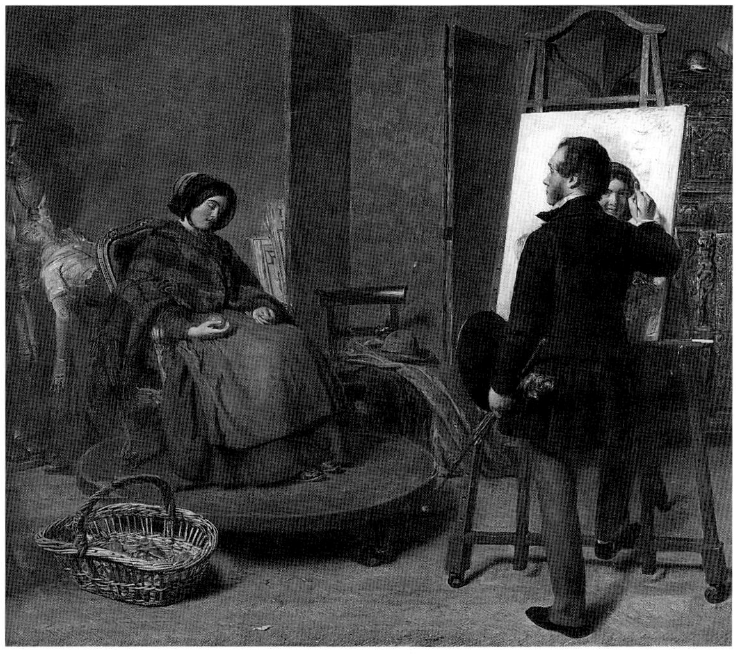

The Sleeping Model was Frith's Diploma work, the picture he was obliged to give (somewhat against his will) as an example of his work to the Royal Academy on his being elected an academician in February 1853. Although there were no set rules as to appropriate subject matter, grand and heroic themes or morally instructive works met with approval. Some academicians would have considered *The Sleeping Model* an unsuitably trifling subject for a Diploma work, but it is typical of Frith not merely in its anecdotal character but in its use of a scene from modern life. Perhaps aware of the Academy's disapproval of self-portraits as Diploma pieces Frith never referred to the picture as such, although there is little doubt that the artist's features are Frith's. He described it in his autobiography as a representation of an amusing incident that highlighted 'one of the difficulties that beset all artists', and one which, as various tales in his memoirs make clear, vexed Frith especially, the problem of finding suitable models.[1] Frith tells how having met a particularly pretty orange-seller in the street and persuaded her into his studio only after gaining, at her request, the consent of her Catholic confessor his intention of painting her captivating laugh was foiled when she fell asleep. The bewildered artist was forced to change his theme from the smiling to the sleeping model. The theme of artist and model was an ancient one, but one which in the Victorian age was charged with sexual unease and ambiguity. Modelling was considered a disreputable activity particularly for young unmarried women, as Frith's anecdote suggests, and the painter's studio was a morally dangerous place. The impeccably dressed and respectably posed Frith has been careful to create in his picture both a physical and social distance between himself and his working-class model. The model may be fully clothed, but she is asleep and unchaperoned and any contemporary viewing the picture would have known that the poor Irish girls who sold oranges two for a penny in the winter were often the spring flower-sellers of low moral reputation.[2] That Frith was well aware of this sexual tension is suggested by the slightly lubricious quality to the story as he relates it in his *Reminiscences*, revealing that in his attempts to talk to her he had asked whether she was ever annoyed by soldiers and street-loafers to which she replied "she was bothered; but it was by swells. Gentlemen is much greater blackguards than what blackguards is". In *The Sleeping Model* Frith covered up a worrying moral anxiety in an amusing story-picture. Whether the underlying tension in Frith's self-portrait reflected his own double-life from the early 1850s, when he kept a mistress and two families is hard to tell, but he returned to a similar theme of the ambiguous relationship between artist and putative model on two separate occasions, in his *The Visit* of 1867 (National Portrait Gallery) and the *Self-portrait with an Italian Flower Girl* of 1875, intended for the Hospitalfield collection of self-portraits 'in character' (fig.37).

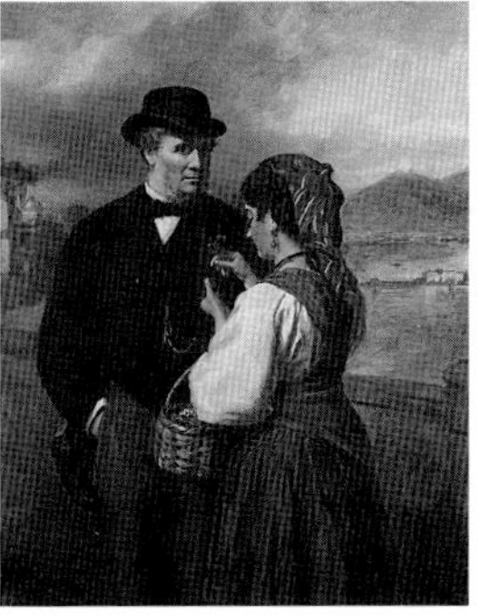

Fig.37 William Powell Frith,
Self-portrait with an Italian
Flower Girl, *1875, (Arbroath,*
Patrick Allan-Fraser of
Hospitalfield Trust)

1. W.P. Frith, *My Autobiography and Reminiscences*, 1888, pp.165-167, 188, 299-300.
2. Henry Mayhew, *Survey of Labour and the Poor*, (1849) republished 1980, vol.1, p.269; vol.2, pp.7-8, 64-65.
Lit.: Paula Gillett, *The Victorian Painter's World*, 1990.
Graham Reynolds, *Victorian Painting*, 1966.

47 **William Huggins** 1820-1884
Self-portrait with a Guitar about 1840-1841
Oil on board, 80.6 x 67cm
(Williamson Art Gallery & Museum, Birkenhead, Wirral, inv.1556)

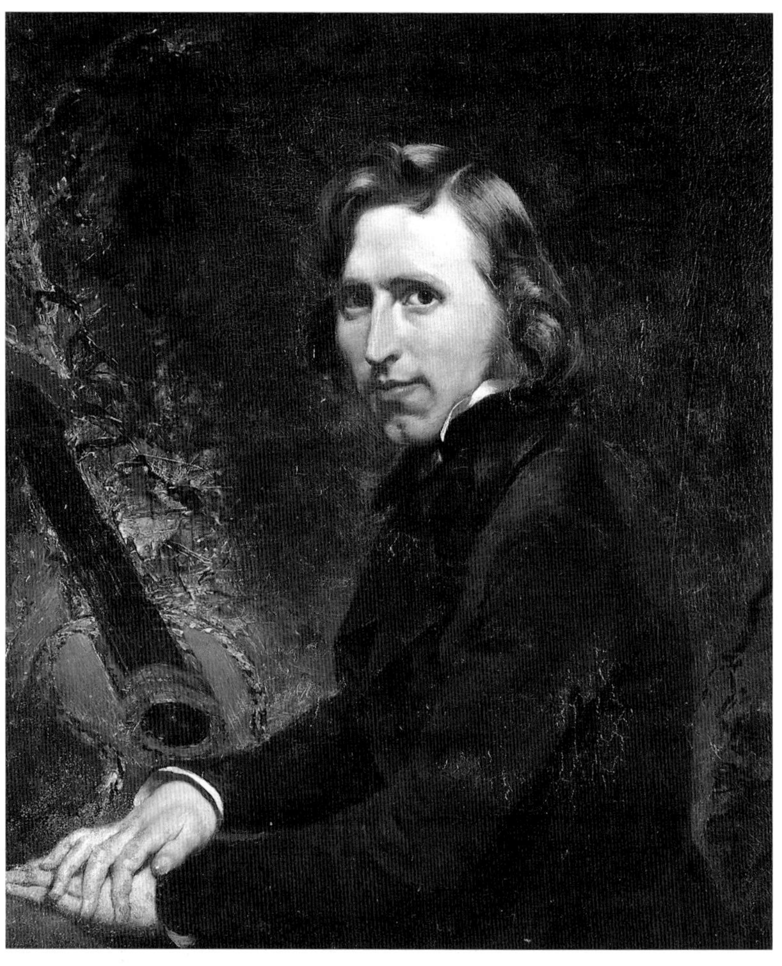

Huggins was an artist of promise winning a prize from the Liverpool Mechanics Institute at the age of fifteen for his ambitious *Adam's Vision of the death of Abel*. From the start he concentrated on painting animals, eagerly studying them in the Liverpool Zoological Gardens, before entering the Liverpool Academy Schools in 1835. He went on to make his mark as a painter of farm and wild animals, but always harboured ambitions to be a history painter. His few early attempts usually included animals such as *Christian and the Lions* of 1848 (Liverpool, Walker Art Gallery). Until at least the early 1850s Huggins also appears to have had an extensive portrait practice and the self-portrait shows his characteristic combination of vigorous brushwork and delicate depiction of features. The self-portrait dates from the early 1840s when he painted in a glossy style in rich deep tones. It may well be the portrait he exhibited at the Liverpool Academy in 1840 or another of 1841 in the hands of a private collector in 1886.[1] Another self-portrait is dated 1842 (Liverpool, Walker Art Gallery). The same long, sensitive-looking face appears on a small bust being modelled by William Spence (1793-1849) in Huggins' portrait, dated 1841, of the Liverpool sculptor, who was his drawing master and friend. The Birkenhead self-portrait appears to have been kept in the family, as a label on its reverse suggests that it was owned by S. Huggins, presumably either his elder brother Samuel (1811-1885), the architect and founder of the Society for the Protection of Ancient Buildings or his sister Sarah (born 1817), an artist herself, who exhibited mainly flower paintings at the Liverpool and Royal Academies between 1853 and 1865. Huggins' self-portrait also celebrated other accomplishments. In the past artists had sometimes portrayed themselves as practitioners of the 'sister art' of music as it symbolised the breadth of their artistic creativity. Huggins was a musician of fair ability, the guitar being his favoured instrument and at least one of his sitters remembered as a child being serenaded with sentimental love songs by Huggins on his guitar in order to keep her amused: 'To this day I believe that the tune of *'Twere vain to tell thee all I feel'* would bring back the figure of the little man with his long light brown hair (long even for that day, and for a painter), his quaint attitudes and his impassioned manner'.[2] His impassioned manner is evident in the handling of his self-portrait. His 'artistic temperament' also surfaced in a touchiness and resentment of criticism which was probably indirectly referred to in his curious tomb epitaph, said to have been composed by himself: 'A just and compassionate man who would neither tread on a worm nor cringe to an Emperor'.[3]

1. Lent to the *Grand Loan Exhibition*, Walker Art Gallery, 1886, cat.no.24.

2. H.C. Marillier, *The Liverpool School of Painters*, 1904, p.147.

3. M. Bennett, *Merseyside Painters, People & Places*, 1978, p.120.

48 **Robert George Kelly** 1822-1910
Inspiration: Portrait of the Artist in the Chamber of the Hibernian Academy dated 1847
Oil on canvas, 82 x 70.5cm
(Williamson Art Gallery, Birkenhead, inv.8042)

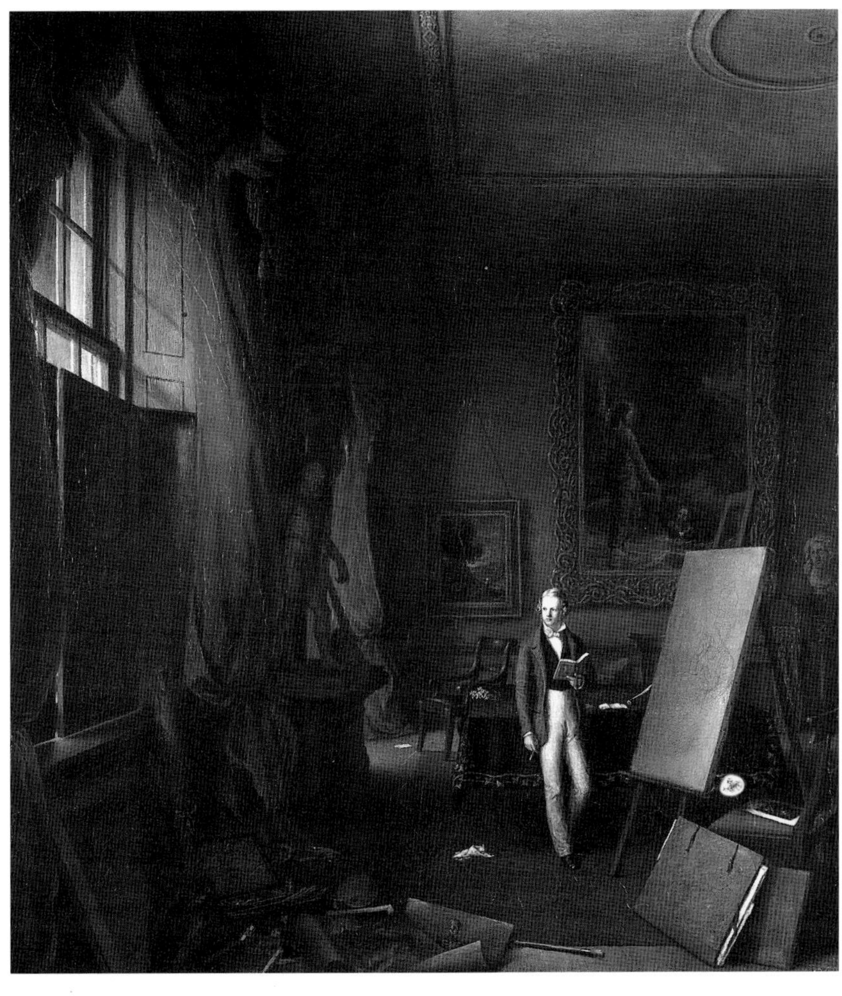

Kelly first exhibited Irish landscapes and views of naval frigates at the Royal Hibernian Academy, Dublin as a student in 1842. The subjects were perhaps influenced by his family background, his father being a Royal Navy Commander. In 1847 Kelly showed at the Hibernian Academy separate portraits of his mother and father and he may have painted the portrait of himself standing in the Academy at the same time. He referred to it as *Inspiration* and passed it on to his son Robert Talbot Kelly, also an artist. The light streaming through the window, spot-lighting the artist, enhances the daydream-like quality of Kelly's self-portrait, as he stands holding a book, as if in reverie, overwhelmed by the grand surroundings of the Academy, and seemingly inspired by the art of his predecessors and contemporaries. In the background one can dimly see examples of his own student work, large history paintings on religious themes such as *The Last Man* and *Christ helping the drowning St Peter*. In 1847 the portrait of Kelly's mother had attracted the attention of commentators, who considered him a young man of promise. The following year he painted *A Tear and a Prayer for Erin: "We are become a reproach to our neighbours"* (also known as *An Ejectment in Ireland*), which became his best known and unwittingly controversial picture when its 'political' content was discussed in the House of Commons after its display in 1853 at the British Institution. In 1858 he settled in Birkenhead, where he lived for much of

his life earning a living as an art master at the local School of Art and eventually became a Conservative alderman. In 1863 he recommended submitting Irish, Scottish and Welsh landscapes to the Academy and continued to do so until 1899. However, the young man of promise and 'inspiration' never lived up to them, to the despair of his wife who blamed much of his lack of success on his being married and having to keep his large family of four sons and seven daughters. In about 1914 she wrote to her son Talbot Kelly, 'Dear old Father had to work for bread and butter, not for fame or for important exhibition pictures and to try to say much about them I fear would do him no good. We all know his work was good, but not what you could publish anything about ... No doubt at all there were great possibilities ... and had he remained unmarried he would have done something worth being talked about and his utter want of business habits with such like men was a great hindrance to him ... If he had married a wife with plenty of money things might have been different, but you see he did not <u>so!</u> alas he had to become just an ordinary plodding Artist.'[1]

1. Letter from Mary Kelly to her son Robert Talbot Kelly undated c.1914 in the artist's file Williamson Art Gallery, Birkenhead.
Lit.: Walter George Strickland, *A Dictionary of Irish Artists*, 1969.

49 **Sir John Everett Millais** 1829-1896
Self-portrait 1847
Oil on board 27.3 x 22.2cm
(Trustees of the National Museums & Galleries on Merseyside, Walker Art Gallery, inv.WAG9240)

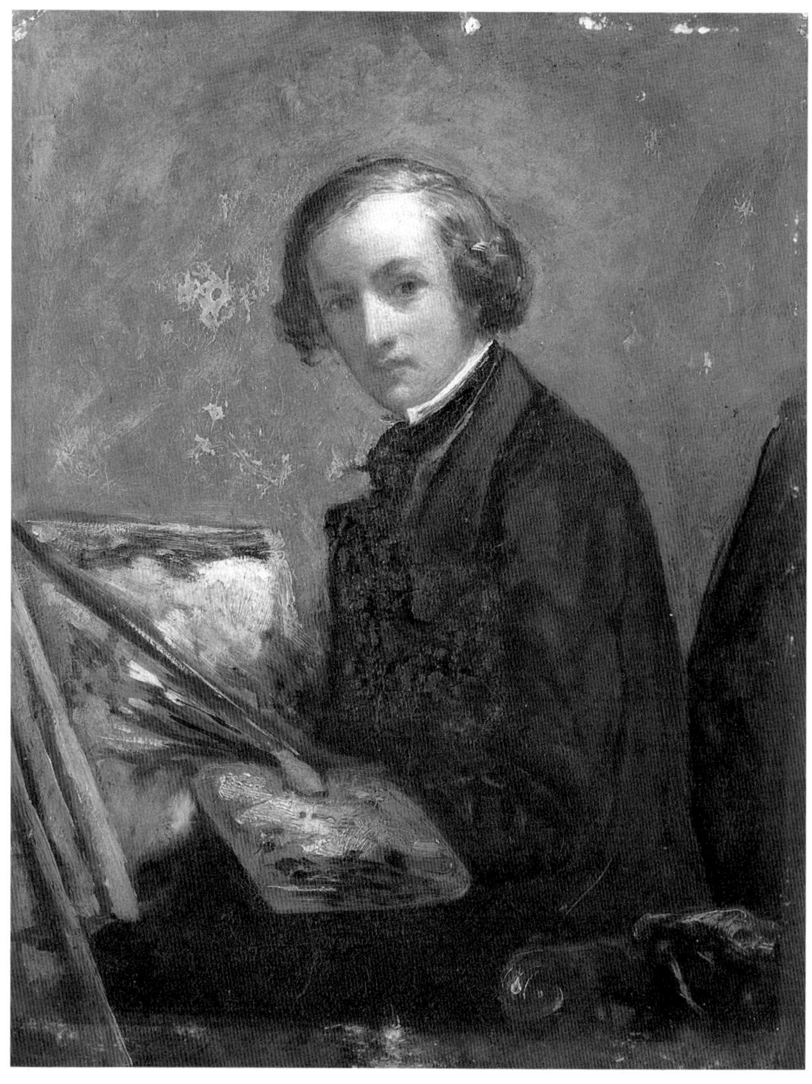

This small fresh-faced portrait of the artist seated with his palette at the easel was his first self-portrait in oil. It was painted when he was only seventeen or eighteen years old and was given by Millais to a teenage friend and fellow student at the Royal Academy, John Kennedy (1833-1904), who later taught at Dundee School of Art. It was presented as a parting gift and was presumably intended as a portable keepsake of a student friendship. He re-used board on which he had already sketched some figures for a large oil painting submitted for the competition to decorate the new Houses of Parliament. Millais had enrolled as a student at the Royal Academy at the age of eleven, the youngest student ever to have been accepted. His precocious drawing and technical skills soon earned him the regard of lecturers, who considered him their star pupil, and of other students who nicknamed him 'The Child' and applauded him vigorously when he received an Academy medal in 1844. In 1847 he had won the Gold medal for his large *Benjamites seizing their Brides*. For a youngster like John Kennedy, Millais would have been a role model and it is evident that Millais took on this role for other young aspirant artists as well. In about 1847 he took under his wing and offerred studio space to his less technically gifted fellow student, William Holman Hunt. The friendship led the following year to a meeting with Dante Gabriel Rossetti, the founding of the Pre-Raphaelite Brotherhood, and a dramatic change in Millais' painting style, away from the Etty-influenced rich, dark tones evident in the self-portrait, to the bright, sharply outlined, minutely detailed manner of his first Pre-Raphaelite masterpiece begun in 1848, *Lorenzo and Isabella* (Liverpool, Walker Art Gallery). Within five years Millais had become the youngest elected associate of the Academy and the most influential English painter of his day. Although the Pre-Raphaelite Brotherhood were in their youthful days at least a closely-knit group sharing ideals, working practices and often studios they rarely produced self-portraits as a way of confirming their friendships. They preferred instead to exchange drawn or painted portraits of each other rather than of themselves.

Lit.: Mary Bennett, *Artists of the Pre-Raphaelite Circle: The First Generation*, 1988.
John Guille Millais, *The Life and Letters of Sir John Everett Millais*, 2 vols., 1899.
The Pre-Raphaelites, Tate Gallery, 1984.

50 **George Morland** 1763-1804
The Artist in his Studio with his Man Gibbs about 1802
Oil on canvas, 63.5 x 76.2cm
(City of Nottingham Museums; Castle Museum and Art Gallery, inv.1904-55)

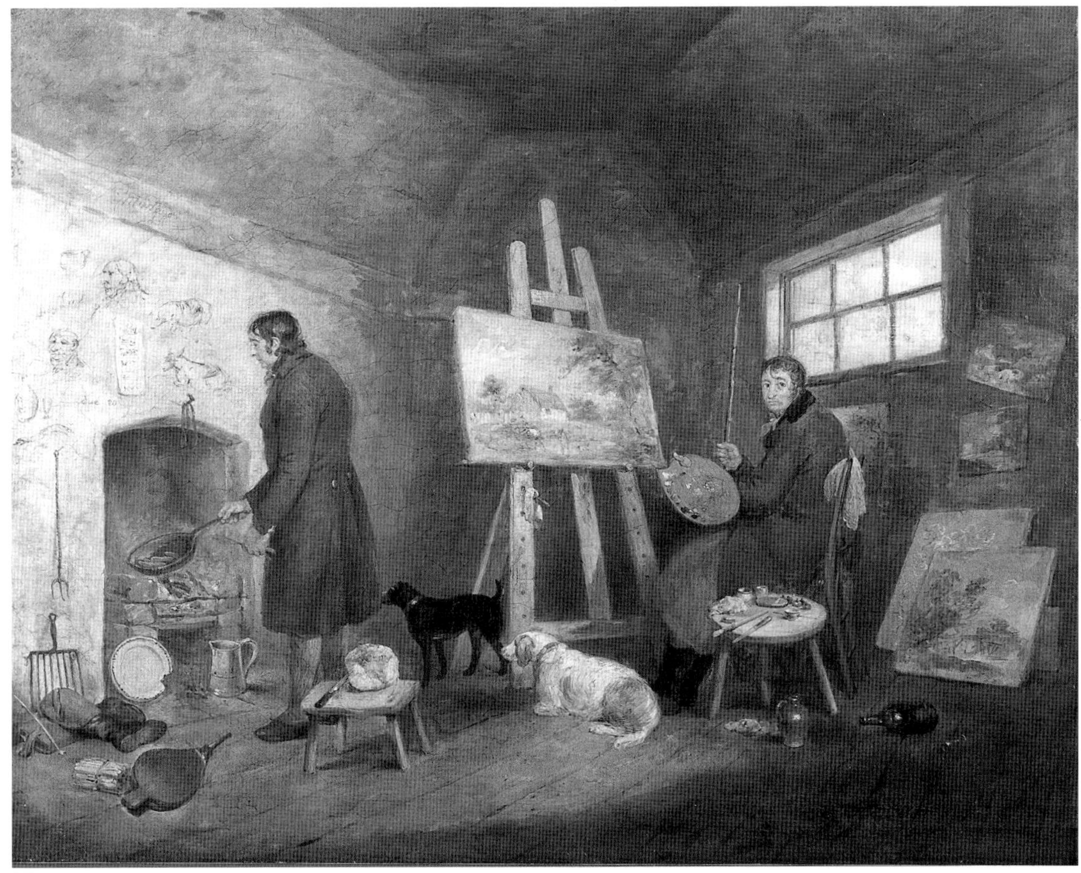

The artist is shown at the age of about forty in the disorderly attic studio of the house in Paddington, rented for him by his estranged wife, after Morland had left the custody of debtor's jail. In order to pay off his debts he had to dash off large numbers of the low-life landscapes which provide the few patches of bright sunlit colour in the grey garret of the picture. The self-portrait documents the actuality of the artist's studio in Morland's typically naturalistic manner, derived from the seventeenth-century Dutch painters by whom he was influenced. Morland's painting is in marked contrast with the self-advertising and status-conscious interiors of Tillemans' and Hayman's pictures (Cat.nos.22, 34), whose antique busts and richly framed paintings emphasise the successful working studio as a suitable venue for a patron's visit. Neither is Morland's picture overlayed with the later romantic imagery employed in Egg's painting where the poor artist closeted in a garret (Cat.no.44) is sustained only by the belief that he may be on the verge of creating great work. The pasty-faced Morland sits amongst the strewn debris of past drinking sessions, which led to his suffering from paralytic attacks. He has surrounded himself with the badly stacked, lopsidedly hung and unframed examples of his work, with which he is

presumably hoping to pay off the debts that are scribbled on the wall, next to the fire-place, amid caricature drawings and other 'inspirational' motifs. That the painting gives an accurate picture is confirmed by contemporary accounts of Morland's last years, slovenly dressed, desperately drunk and often reliant on his man Gibbs to hold him at the easel as he painted.[1] The picture was supposedly inspired by, and intended as a companion to, Sir Joshua Reynolds' picture of his own kitchen in the house which had once been the residence of Morland's father, also an artist.[2] Yet into what could be a depressing image Morland injected humorous elements; the dog studiously watching the sausages cooking and the smoke which rises from them in the form of a flabby-faced caricature of Morland's own face, as if to imply that it is something as mundane as food that truly inspires the artist.

1. G. Dawe, *The Life of George Morland*, 1807, p.165
2. Dawe, as above, p.168. However, no such painting by Reynolds is known to exist and it would have been quite in character for Morland to pull his biographer's leg over the source of his inspiration.

51 **John Phillip** 1817-1867
The Evil Eye: Self-portrait of the Artist sketching in Spain signed and dated 1858
Oil on canvas, 76.2 x 63.5cm
(Trustees of Patrick Allan-Fraser of Hospitalfield, Arbroath, inv.21)
(colour plate 16)

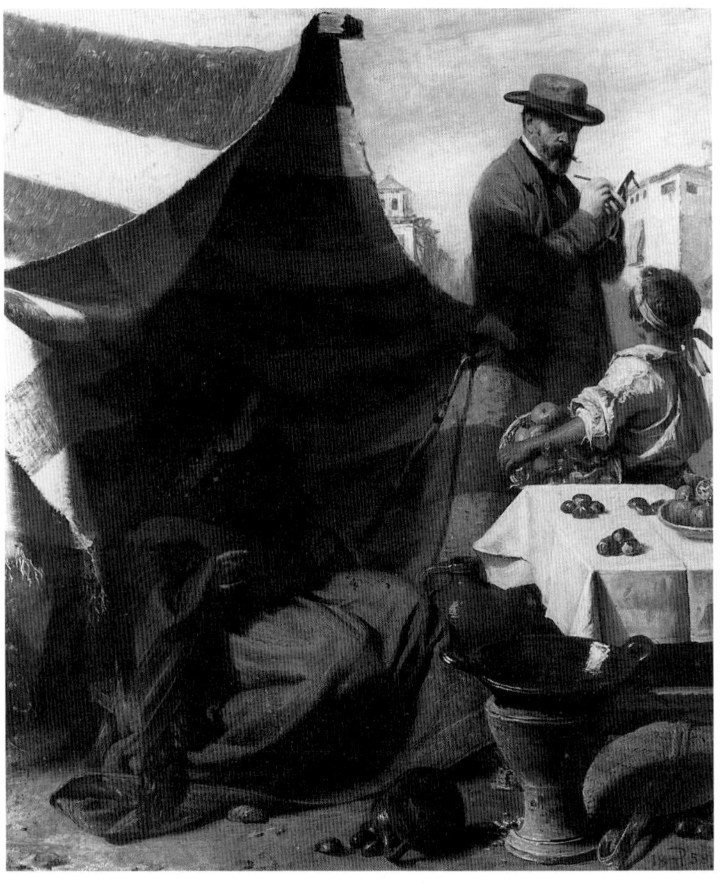

The picture is one of a group of self-portraits 'in character' that Patrick Allan-Fraser commissioned in the 1850s from his former colleagues in the 'Clique' to decorate his house at Hospitalfield (see also Cat.no.44). Along with Egg and Frith Phillip had been one of the members of the 'Clique', founded in 1837 by a group of close friends to sketch incidents from literature and mutually criticise their work. Phillip had begun by painting scenes from Scottish history and contemporary rural life, but after the success of his first visit to Spain in 1851, several of the fruits of which were bought by Queen Victoria, he turned his attention to painting scenes from Spanish contemporary life. After his second trip in 1856 his work focussed so whole-heartedly on that country that he was nicknamed 'Spanish' Phillip. It was the second visit that had the greatest impact on his work, thereafter he showed a finer ability to capture the dramatic possibilities of the country's light and colour, and a new feeling for the mood of his Spanish subjects. Although he painted many purely picturesque costume pieces, peopled with beautiful women and handsome swarthy men, Phillip was especially fascinated, as was his audience back home, by scenes which though taken from modern-day life in Spain still showed its ancient customs and traditions, and which conveyed its seemingly alien character. Not unsurprisingly Phillip chose just such a theme to comply with his friend's specific request for a self-portrait 'in character'. The demand required more than a mere depiction of an artist's features and positively encouraged the autobiographical, narrative composition that resulted. Phillip depicted himself at work in the streets and squares of Seville sketching a market-boy, while in the foreground in the deep shade of her market-stall awning a young woman cowers away from the artist and makes a sign to avert the effects of his concentrated stare, his 'evil eye'. Phillip's hispanophile friend Richard Ford had warned in his *Handbook for Travellers in Spain* (1845) that the Spanish disliked being drawn, partly because their experiences with French military spies during the Napoleonic invasion (1808-12) had taught them to be wary of anyone sketching, but also because of their half-magical awe of the artist, who they feared might capture their soul along with their features. By painting this autobiographical incident Phillip indirectly highlighted the primitive power of the artist in society, as the only person who could reproduce your features and make them live on long after death. Phillip's fascination with this topic, and its popularity with his public, is suggested by the fact that he produced three versions of the scene in the two years after his visit.

Lit.: David & Francina Irwin, *Scottish Painters at Home and Abroad*, 1975.

William Payne, *Hospitalfield: Patrick Allan-Fraser and his art collection*, 1990.

Self-portrait in a Studio about 1840-42?
Oil on millboard laid on canvas, 60.3 x 45.4cm
(National Portrait Gallery, inv.NPG4093)

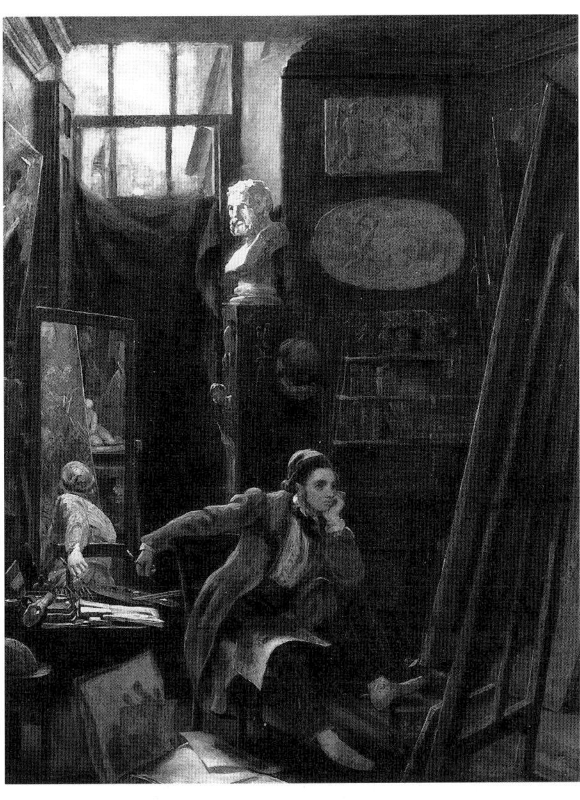

The *Self-portrait* was perhaps painted shortly after Sant had entered the Royal Academy schools in 1840 or when he began his career as a professional artist in 1842. From the start he concentrated his attentions on society portraits and sentimental subject paintings of children as biblical characters. These were often engraved and were greatly appreciated by middle class society. He enjoyed a long and successful career as a portrait painter, his ability in painting children led to his engagement as Principal Painter to Queen Victoria in 1871. For most of his career his public persona was far from the moody young man of this self-portrait who stares rather disconsolately at a huge, unfinished canvas, part of whose ambitious design is cleverly reflected in the full length mirror behind him. Instead his public image was represented by his carte-de-visite photograph (fig.38). Both the photograph and painting share a similar pose of hand to cheek but in the painting the pose's derivation from Dürer's figure of *Melencolia* (fig.6) is still clear and significantly reflects the picture's whole brooding mood, whereas the photograph presents us with a businessman-cum-gentleman in his velvet jacket. The photograph provided a more prosaic view of the artist, taken by an objective observer, whereas Sant's painting reflected how he imagined himself to be. Sant shows himself neither at work (his palette has been laid aside) nor at rest, but chalk in hand waiting for inspiration to strike, should it strike at all. He has surrounded himself with all the props of an artist's studio, scattered across the floor are his sketches, on the walls hang paintings alongside the plaster casts and armour which provide models and accessories for his compositions, and placed on pedestals and tables are classical busts and nude statuettes. He has even included the mirror, which from the

fifteenth-century onwards, had been considered an essential studio tool useful for checking work for compositional defects. As Vigée Le Brun wrote, 'You should always have a mirror positioned behind you so that you can see both the model and your painting at the same time ... it is the best guide and will show up faults clearly'.[1] In Sant's picture the mirror also serves to emphasise the extent to which he leans anxiously forward towards the canvas as he considers his next move. The mood of despondency is intensified by the gloomy interior artificially created by the blanket hanging across the lower half of the studio window. Sant soon shed all traces of despair, but in this youthful self-portrait he created what became the archetypal image of the artist.

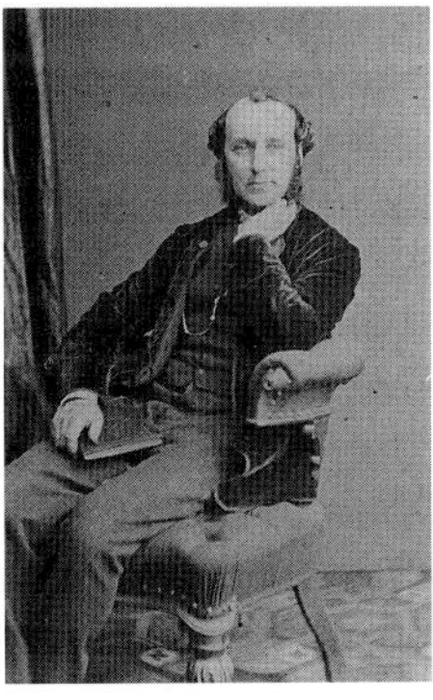

Fig.38 Carte-de-visite photograph of James Sant, by J&C Watkins, (London, National Portrait Gallery)

1. In her *Advice on the painting of portraits*, in *The Memoirs of Elisabeth Vigée Le Brun*, (1835-37) trans. Siân Evans, 1989, p.354.
Lit.: Sir Oliver Millar, *The Victorian Pictures in the Collection of Her Majesty the Queen*, 1992, p.224.
The Victorian Art World in Photographs, National Portrait Gallery, 1984.

53 **Walter Sickert** 1860-1942
Self-portrait about 1896
Oil on canvas, 45.7 x 35.6cm
(Leeds City Art Galleries, inv.13.1/42)

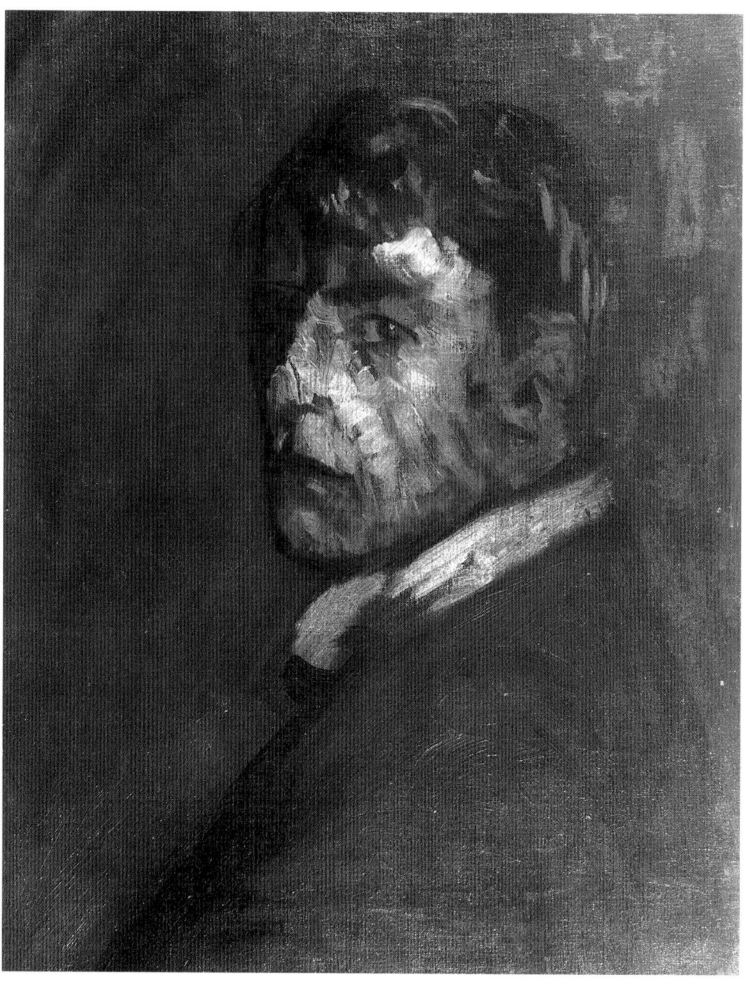

The self-portrait is one of a group of paintings and drawings which Sickert gave in 1896 to Miss Ellen Heath, a friend and informal pupil of his in the mid 1890s. Throughout his life Sickert enjoyed painting informal portraits of friends and artists and his oil painting of Ellen (Leeds City Art Gallery) shows her in profile view to the right, mirroring the position of Sickert in his self-portrait. In 1896 another companion of Sickert's, the caricaturist and essayist, Sir Max Beerbohm had commented on the artist's 'charm- for *all* women - Duchess or model' and noted his 'Cruel mouth - kind eyes'.[1] The dramatic fall of light Sickert has used certainly brings out the cruel mouth but adds a sinister red-eyed presence to the one visible, glaring eye. The year 1896 was not a happy one for Sickert. His attempts to establish himself as a money-earning portrait painter through contacts made via his wealthy and politically well-connected wife had foundered. His marriage also was failing, due to his promiscuity, leading to a final separation in September. Lacking her money Sickert was forced to financially support himself through journalism and teaching. As Wendy Baron has suggested the bitter mood emmanating from the self-portrait reflected his disillusion and depression. Sickert's hostility is emphasised by the coarse block-like web of brushmarks with which he has modelled his face. The dark tones and dramatic lighting which highlight Sickert's basilisk-like, gimlet-eyed stare also add a perceptible theatrical mood

to the picture. Sickert's numerous self-portraits, from the earliest in 1882 to the last in 1940, often reflected his propensity to self-dramatisation. He never lost the sense of theatre nor the theatrical contacts which he retained from his early and brief career as an actor in the early 1880s. The ironic title given to one of his self-portraits *The Juvenile Lead* (Southampton Art Gallery), painted when he was aged 47, refers directly to this period of his life which had included an appearance on the stage at the Merseyside resort of New Brighton in a tour of *Henry V*.[2] Many of the late series of self-portraits also found their expression in dramatic or narrative compositions. In this penetrating, early self-portrait, intended for a friend and artist companion, he focussed instead on his head alone. His expressive features, revealed by a dramatic fall of light, both expose his inner turbulence and create an image of tormented genius.

1. Quoted in Richard Shone, *From Beardsley to Beaverbrook: Portraits by Sickert*, Victoria Art Gallery, Bath, 1990, p.14.
2. Photograph illustrated in frontispiece, *W.R. Sickert*, Tate Gallery, Liverpool, 1989 (Barbara Bagenal Collection, Tate Gallery Archives).
Lit.: Wendy Baron, *Sickert*, 1973.
W. Baron & R. Shone ed., *Sickert Paintings*, Royal Academy, 1992, p.102 cat.no.19.

54 Philip Wilson Steer 1860-1942
Self-portrait Aged Eighteen 1878-79
Oil on board, 76 x 63.5cm
(Williamson Art Gallery & Museum, Birkenhead, Wirral, inv.8157)

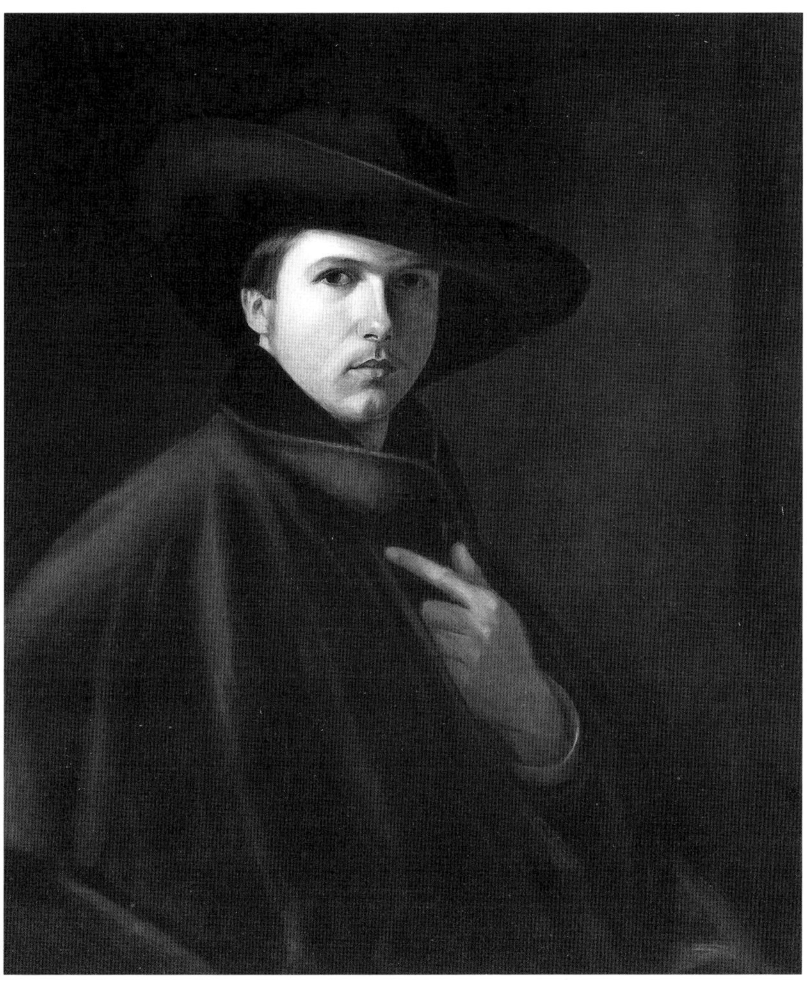

The *Self-portrait* dates from a period in Steer's life when he had not yet decided to take up an artistic career and was still attempting the Civil Service entrance exams required for a job at the British Museum. The portrait was a novice provincial painter's cautious entry into the artistic world, as such it was partly dependent on the example set by his father Philip, a portrait painter who had moved from his native Devon to Birkenhead on his marriage in 1853. In the 1850s the father had portrayed himself debonairly dressed in a short cloak with a palette and easel (Birkenhead, Williamson Art Gallery). The younger Steer in his self-portrait has solemnly donned the mantle of his deceased father. Though the cloak may have been borrowed from his father the pose, hand on chest, derived from Reynolds, another Devonian artist, who had painted himself wearing a red academic gown and cap (Tate Gallery). In 1878 the Reynolds hung in the National Gallery where Steer would have seen it during his studies. The choice of Reynolds as a model might appear somewhat traditional for someone who within the next decade was to become part of the English avant-garde of artists influenced by Impressionism. But once again his father's activities had set a precedent. In 1836 Steer senior had been advised to gain entrance into the art world by copying Reynolds' self-portrait in nearby Plympton, as this was as good a way as any of demonstrating one's skills.[1] A portrait of the first professional head of English artists was still a marketable image. The choice of Reynolds may therefore have been made both as a tribute to a great artist and a nod in the direction of familial tradition. However, the picture's overall mood, set by Steer's dress and the sharply accentuated contrasts between dark and light tones, neither refers back to the fanciful Italianate expression of his father's self-portrait, nor to the mellow Rembrandtesque qualities of Reynolds' work, it is the product of Steer's own impressionable imagination. On his first trip abroad to Paris, aged sixteen, he had written of the favourable impression left by the Spanish paintings in the Louvre, especially those by Murillo.[2] The dark cloak and collar held tightly against the brightly lit cheek and chin and the wide-brimmed slanting hat, which isolate his head from his body, recall paintings by seventeenth-century Spanish artists which Steer would have seen in the Louvre. Steer's satisfaction with his experimental self-portrait encouraged him in his choice of career, and sometime in 1878 he started studying at Gloucester School of Art.

1. Letter from Sir William Elford to Philip Steer 2nd December 1836 quoted by Bruce Laughton, *Philip Wilson Steer*, 1971, p.1.
2. Letter to his mother quoted in Laughton, as above, p.2.
Lit.: D.S. MacColl, *Life, Works & Setting of Philip Wilson Steer*, 1945.

55 **George Frederick Watts** 1817-1904
Self-portrait 1904
Oil on canvas, 66 x 52cm
(Trustees of the Watts Gallery, Compton)

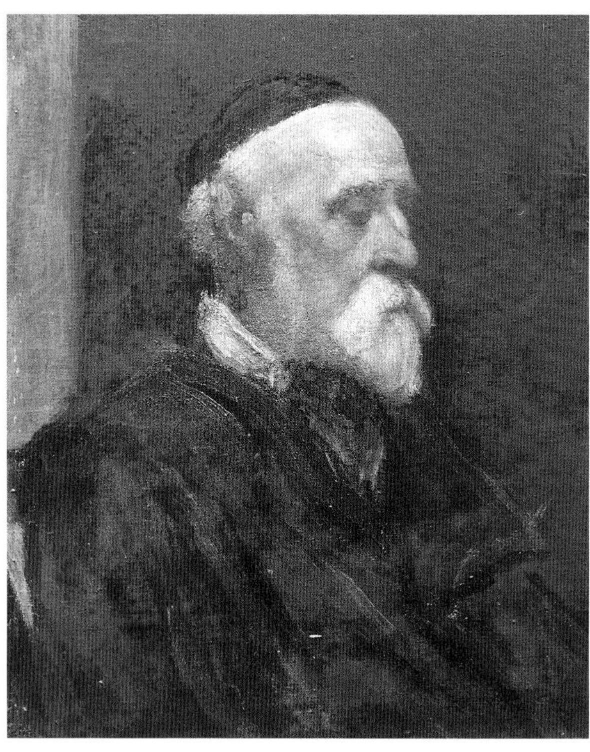

According to the catalogue of the Watts Gallery compiled by Watts' wife this unfinished self-portrait was begun only a few weeks before his final illness struck on the 4th of June 1904. On that day he had still been hard at work in his studio, still proud of his ability at the age of 87 to paint without the need of a mahlstick to steady his hand. In order to draw the distinguished profile view which dominates this self-image he had made use of a photograph, rather than mirrors. According to his wife 'to this is owed the contemplative expression', which was her description for the closed eyes that Watts would have found impossible to paint without the help of a photograph. It was his intention to use the portrait to experiment anew with 'a former method of under painting in tempera'. In this respect he was following his usual practice, as he wrote to a patron: 'I paint myself constantly; that is to say, whenever I want to make an experiment in method or colour, and am not in a humour to make a design'. The images that resulted from such experiments were not, as he made clear in his letter, considered suitable for exhibition: 'I should feel a sort of absurdity attaching to such a proceeding.'[1] His technique had always been idiosyncratic, due perhaps to his being mainly self-taught. The lively surface texture, rich glowing colours and painterly effects of his pictures derived much from the work of Venetian artists, whom he had admired ever since his first stay in Italy in 1843 to 1847. Throughout most of his life he was known mainly for his portraiture, but in the 1880s his large scale mural cycles, idealistic allegorical works and sculpture were finally appreciated and brought him increasing fame, culminating in a personality cult in which Watts became the revered sage and grand old man of High Art. For Watts the Uffizi's self-portrait gallery was the most interesting he had known. The self-portrait he sent to join the collection in 1879 was modelled, as was this his last, on that of Titian (Florence, Uffizi). Watts' personal self-identification with Titian had grown stronger as he grew older. The academic robes worn by Watts in his final self-portrait even looked like the coats worn by the Venetian artist. He constantly wore a skull-cap in his studio, and along with his beard and his noble features this made him look even more like Titian (fig.39). Even Watts' insistence on continuing to work well into his old age was reminiscent of Titian, still at the easel in his nineties. But Watts's last self-portrait reflects more than an artist seeking to pay homage to another. The downcast eyes and the close-up focus on the head, so typical of Watts's work, transforms the portrait into a monumental prophet-like image, distilling the introspective mood of someone all too aware of approaching mortality.

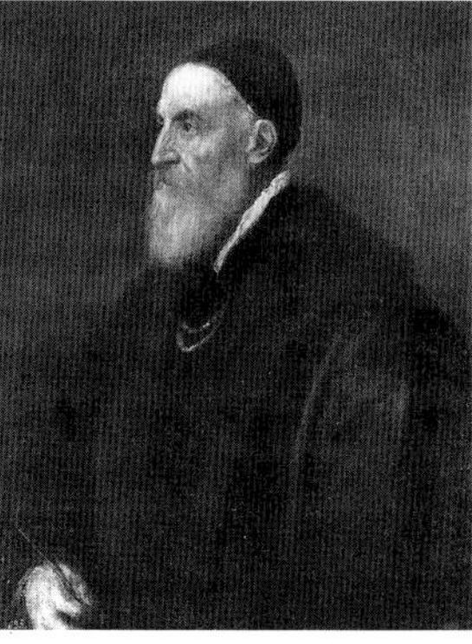

*Fig.39 Titian, **Self-portrait**, about 1558, (Madrid, Prado Museum)*

1. Mary Watts, *George Frederic Watts: The Annals of an Artist's Life*, 1912, vol.1, p.245.
Lit.: Mrs. Russell Barrington, *G.F. Watts Reminiscences*, 1905.
W. Blunt, *England's Michelangelo*, 1975.
Chris Mullen, 'Introduction' to *G.F. Watts A Nineteenth Century Phenomenon*, Whitechapel Art Gallery, 1974.